Mississippi Mind

Mississippi Mind

*A Personal Cultural History
of an American State*

Gayle Graham Yates

The University of Tennessee Press / Knoxville

Frontispiece: Tall Pine Trees on the Natchez Trace Parkway
in Mississippi. Photo by Gayle Graham Yates.

Library of Congress Cataloging in Publication Data

Yates, Gayle Graham, 1940–
    Mississippi mind : a personal cultural history of an American
state / Gayle Graham Yates.—1st ed.
        p.   cm.
    Includes bibliographical references (p.).
    ISBN 0-87049-643-3 (cloth: alk. paper)
    1. Mississippi—Civilization—20th century.   2. Yates, Gayle
Graham, 1940–   .   3. Mississippi—Biography.   I. Title.
F345.Y38   1990
976.2′063—dc20   89-28630   CIP

To the women
of my family

    Natasha Yates
    Gertrude Wilson Yates
    Erma Gay Mathers

and in memory

    Gleta Jones Graham
    Bessie Graham
    Lucile Graham

Contents

Acknowledgments   xi

Introduction   xvii

1.   Allegiance and the Land   1

Preface   1
Mississippi: The Home Place   4
My Day on the Old Natchez Trace   16
Interviews with Mississippians about Their Mississippi   33
Philadelphia, Mississippi: A Prism for Light
   on the Mystery of Meaning   50

2.   Race   53

History of Race Relations   54
The Civil Rights Movement   64
After the Movement   78
One Sociologist's Experience   87

3.   Politics   94

William Winter: A Political Life   97
Cora Norman and the Mississippi Committee
   for the Humanities   106
A Meeting of the Mississippi NAACP   116
Mississippi in the Two-Party South   125

4.   Knowledge, Arts, and Education   133

The Oxford Courthouse Square, the Human Spirit, and
    Benjy Compson   134
My Visit with Eudora Welty   141
James Curtis, Modernism, Postmodernism,
    and Elvis Presley   159
The Arts and Education in Mississippi   164

5.   Gender and Sexuality   194

Miss Ruth's Wedding   200
Julian Rush   211
Beth Henley, Mississippi Playwright   219
Boys and Men   227
Peggy Prenshaw: A Woman's Way   239

6.   Spirituality, Religion, and Belonging   247

Language, Images, and the Civil Religion in Mississippi   252
A Gender Journey to Vicksburg   257
The Civil Religion and Founded Religion   263
Fannie Lou Hamer's Mississippi Spirituality   266
Mississippi Christianity   270
Epilogue   277

Notes   281

Index   291

Illustrations

Tall Pine Trees on the Natchez Trace   frontispiece

Outline Map of Mississippi   xxi

Hebron Cemetery   5

Natchez Trace Map   18

Dog Trot House, French Camp, Old Natchez Trace   28

Erma Gay Mathers   34

Jeannie Griffith   40

Martha Bergmark   45

Anne Moody   79

Vaughan Grisham   88

William Winter   98

Cora Norman   107

Aaron Henry   118

Margaret Walker   123

Oxford Courthouse   135

Statue of Confederate Soldier, Oxford Courthouse Square   136

Eudora Welty   142

Alferdteen Harrison   185

Charles Sallis   188

Ruth Winfield Love   199

Peggy Prenshaw   241

"Welcome to Mississippi" Sign   278

Acknowledgments

To many people I want to express heartfelt thanks for their help and encouragement and for their preliminary readings of this book. The first is Bill Ferris, who asked me, when he and I were serving together in 1980 on the American Studies Association convention program committee, "Why don't you write a book about your growing up in Mississippi and your work now in the academic women's movement?" His casual proposal served as a kind of psychological permission-giving and freed me to write the book that I most wanted to write. He and his colleagues at the University of Mississippi and its Center for the Study of Southern Culture, particularly Ann Abadie, Jo Ann Hawks, Dorothy Abbott, Charles Reagan Wilson, Ron Bailey, Maryemma Graham, Lisa Howorth, and Martha Doyel helped me a great deal with my research, especially during the 1984–85 sabbatical year when I was a fellow at their center. Cora Miner Jordan, my close friend from college, and her husband, Winthrop, were warm and gracious hosts many times on my research trips to Oxford.

Professors at Cora's and my alma mater, Millsaps College, also were enormously helpful. The late Professor Ross H. Moore served as my eighty-plus-year-old research assistant, giving me much information and opening many doors to me, including Eudora Welty's. Just as he taught us students to think critically in his current history class (and made us Mississippi adolescents avid readers of the *New York Times*) nearly three decades ago, he again taught me about Mississippi and the wider world as I worked on this book, and I remember him with thanks. Robert E. Bergmark and Charles Sallis of Millsaps also were quite helpful. Professors Moore and Bergmark read a draft of the entire manuscript, and Bob and Carol Bergmark were often my hosts in Jackson during the research phase of my project.

To the Mississippians whom I interviewed I owe a deep measure of thanks. They all were kind, self-giving, and cooperative with my effort to gain an accurate and vital understanding of the contemporary and past culture of Mississippi. I want to thank Martha Bergmark, Jeannie Griffith, Alferdteen Harrison, Ruth Winfield Love, Erma Gay Mathers, Cora Norman, Peggy Whitman Prenshaw, Charles Sallis, Eudora Welty, and William Winter for permission to publish directly from their interviews.

Other friends and colleagues who have read chapters of this material and given useful responses include Mary Farrell Bednarowski, Alla Bozarth, George Lipsitz, David W. Noble, and the late Lois Noble. The complete manuscript was read with care and thoughtfulness by James B. Nelson of the United Theological Seminary of the Twin Cities and by my "academic father-in-law," my husband's mentor at Harvard University, James Luther Adams. Joy Kasson of the University of North Carolina and Bill Ferris did the most gratifying readings of all, when they served as reviewers for The University of Tennessee Press and recommended publication.

I thank the Bush Foundation and the University of Minnesota for giving me a Bush Sabbatical Fellowship for 1984–85 to support this book project and my parallel teaching development on the South. During 1987–88, the Graduate School of the University of Minnesota awarded me a Grant-in-Aid-of-Research, which helped to complete this project.

Sherry Linkon and Scott Kassner were my research assistants in 1987–88, during the writing of my final draft. Both contributed ideas, did library research, provided criticism and editorial assistance, typed and ran off manuscript copy on the computer, gave me moral support, and in general aided the completion process most generously. Two colleagues who served as chair of American Studies while I worked on this book, Edward M. Griffin and David W. Noble, thoughtfully helped me arrange research and writing time. Our secretary at American Studies, Betty Agee, gave her usual considerate, thorough, and loving care to me and my work with this book as she does to all of us American Studies people, and I thank her with deep appreciation for her support. Equally competent and caring, Theresa Miller did the laser printing of my final manuscript and very meticulously attended to details of manuscript style and permissions requests for me, not an easy task in any case but one made more complex in this instance because I left for a term in Munich, West Germany, before it was done, and she had to handle much on her own. I thank them all and all of the other Minnesotans—faculty, students, and friends—who have aided me in my work through the years.

I also wish to thank Carol Wallace Orr, Dariel Mayer, Lee Campbell Sioles, and Mavis Bryant at The University of Tennessee Press for their work on behalf of this book. They have given my work extraordinary care and have given me wise counsel as they tended the publication process.

The mistakes, errors, and lapses of judgment here are my own. "To err is human," Martha Ray, my Millsaps College roommate, inscribed in the cookbook she gave me as a wedding present. I hope my readers will grant the deficiencies of this book the sort of advance pardon she gave my cooking. I know well that there would be many more mistakes here if the people named above had not helped me as they did.

As always, it is to my family that I am in the deepest debt. Wilson, my husband, and Natasha and Stiles, our young adult children, have been enthusiastic about my Mississippi project and have been my bedrock support system, day by day, year in and year out. Stiles, a college English major, suggested the title. Natasha took the pictures of me for the project, and Wilson served as a kind of editorial assistant, doing everything from tracing missing footnotes sources to relaying phones messages to my editors when I was in Munich. To the three of them I have a debt of gratitude which I gladly pay with love.

I acknowledge and thank the holders of copyrights on the following previously published materials for allowing me to quote from them:

Excerpt from Alice Walker, *The Color Purple* (copyright © 1982 by Alice Walker), reprinted by permission of Harcourt Brace Jovanovich, Inc., by permission of the Wendy Weil Agency, and by permission of The Women's Press, London.

Quotations from William Faulkner, "Nobel Prize Speech" (© 1950), *Absalom, Absalom!* (© 1936), and *The Sound and the Fury* (© 1929) by permission of Random House.

Excerpt from Eudora Welty, *The Wide Net and Other Stories* (copyright © 1942 and renewed 1970 by Eudora Welty), reprinted by permission of Harcourt Brace Jovanovich, Inc.

Quotations from Willie Morris, *The Courting of Marcus Dupree* (© 1983), reprinted by permission of Dell Publishing Co.

Quotation from James Curtis, *Culture as Polyphony* (© 1978 by the Curators of the University of Missouri), reprinted by permission of the University of Missouri Press.

Quotation from David Sansing, *Mississippi: Its People and Culture* (© 1981), reprinted by permission of T. S. Denison and Co.

Quotation from Alexander P. Lamis, *The Two-Party South* (© 1984), reprinted by permission of Oxford University Press.

Quotation from R. Edwin King, Jr., "Foreword," in John R. Salter, Jr., *Jackson, Mississippi: An American Chronicle of Struggle and Schism* (© by John R. Salter, Jr., 1979, reprinted 1987), reprinted by permission of Krieger Publishing Co., Inc.

Quotation from Anne Moody, *Coming of Age in Mississippi* (© 1968), reprinted by permission of Doubleday and Co., Inc.

Quotation from *Atlas of Mississippi* (© 1974), reprinted by permission of the University Press of Mississippi.

Quotation from Alferdteen Harrison, *Piney Woods School, An Oral History* (© 1982), reprinted by permission of the University Press of Mississippi and of Alferdteen Harrison.

Quotation from record jacket texts from "Mississippi Folk Voices" and "Hobo's Meditation," in *Mississippi Folk Voices*, Southern Culture Records, SC 1700, by permission of the Center for the Study of Southern Culture, the University of Mississippi.

Quotation from T.S. Eliot, "Little Gidding," (© 1950), reprinted by permission of Harcourt, Brace, Jovanovich, Inc.

Quotation from Charles Reagan Wilson, *Baptized in Blood: The Religion of the Lost Cause, 1905–1920* (© 1980), reprinted by permission of the University of Georgia Press.

Quotation from Andy Kanegiser, "Textbooks Now Giving Blacks Fairer Shake," The *Clarion Ledger and Jackson Daily News* (© 1984), reprinted by permission of the Clarion Ledger and Jackson Daily News.

Quotation of the poem, "My Mississippi Spring," from *The Southern Review* 23:1 (Summer 1985), reprinted by permission of Dr. Margaret Walker Alexander.

Quotation from *The Afro-American Quilters Exhibition Catalogue* (© 1983 by Maude Southwell and Ella King Torrey), reprinted by permission of the Center for the Study of Southern Culture, the University of Mississippi.

Quotation from the Vicksburg Park brochure, U.S. National Park Service, by permission of the Vicksburg National Military Park.

Quotation from Florence Mars with the assistance of Lynn Eden, *Witness in Philadelphia* (© 1977), reprinted by permission of Louisiana State University Press.

Quotation from "Beth Henley," in John Griffin Jones, ed., *Mississippi Writers Talking*, volume 1 (© 1982), reprinted by permission of the University Press of Mississippi.

Quotation from Darryl Warner, "Interview with Mrs. Artemesie Brandon," *I Ain't Lying*, volume 1 (© Winter 1982), reprinted by permission of Mississippi Cultural Crossroads, Patricia Crosby, editor of *I Ain't Lying*.

Quotation from Dr. Sarah Rouse's speech in Thomas H. Brown, ed., *Ingredients for Survival: The Mississippi Committee for the Humanities Tenth Anniversary Conference*, reprinted by permission of the Mississippi Humanities Council.

I acknowledge and thank as well the following individuals and archives who have given me permission to quote from their archival material, previously unpublished material, or my notes from their lectures:

Dr. Margaret Walker Alexander, lecture at 1984 Mississippi state NAACP convention.

Vaughan Grisham, classroom lecture given at the University of Mississippi, 1985.

Mississippi State Department of Archives and History, diary of Emma Balfour, 16 May 1863–2 June 1863.

Julian B. Rush, letter to Gayle Graham, July, 1961.
Sarah Isom Center for Women's Studies, University of Mississippi,
    interview of Vassor Joiner by Edwin Fox.
Yi-Fu Tuan, "Concepts of Region: A Commentary," paper, 1981.

Introduction

Mississippi Mind is about the culture of the state of Mississippi since the civil rights movement publicly began there in 1961. It is about Mississippians, whether they live within the geographical boundaries of their state or abroad. It is written in a personal voice out of my own experience as a Mississippian. Its background is my growing up time in the 1940s and 1950s in Mississippi. Through literature and arts, archival materials, scholarly works on features of Mississippi life, travel observations and interviews, I studied contemporary Mississippi culture and society in order to discover their meanings. I compare my childhood Mississippi with the state in the recent past and in the present.

My book is a research report in the American-Studies scholarly mode on the aspects of Mississippi life, work, and organization that constitute the state's unique features and that make Mississippi what it is today, symbolically, emotionally, politically, and historically. At the same time, in this book I wish—sometimes implicitly, sometimes overtly—to compare and contrast Mississippi and a Mississippi mentality with other human forms of action and engagement, those which are southern, American and international. The civil rights movement contributed a social, cultural, and personal watershed, as well as a political one, for many Americans; and it is that change in the times, as well as that time-period location in Mississippi and in the United States, on which I focus.

This book is also personal. It is my own story. I have come to believe that any book that any of us writes is our own story. That is, whether writing mathematics or physics, poetry or sociology, we humans are trying to explain ourselves and life around us to ourselves and to one another on this planet Earth. While I do not want to subscribe to a fallacy of exaggerated American individualism, I tell my own story in order to illuminate the meaning of the experience of my people. I introduce my own story as one source of understanding, through which the larger story may unfold. This personal work is of a sort which many American women have, through feminism, begun to do, for feminist scholarship has legitimated the authority of the personal narratives of women.

I use the literary journey motif, collapsing what in fact were several trips into the appearance of one. Thus, the literary and personal journey reported in a section in the first chapter, "My Day on the Old Natchez Trace," an account of a literal trip and the reverie it evoked, is crucial to establishing the texture of my work as well as its themes. The other dominant motif, that of reading, suggests a theme already very familiar in the tradition of intellectual historians. But I am trying to use reading in a fashion more elemental than the way scholars usually use it. That is, I am using reading, too, as a form of experience. The very reading that I record here gives shape to identity that is at once both personal and collective, individual and cultural. In fact, one alternate title might be "An Autobiography of a Reader and Her Community." The child who I was, was too close to illiteracy ever to take reading for granted.

Arguably, since the coming of television, reading is no longer the primary American means of learning, but it was for my generation, and I am only a second-generation reader. I introduce reading here as fundamental to the impetus for the "journey" toward greater understanding, toward knowledge, toward truth. It is central to my story as one woman. It is also central to the meaning I can draw in order to interpret Mississippi and thereby a portion of the culture of the United States.

I came to this book, as a research project, by way of my two
earlier books and my work as a professor of American studies
and women's studies. In my 1975 book, *What Women Want*, I
studied the ideas of contemporary feminism, in which many of
us were caught up at the time. Taking as a framework the paradigm analysis outlined in Thomas Kuhn's *The Structure of Scientific Revolutions* and applying it socially, in that book I suggested
that our feminism was a new gender paradigm for American
society. I analyzed three competing premises for the emergent
feminist paradigm that I saw in the women's movement of the
1960s and early 1970s. After that, I sought further to ground
my feminist theory in historical and international perspectives.
Believing our feminist thought in the United States to be domi-
nantly Anglo-American and rationalist, I studied the works of
nineteenth-century British feminist activist and theorist Harriet Martineau. Viewing her thought as an antecedent of
present-day Anglo-American mainstream feminism, I published
a volume of her works on women and feminism, called *Harriet
Martineau on Women*.

While I am proud of my earlier work, this book is not a logical
consequence of nor even a sequel to it. Rather, the opposite is
the case. I have chosen to leap from the rational and analytical
presentation that I garnered so carefully in the earlier two
books and to attempt here to meld intuitive and analytical meth-
ods of presentation. I chose to focus on Mississippi since the civil
rights movement because this topic, like feminism, matters to
me. Mississippi is my birthplace, and I was a marginally involved civil rights activist as a young adult. More important,
however, the civil rights movement played an enormous role in
shaping my world as well as my personality. It set the social
agenda in which my generation of Americans grew up. Yet,
when I started this project, I did not know much that was factual about Mississippi. For nearly a quarter of a century, I have
been away from Mississippi, living in Nashville, Boston, Minneapolis, and Cambridge, England. Those intervening years
had been busy years for me personally, during which I was oc-

cupied with my graduate education; my adaptation to life in two unfamiliar regions of the country, New England and the Midwest, and one foreign land, England; feminist scholarly efforts as a part of establishing the field of women's studies; and child-rearing and family life. Therefore, for a long time I had not paid much attention to Mississippi, and, just as an outsider would, I had to return to do scholarly research to find out much information. Still, the root source of initial understanding, my childhood imprinting, remained available to me. The resulting blend of the personal and the intellectual, the folksy and the erudite, the political and the practical, as they came together in my writing as a book, was the most satisfying work I have ever done.

This resulting volume, *Mississippi Mind*, I offer to readers as a presentation of culture, community, criticism, and remembrance—and also as an invitation. I invite readers to come home with me to Mississippi on an intellectual, spiritual, and literary journey. I would be pleased if, in these pages, readers can find as well glimpses of themselves and also perhaps some slight recognition of their own homelands.

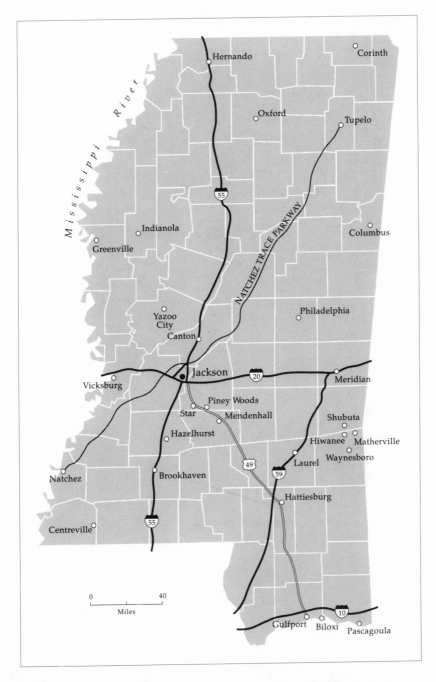

Outline Map of Mississippi with Locations Named in *Mississippi Mind*. Map by University of Tennessee Cartographic Laboratory.

We shall not cease from exploration
And the end of all our exploring
Will be to arrive where we started
And know the place for the first time.

T. S. Eliot, "Little Gidding,"
Four Quartets

1

Allegiance and the Land

And the Lord God said to Moses, Take off your shoes,
for the place on which you stand is holy ground.
                                    Exodus 3:5, King James Bible

Preface

When I was twenty-three and pregnant, newly living in Cambridge, Massachusetts, only my second year out of the South, fresh from the front lines of a summer voter-registration drive for the black civil rights movement in Nashville, I read nearly everything that William Faulkner had ever written. During the weeks, the days, late into the nights before my first baby was born, I devoured Faulkner's works. I do not yet understand the synchronicity or compulsion or subliminal drive that pressed me to it, but by a similar coincidence, I read Eudora Welty's *The Optimist's Daughter* in a Charleston, West Virginia, motel near a place from which one of the characters of that book and Welty's own mother had migrated. During the first weeks of my residence as an alien in England, in Cambridge I picked up to read for the very first time Virginia Woolf's feminist classic, *A Room of One's Own*, although as I did it, I had no factual knowledge of the book's locale in that Cambridge, only a ravenous hunger for its message of female authority and justice. Such have been the chance juxtapositions that have formed my life. I needed to know with a life-and-death passion, and something inside me, intuitive, compelled me to read and selected the volumes for me.

I read Faulkner as if his fiction were milk and bread, wine and cheese, fruit and meat, as I struggled to overcome the strangeness of the Massachusetts land where Yoknapatawpha's Quentin Compson died, as I watched the evening sun of my own Mississippi childhood go down, as my body prepared me for the irrevocably female new life that was to come in the aftertime for both me and my firstborn.

Never have I been an ordinary student despite my professorial appearance. The classroom has seldom sufficed. I learned most of the things that I know out behind some barn or other, passing in some corridor, sitting by some sickbed or on some kitchen stool, acting on a traveler's impulse, or overhearing some chance remark. Talking to people; watching them, if shyly; and observing organizations and how things are done in them have been instructive for my life. But, most of all, books have taught me. Books I have had faith in, a faith that has never failed me as people sometimes have. With that faith, I have read every word that Faulkner wrote—well, almost every word, even some of them one spring in fellow southerner Allen Tate's classroom. Yet it *took*, that reading of Faulkner, like some powerful vaccination against disease, that autumn in Cambridge when I was very young and very heavily pregnant, a pure-bred southerner who did not yet know her home. I have a very literal mind. What I learned from Faulkner was who I was.

Many years later, the daughter born from that pregnancy said to me, "It was your mother you got it from. Don't you remember than summer we found those scrapbooks she made when she was fifteen, and on all the clippings she had scratched out all the words 'men' and written in 'people'?"

I had forgotten.

My mother, my daughter, and I all have lived by the same strange urgency, full of contradictions, rich with synchronicity, that propels us to places we do not know and do not even think we want to be. My mother had retired by the time I had followed her literary teacher's lead and had written a book. Away from her and Faulkner's Mississippi, I wrote a whole book about scratching out men and writing in people. It was published in Cambridge, Massachusetts. At the time I did not think it pertained to Mississippi. That place of publication, too, was an instance of synchronicity, of strands of my life coming together in ways that I did not see fully at the time.

Given my oblique understanding of the ways of the world, then, it is not at all strange that here in the middle of things, in a winter of my mid-life, I went to Mississippi to find out what I know. Call it writing in people. Call it the education of a Mississippi woman. Call it a rebuttal to Thomas Wolfe: you can, too, go home again; with a woman it is different. Call it Willie Morris revisited. Starting north, going south. Whatever its name is, it had something to do with books, learning, and figuring out life. It was time. It was high time. When I was forty-four and at last a real grown up, with winter established in the frozen north, I got in my car in Minnesota and drove south toward home. I had waited a long time for this journey. All my life. As I started out of the midwestern city where I live my normal life, I was exuberant. I opened the car window and let in the cold winter wind. I turned the music on my car's tape player as loud as it would play. As the music swelled and fell and as the icy wind blew through my hair, I cried, "I'm going home. It's okay now. I am going home."

Never mind that every literary southerner who ever lived has done it before me. This is my life.

Passersby would have seen a silly grin on my face. I had learned the hard way that book learning isn't all there is. I was going home perhaps to discover some more books—that I had learned in part from books. I was going back to my place, the homeplace South once again to hear its songs, to march to its drumbeats, to raise its hymns, to listen to its dissonance, perhaps once more to be quieted by its lullabies, maybe even to face the music. This time, though, whatever was playing, it would be my song. Back in the red clay hills from whence I came or in the Mississippi towns where I first knew the world, I was hoping to hear a new chorus and to record it in a way that had not been heard before, to record it for me and also to record it for you, this time to remember and to get it right. What follows is what I saw and heard and learned on my journey.

Mississippi: The Home Place

Down the red clay graveled road, far back in the thick woods where very few people travel anymore, in a place of incredible beauty and sheer tranquility, the white frame Hebron Church that still stands has sat peacefully and solemnly since 1880. And, more important to this story, since sometime in the 1840s, when, according to the courthouse records, one of my great-great-grandfathers, Samuel Jones, organized the Methodist congregation in the log house "eight miles northeast of Waynesboro on the Matherville road," the Hebron cemetery has received the mourned dead of my people for five generations.[1]

In my memory, Hebron, albeit a graveyard, is the wonderful, lush out-of-doors of my Mississippi childhood. I associate it with springtime, discovery, warm breezes, oyster shells, flowers blooming, children playing, dinner-on-the-grounds, families visiting, and the celebration that only nature can bless, perhaps only nature on a spring morning when the sun is shining and the sweet blossoms and abundant foliage already have come to the trees. A graveyard, Hebron was a vibrant part of life, and the annual liveliness of the festive graveyard-working-day on the first Saturday in May is more vivid to me than the occasional somber times of burial to which I was also taken as a child. Every year on graveyard-working-day, we cleared the earth-covered graves with rakes and hoes, replaced the shells that were coverings for some of the graves, placed fresh flowers on all the graves, and planted azaleas or roses on certain ones. It was rather like a gardening-gathering of huge families of neighbors and kin.

Having gathered large buckets of pink rosebuds from our family's bushes so early in the morning that there would still be

Hebron Cemetery. Photo by Gayle Graham Yates.

heavy dew on them and dew wet on our bare feet as we carried the roses into the car, my brother and I set out eagerly as full participants in the annual ritual. We would participate in the graveyard-working as workers, pulling weeds, raking, laying shells, and placing our pink rosebuds. However, before our elders had finished their tasks, we would drop our chores and run around merrily, taking care not to step on any grave directly, and identify the relatives and ancestors and neighbors who were buried beneath us: "That's Grandpaw and Grandmaw." "That's Aunt Ida's mother and daddy." "That's Miss Ada Gray's folks." "This is our little baby brother who died before I was born." "That is Daddy and Aunt Bessie and Aunt 'Cile's brother that got blood-poisoning." "That's Uncle Jim and Aunt Larkie's little boy that died." With children's abandon, we were curious and fascinated about what knowledge the cemetery held, but we had little sensitivity to the painful memories of loss our mother and father, aunts and uncles rekindled each spring on cemetery-working-day. Some years our mother would not go, murmuring ineffectually to our deaf ears about "folks eating and laughing and having a party over the dead." (She mentioned her infant William when she phoned me to wish me happy birthday on my forty-fifth birthday, telling me it was forty-seven years since his death and telling me as she had countless times before what a welcome healthy, happy, beautiful baby I had been after his death.) But sometimes Mother did go to Hebron with us, and Merrell and I always felt better when we all set out together, not missing any member of our family: Daddy, Mother, and Merrell in the front seat of our Willys car, Aunt Bessie, Aunt 'Cile, and me in the back seat.

Dinner-on-the-grounds was the very best part of the festivities. The men would have set up sawhorses with boards across them to make ample tables under the trees in the side church-yard in front of the cemetery. Some families would have brought ice from the ice house to chill the drinks, and, more importantly, to pack around the ice-cream buckets for the hand-turned ice-cream freezing. The women would have cooked plates and platters and pans of wonderful food, all put on the table at once and all available for all-you-can-eat: fried chicken—*several* platters of fried chicken for comparing the merit of the women's culinary talents; hams, cold roast beef, pimento-and-cheese sandwiches, tunafish sandwiches, stuffed eggs; potato salad, coleslaw, carrots-and-raisin salad, Waldorf salad, Jello salads, lettuce-and-tomato salad; all manner of pies and cakes and cookies, especially ones made with molasses and pecans, coconut and eggs. Aunt Bessie always made a three-layer coconut cake from a fresh coconut that Merrell and I had gotten to crack, drink the milk out of, and grate the day before. For drinks, we always had iced tea, presweetened at home while it was still hot. There may have been something else to drink for children or adults other than sweet iced tea, sometimes with lemon, but I do not remember it. My people were teetotalers, and at the time Mississippi was a dry state, so there would have been no beer, no wine. If any of them did drink, and my own family decidedly did not, it would have been thought sinful and outrageous to have alcohol at the church. And while there might have been milk for the children or lemonade, I doubt it, for I have no memory of it at dinner-on-the-grounds. In my memory at least, we all drank big icy glasses of sweet tea, ate fried chicken and ham and stuffed eggs and potato salad until we said we thought we would pop. (Some of the boys would say they were going to bust, but the ladies frowned on that, and, in those days, I was in training to be a little lady. In college, Mrs. Coullet, our Latin teacher, told us that, when we were happily full of food, we should say we were replete.) And then there would be dessert, two or three desserts for everybody, ending with the finale of ice cream from the big wood buckets now packed down with ice and salt to keep the frozen custard solid and smooth.

Never so replete have children been, replete of food, replete of iced tea, replete of pink-rose-fragranced morning dew, replete of sanctity of community, replete of contentment, replete of order in the universe, replete of a place in the sun, as these children were at dinner-on-the-grounds at Hebron on graveyard-working-day on the first Saturday in May in the 1940s.

Merrell and I attended church somewhere other than Hebron. Then we left home, and home was somewhere else, and then our loyalties lay elsewhere. So it was many years before we returned together to Hebron cemetery. I had learned from an internationally famed geneticist that our prematurely gray hair and blue eyes were characteristic of our Irish forebears. Even so, I was startled when, in our thirties, after four years had passed without our seeing one another and he came home from Texas and I from Minnesota, Merrell's dark curly hair had become snow white. When we were next at Hebron cemetery, with his hair white and mine graying, we were there to bury one of our parent-women, Aunt Bessie. By then, Merrell's occupation was growing roses. By then we were neither one carefree to run merrily among the graves. We had brought children's deepest sorrow to that familiar soil. "Remember us," we cried to the land in our grief. We planted rosebushes from Merrell's nursery at her grave. The last time I saw her she wore a bit of lace I had brought her from Belgium. While she had gone away from Mississippi no farther than eastern Alabama, except once to visit relatives in Rock Island, Illinois, and eastern South Dakota, she sent me out into the world prepared to go, and I came back to Hebron cemetery her reverent child.

Once visiting Aunt Bessie's grave in the Hebron cemetery, I saw for the first time that my great-grandmother Graham's tombstone has no birthdate on it. Rather, it says, "Moved from Ireland in 1850." Her husband beside her has a C.S.A., Confederate States Army, grave marker.[2] Aunt Erma told me that our great-grandparents were newly married when they came to this country. It astonishes me that there is no birthdate recorded for our great-grandmother over her grave. Instead, we have her first and only as a full-grown adult, giving her no childhood, no youth. Perhaps she boarded the boat a mere girl, hopeful and expectant, with her bridegroom. Perhaps she was an older woman with a past. Perhaps the Irish girl and boy had grown up together and had shared the hard poverty of the Irish potato famine, fashioning love out of the convenience of a fresh start in a new land. Perhaps she was sickly and one too many among the mouths her parents had to feed, so she was sent freely but unwillingly to the boat for New Orleans with James Graham. We do not know any of these things. Life begins in America for my great-grandmother Graham. Life begins in America. Or life as we know it.

Adult now, I have stood before the grave of this foremother of mine knowing, full of knowledge, brimming with comprehension, having read the immigration accounts, having read well my American history, having searched the archives in this country and abroad. Yet none of my latter-day erudition will yield her date of birth, nothing I can do will bring her back. Her birth is hidden from me, shrouded in my ignorance and that of my people, my country, my America.

When I went to Mississippi in 1985, I at last felt at home in the world. I had made my peace with myself and my America. And I went to Mississippi to make peace at last with it. *Let me be alien no more in my homeland,* I asked it. I hoped for the shrouded shadow of Great-Grandmother Graham for my companion. *Let us both have birth before we have death,* I asked.

When I went to Mississippi, I wanted to capture life there. Instead, it captured me. Once, essential to my survival as a proud American, I had believed that time and place do not matter. Rather, I had been taught and had affirmed as my own the doctrine of leveling, the belief that all people are the same in this America, this democratic land of opportunity.

Yet, wherever I went or whatever I presided over, I had to start over each time with each new person, someone asking, "Where are you from?", "What does your father do?", "What does your husband do?", "Who are your people?", "Where did they come from?", no matter what I said or did. There are markers to how a person is known, however great her protest, that have to do with her era, her location, her color, her gender— that have to do with who her people are. These are matters about which she has no choice. Even when the markers give false impressions or are hurtful, she or he is still unable to have a say in what they will be. That is why I settled for trying to understand mine. That is why I went to Mississippi to try to find out what mine were. I went to Mississippi to discover the quality of the human spirit that inhabits that place; and Mississippi, just as it had on that May morning when I first saw the light of day there, reminded me that the markers of place do matter, that time and place do matter terribly, that they are decisive for who one will be.

So let me begin again. I was born into a poor farming family on a May day in 1940 in the piney-woods section of southeastern

Mississippi. My mother was a teacher. She resented strenuously having to earn a livelihood to supplement the meager income Daddy could earn from plowing his mules on his inherited farm. She much would have preferred to be a housewife, but the housewifely work of cooking and canning and milking and churning, of sewing and quilting and crocheting and embroidering was done with extraordinary competence by my father's two older sisters, Aunt Bessie and Aunt 'Cile, who, although inhabiting a house separate from ours across the driveway of our farmhouse road, were fully participating adults and parent-figures in our household, my father's "dependents," the income tax documents would call them.

When I was three, I learned to read, not from my teacher mother, but by taking my older brother's school reader to Aunt 'Cile and saying, "Show me how to read." Thus it was that I became a reader, and the story of my independence as a human soul began.

There is no question in my mind about what was the most important thing I ever did in my life: I learned to read. Such literacy is the key to liberation for millions of us citizens of this planet, whatever backwater or tenement or desert chance may have destined us to be born into. Our Gold-Coast and silver-spoon fellow travelers have influence, power, travel, and connections to get them where they want to be. Those of us born poor have to rely on reading to get us out of there.

Back in the red clay hills, deep in the lush green woods, listening to the cotton-pickers singing in the distant fields, smelling the rich aroma of Aunt Bessie's daily baking, hearing the rhythmic clicking of Aunt 'Cile's foot-pedaled sewing machine, I lounged through childhood curled up in a porch rocking chair reading book after book after book. And by that means I became acquainted with the world, with far-distant places, unusual people and times, and unseen events. In an intensity with which I did not even know the inhabitants of my daily life, my reality became what was on the printed page. By means of reading, I innocently forged the distance that would expand between me and my people, the root conflicts that would set father against child, child against father, as forever alien, if beloved. My mother would mail-order books of my reading level for me from the state library in Jackson, and I would read them so fast she had to set quotas on how many we could order at a time. Sometimes my eyes would be sore from so much reading. I neither cooked nor sewed nor picked cotton. I read books. Sometimes my father would yell at me in exasperation, "I don't know what is ever going to become of you!", and I knew then, most severely of all, that in his eyes and by local standards, mine was a good-for-nothing pursuit. He was ashamed of me for what I did best.

My rebellion against such an attitude lasted well past adolescence. I not only read books, I made my living reading them. Yet some of the most significant books that I read when I had left home were books by Mississippians and about Mississippi. I knew I had missed something, but it took me a long time to figure out what.

In the world's opinion, Mississippi is probably one of the most despised of all places in the United States. It is an easy scapegoat in American society, for it readily exhibits the sins of the nation—poverty, prejudice, racism, sexism, war, arrogance, narrow-mindedness, both religious and political fanaticism, radical individualism to a flaw, recalcitrance in accepting ideas or items not made in America. Even in the South, its own region, it is often represented as the extreme negative example of the South's limitations—rural dominance, slowness in technological progress, social isolation, personal and social conservatism. It is a symbol, like a magnifying mirror that outsider-Americans can hold up to themselves and say, of the reversed image, "Thank goodness, we are not like that!"

Mississippians, too, have held up that mirror and said, "We do not see ourselves there."

Yet I have come to believe that Mississippi as a whole, as a culture unto itself, while exhibiting its own unique, peculiar, unusual features, also is a prototypical culture within the United States, an example of how America can be characterized, both at its best and at its worst.

Therefore, in a very American mood, like Walt Whitman in his "Song of Myself," I tell you the story of my Mississippi to tell you the American way.

In the United States, even though the broad canvas of American culture is one, the details are quite different from place to place. *E pluribus unum* long has been the motto. As with snowflakes and human fingerprints, "the many" all look alike from a distance, for they all belong together in the same clan. But up close and magnified, each has lines and shapes and design unique to itself. Speaking of Birmingham, Alabama, Rosellen Brown captures this sense of regional difference and likeness in her Mississippi novel, *Civil Wars:* "Provincial cities are so much like provincial people, eager to announce their similarities when it is in fact their idiosyncrasies that make them interesting."[3]

To speak of the uniqueness of a place while maintaining awareness of its essential connectedness with other places and their people, geographer Yi-Fu Tuan has described the purpose of the study of a region this way:

> Scientists and scholars, driven by their enthusiasms, too readily forget the truism that there are different paths to knowledge, and that one path can claim superiority over another only if the aim or purpose of an enquiry is the same. Before we can consider the validity of an answer, we must first ask, what is the question? . . . What is the purpose of a regional narrative? . . .
>
> Regions and provinces are created for reasons of efficacy and of power, whether this step be taken by central authority or by the people themselves as they find it expedient to expand their awareness of space and of people beyond the strictly local. Recall that the root meaning of region is *regere*—to command, and that the root meaning of province is *vincere*—to conquer . . . [Cultural] personality is made up of associated cultural traits. . .
>
> [T]o the humanist, the cultural and behavioral traits are constituent of personality, not a superficial layer that can be discarded in the interest of arriving at some general, statistical measure.
>
> Regional personality can mean something quite different from the personality of the people living in a particular area. Regional

personality, to a geographer, is the "personality" of a region; and to appreciate that personality we would need to know not only the psychological traits of the people, but also the ties between people and region—for instance, whether the inhabitants have to wear mittens in January—and also something about the character of the region itself—its climate, vegetation, and topography; its odor on a hot summer afternoon, and the color of the sky at twilight.[4]

To reach an understanding of its culture, in Mississippi, one's first thought is of the land.

James Meredith, the black leader who as a student desegregated the University of Mississippi, has written of his love of Mississippi's land:

> I can love Mississippi because of the beauty of the countryside and the old traditions of family affection, and for such small thing as flowers bursting in spring and the way you can see for miles from a ridge in winter.
>
> Why should a Negro be forced to leave such things? Because of fear? No. Not anymore.[5]

Margaret Walker, also black and also a famous Mississippian, is author of a bestselling novel, *Jubilee*, and the volumes of poetry *For My People* and *Prophets for a New Day*. She too has written of Mississippi's natural beauty and of it powers of regenerating the human spirit, in her poem, "My Mississippi Spring":

> My heart warms under snow;
> flowers with forsythia,
> japonica blooms, flowering quince,
> bridal wreath, blood root and violet;
> yellow running jasmine vine,
> cape jessamine and saucer magnolias;
> tulip shaped, scenting lemon musk upon the air.
> My Mississippi Spring—
> my warm loving heart a-fire
> with early greening leaves,
> dogwood branches laced against the sky;
> wild forest nature paths
> heralding Resurrection
> over and over again
> Easter morning of our living
> every Mississippi Spring![6]

Doubtless the same awareness and love of the land prompted William Faulkner to make his famous statement about "my own little postage stamp of native soil."[7] The myth of Yoknapatawpha County that he invented through nearly the entire body of his work is thoroughly grounded in Mississippi, and, according to all the stories, Yoknapatawpha is a Mississippi county. And Faulkner's white female counterpart, Eudora Welty, using as illustration Faulkner's creation of Yoknapatawpha gave the literary world a classic interpretive essay in the piece, "Place in Fiction." She writes, "It is by the nature of itself that fiction is all bound up in the local. The internal reason for that is surely that *feelings* are bound up in place. The human mind is a mass of associations—associations more poetic even than actual. . . . The truth is, fiction depends for its life on place. Location is the crossroads of circumstance, the proving ground of 'What happened? Who's here? Who's coming?'—and that is the heart's field."[8]

One of the women I interviewed on my trip, Mrs. Jeannie Griffith, black, a retired maid and school lunchroom cook who grew up near Star, Mississippi, and who lives in Jackson now, expressed her attachment to Mississippi, in contrast with other places good to visit, this way:

> Well, we went to San Francisco, Los Angeles, and Pine Bluff, Arkansas, and Birmingham, Alabama. Out of Mississippi? Yeah, we had people there. His [her husband's] brother lived in San Francisco, and I have some relatives in Los Angeles. And I went to Birmingham with friends, with my friends. And his brother lives in Pine Bluff—his nieces live in Pine Bluff; his brother lives in Campbell, Arkansas. We go there often. Not to live. Do I like Jackson? I like Jackson. Now, I like San Francisco to visit, but I like Jackson to *live*.[9]

Another of my interviewees, Martha Bergmark, is white, a lawyer, and at the time of the interview was director of a federal legal services program in Hattiesburg. The program offered free legal services to people below the federal poverty line, meaning that a great many of her clients were black as well as poor—a situation of professional service and social interaction by a white woman unthinkable before 1960. She described her love for Mississippi in terms of both her growing up in the civil rights movement and the state's natural beauty:

> I feel such a strong attachment to the place. I sometimes wonder why that is. I don't have generations of roots here. My own theory on it is that the time when I grew up here was a really strong influence on that. The civil rights movement—I grew up with that movement. That social change. And I was even then so committed to that goal, which has been grossly unachieved. I think perhaps I want to see that through. And yet I think there is more to it. I think there is more to it. I guess I'll never know, if I grew up in Indiana, say, if the same ties would exist. It's really to the soil. I know that's crazy to say that. I grew up in the city of Jackson! I'm not a gardener! I can't stand mowing the yard! But I really can't drive to Laurel or to Jackson or to State Line or to Waynesboro without at some point during that trip, no matter how preoccupied I am with why I am going, think[ing] about how beautiful it is and—and that I love it.[10]

William Faulkner prophesied such ambivalence concerning Mississippi in his 1936 novel, *Absalom, Absalom!*, although, in his Harvard student Yoknapatawpha aristocrat, Quentin Compson, he created a Mississippian much more tortured about the South than either Jeannie Griffith or Martha Bergmark now seems to be. Quentin's "confessor" is his Canadian friend at Harvard. Faulkner describes the two of them: "Shreve, the Canadian, the child of blizzards and of cold in a bath robe with an overcoat above it, the collar turned up about his ears; Quentin, the Southerner, the morose and delicate offspring of rain and steamy heat in the thin suitable clothing which he had brought from Mississippi, his overcoat (as thin and vain for what it was as the suit) lying on the floor where he had not even bothered to raise it."[11]

The book ends:

> "Do you want to know what I think?"
> "No," Quentin said.
> "Then I'll tell you. I think that in time the Jim Bonds [Bond was a black of mixed racial ancestry] are going to conquer the western

hemisphere. Of course it won't quite be in our time and of course as they spread toward the poles they will bleach out again like the rabbits and the birds do, so they won't show up so sharp against the snow. But it will still be Jim Bond: and so in a few thousand years, I who regard you will also have sprung from the loins of African kings. Now I want you to tell me just one thing more. Why do you hate the South?"

"I don't hate it," Quentin said, quickly, at once, immediately; "I don't hate it," he said *I dont hate it* he thought, panting in the cold air, the iron New England dark; *I dont. I dont!! I dont hate it! I dont hate it!*[12]

All of this reminds me, emotionally, poetically, that we American-Mississippians belong to what sociologists have named a pluralistic society. We are different groups of people coming from many different origins with different slants on life, yet we are put together in one place, sharing our variant forms of human life in one space. Our life in Mississippi, as well as perhaps in other places, is often hateful as well as beautiful, often lovely as well as mean. Yet we all belong to it and it to us. We are its, and it is ours, all of us, all of it.

On my journey into seeing our collective past for myself, I came to a better understanding of this ambiguity of love and hatred, of this mix of the commonplace and the ecstatic, of the balance of the weights of history and the present, and of despair and hope on a Mississippi drive from Jackson to Tupelo.

My Day on the Old Natchez Trace

One February Sunday morning I drove my car out of Jackson bound for Oxford. I had had a huge, leisurely, restaurant breakfast of grits and eggs, bacon and biscuits, fresh fruits, and tea on my way out of town; and I had nothing to do all day but to get to Oxford, a three-hour drive north on Interstate Highway 55. I was driving along mindlessly, content, when I noticed the brown road sign, "Natchez Trace Parkway." I drove on past it but then slowed down. I had never been up the Natchez Trace in my entire life, it occurred to me, yet that important road had been somewhere in my consciousness all of my life. Oh, maybe I had gone a short distance out onto it when I was a college student in Jackson, maybe the Natchez Trace, the two-laned parkway road locally called "the Trace," was one of the quiet, velvety dark places to which I had a few times ridden out of town and sat parked in a lone car with a young man as earnest and intense as I, engaged with soft kisses and sexual limits and dappled black shadows of trees by the secluded roadside. But I had never *really* been on the Natchez Trace, never seen what was there in the daylight, never paid attention, never driven its length, never taken in its beauty deliberately, never absorbed its history or its meaning, never gotten out of the car and walked along the old road with my own two feet.

This time I changed my mind. It is hard for me to turn back, to turn around and go back, but this time I did it! I turned the car around and went onto the parkway. And that day became one of the High Holy Days of my solitary journey back into my homeland.

The Natchez Trace Parkway is in the national park system maintained by the U.S. Department of the Interior. It begins as a roadway that runs from what is now Natchez on the Mississippi River in southwestern Mississippi and goes sharply north-northeasterly across the full distance of the state through Jackson and Tupelo and on into Alabama and through Tennessee to Nashville. It has been a road since, among Mississippi Indians, it connected the Chickasaw nation in the north to the Choctaws and the Natchez people in the south. The *Atlas of Mississippi* says of it:

> Probably the most scenic of the four [parks maintained by the National Park Service in Mississippi "dedicated to conserving the scenic, scientific, and historical heritage of the United States for the benefit and inspiration of the People"] is the Natchez Trace. . . .

Today the Natchez Trace is a major tourist and recreational high-

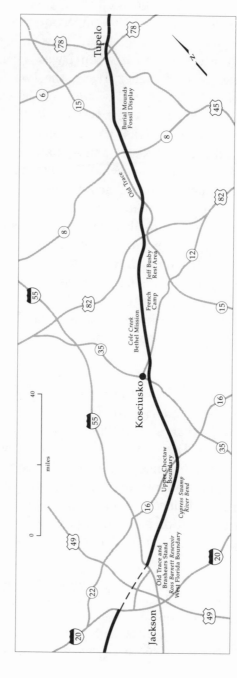

Natchez Trace Map Showing Selected Locations between Jackson and Tupelo, Mississippi. Map by University of Tennessee Cartographic Laboratory.

way . . . Each mile of the completed trace is flanked by approximately 100 acres of land which is in a completely natural setting with no roadside signs or other distractions. Numerous facilities such as camp grounds, picnic areas, visitor centers, historical sites, and trails are located along the entire length of the highway. Two major park developments are also located on the trace.[13]

Historians say that there have been four periods in the road's life, five if you count the years it really was a "trace," an unused webway of paths and trails more useful for legend and memory than for transportation.[14]

First, it was an Indian road. Second, it was a road used in the early 1700s by French colonists, traders, and explorers and by their Spanish and British successors to gain access to the North American "West," connecting overland to and from Tennessee with the Mississippi River. In the early years of the United States, the earliest 1800s, the road was put to its third use, that of post road or U.S. government road in the Mississippi Territory. It was most used by, and best known as the road of, the "Kaintuck" boatmen, tough, rowdy, white fellows from Kentucky, Tennessee, and Ohio, who floated goods south down the Mississippi River in flatboats in those days before steam or electrical power and had to walk or ride horseback on their return trips from Natchez or New Orleans. By European, though not Choctaw, reckoning, New Orleans was in Spanish territory until after the War of 1812, and the "Kaintucks" got their pay in Spanish gold and silver and took it back to Tennessee on the Natchez Trace, often terrorizing the people along the way and with their payloads tempting bands of thieving bandits even rougher than they along the road that they traveled.

For a good part of the nineteenth century, what is now the Natchez Trace was a frontier road, one that was often dangerous to travel. It saw the Civil War, with decisive battles fought near it. The Battle of Shiloh in Tennessee, near Corinth, Mississippi, took place not far from it. Also close was the scene of General Grant's 1863 victory in Jackson that preceded the war's decisive Mississippi siege at Vicksburg, the road's terminus upriver seventy miles from Natchez. One battle on the way to Vicksburg, the Battle of Raymond, is commemorated on the parkway. In the twentieth century, the road fell into disrepair and was brought back to life as a national parkway through a series of coincidences of popular attention, efforts of the Daughters of the American Revolution, a WPA project in the Roosevelt administration, and cooperation among members of Congress from three states. Now, for these many years since the 1930s, it has been a recreational and historic-preservation roadway.

When it originally was an Indian road, it was more precisely many passageways. The paths and trails probably were hunting and trade routes for the three largest Mississippi groups of Native Americans. In what is today the state of Mississippi, the Chickasaw nation in the north, the Natchez people and the Choctaw nation to their south, and some smaller Native American tribes such as the Gulf-Coast based Pascagoula and Biloxi hunted, made connecting routes among their own villages, and explored the surrounding lands, as well as traveling to the south and north to trade with the other nations.

The first white people the original Mississippians saw probably were Hernando De Soto and his fellow explorers in 1540. These Spaniards spent the winter of 1540–41 in makeshift housing near what is now Columbus among friendly Chickasaws. However, when De Soto ordered the Chickasaws to become servants for his group, they became exasperated and burned down the Spaniards' camp-buildings, causing De Soto and his group to fight and flee and in so doing to lose forty men. After two years in the Mississippi Delta and in Arkansas in a futile attempt to reach Mexico, the Spanish band came back to Mississippi, De Soto died, and his men buried him in the Mississippi River.[15]

A century later, French explorers were the first Europeans to come into, assert control over, and settle the land bounded by the waters of the Gulf of Mexico and the Mississippi River, which is now southern Mississippi. Explorers Father Pierre

Marquette and trader Louis Joliet had come down the Mississippi in 1673, and La Salle had traveled all the way down to the mouth of Mississippi River, and thus had passed through "Mississippi," when he claimed and named "Louisiana" for his French king in 1682. However, it was after the French arrived as colonists, in 1699 at Fort Maurepas near Ocean Springs, and in 1716 at Fort Rosalie on the Natchez Bluffs, that their traders, missionaries, and military men pounded the old Indian roads into their own pathways. A French map of 1733 shows the road connecting Natchez Indian villages to Choctaw ones around what is now Jackson, and both to Chickasaw settlements to the northeast. After 1763, when the French turned over their claim to the land to the English, British maps show the same trail, calling it the "Path to the Choctaw Nation."[16]

After the American Revolution, Spain owned the southernmost portion of present-day Mississippi. To the government of the United States, the rest of it was technically western Georgia until the Mississippi Territory was established in 1798.[17] All this time, to the Indians who had long inhabited it, the area was still *their* land. The Central Southeast of that time was West Florida, and the Natchez Trace entered its third phase, that of the trail for the northward journey of "Kaintuck" boatmen. Produce such as flour, pork, tobacco, hemp, and iron was floated down the Mississippi River to markets in Natchez and New Orleans from U.S. western frontier places such as Ohio and Kentucky, earning Spanish coins for the owners of the produce. The only way home was on foot or horseback along the 450-mile route of formerly Indian-controlled paths from Natchez to Nashville.

The most recent life of the Natchez Trace, including its capitalized name and, with that, its symbolic authority, began inauspiciously in 1909, when the Mississippi Daughters of the American Revolution (DAR) placed a monument commemorating the road on the Natchez bluff of the Mississippi River where the road must have begun. It is likely that this fresh interest was instigated by an article, "The Natchez Trace," in a 1905 *Everybody's Magazine*. In the subsequent twenty-five years, the DAR sponsored monuments that were set up in all counties except one through which the Natchez Trace ran, through Mississippi, Alabama, and Tennessee. When these monuments were erected, there were speeches and civic celebrations, arousing a great deal of public interest in the history and legend surrounding the road. A large number of widely read accounts of these matters were published in sources ranging from scholarly journals to city newspapers. With the coming of the New Deal in the 1930s and the federal government's involvement in jobs programs for the unemployed, Congressman Jeff Busby of Mississippi, with his congressional counterparts from Alabama and Tennessee, noting the efforts of the DAR and those of journalists and state and local historians in the region to build interest in the Natchez Trace, introduced legislation into Congress to have the old road surveyed and made into a national parkway. The Natchez Trace Parkway was officially added to the National Park System by action taken on 18 May 1938, and the U.S. government proceeded to acquire the land and to build the paved road with its historic markers alongside the "trace" of where the old road had run.[18]

As I turned my car onto the Natchez Trace Parkway that February Sunday morning in the 1980s, I was happy. The summer before this trip, I had read the book *Blue Highways* by William Least Heat Moon, [19] an account of the mixed-blood Osage Native American author's journey in his truck named Ghost Dancing along the back roads of the United States, colored blue on his map, in a solitary quest for the common people and out-of-the-way places all over this country. Not incidentally, his was a journey of *self*-discovery, he having a hearty case of the blues over losing both his job and his Cherokee wife. I fancied this brown-labeled park-road a sort of blue highway of my own. I too was a solitary journey in search of psychic peace, but the course of my journey, unlike that of Least Heat Moon, was back to my roots and back to the books where I was most at home.

In this happy state, mind altered by the open road, at first I did not think of history but, free-associating somewhere in a spiritual sanctuary beside or above or beyond or within, but still on the road, I thought of another American Indian, a colleague who used to teach at my university.

Natchez Trace. Indian road. Native American colleague.

My colleague once had played a part in saving my professional life. We had not known one another well. We had sat together at a few meetings. I once had told him a touching story of my son at fourteen taking a girlfriend five fresh roses, all that he could afford, under his zipped-up coat in a most frozen Minnesota winter; and my colleague, showing me that he remembered how a boy feels, had told me back a story about trying to make a girl a Valentine and messing it up. We were in similar spots in our university, and in the very month that he was leaving the university, he stood up for me in a meeting. "Eloquent," said one of our other colleagues who phoned to tell me about it. "He said, 'You seem to forget that you are dealing with the life of a *human being.*'"

Like William Least Heat Moon's hopeful book, that message from my Indian colleague comes back to me on the road: *somebody understands, someone whose broken spirit is healing. "This is the life of a human being."* This road, memory tells me, can be healing like the ocean I love, with its soothing roar and crash, repeated, repeated, repeated, ever different, ever the same, reliable for quiet harmony, for thought, and for concentration. This road is the avenue to contemplation.

As the contemplative, I drive my car forward eagerly.

After I join the Trace, the first stops indicated by the neat official roadside signs seem to emphasize nature. I stop at the picnic area on the Pearl River and walk along the edge, down to the sandy riverbank, enjoying the sight of the black, deep, pooling water. I stop at a cypress swamp, beautifully marked for the lay naturalist, appearing as southern exotica for the outsider. But for me, the native, the cypress trees are childhood familiars—sturdy gray ghosts of wood—the "knees," tough, gnarled root sections growing up out of the water some distance from the trunks of the cypress tress which also rise in the deep shade from their watery source.

For a while the road goes along the shore of the vast Ross Barnett Reservoir, a human-made lake dammed up on the Pearl River near Jackson and named for the governor of Mississippi who, in the official name of the state government, from 1960 until 1964 presided over the height of outspoken public antagonism to black civil rights, lawlessness in the name of states' rights, and brutality toward black people and advocates of their rights.

My first sight of the actual trace road as it is preserved comes soon out of Jackson, soon after my reverie on my sense of connectedness to the two Indians, one from literature, one from university meetings. Human beings. It is a roadside stop by the paved road like the others—one among many, I was to learn—and there are picnic tables on its banks. I walk out into the deep sunken path channeled through the woods. I am satisfied, deeply satisfied. "I'm home! I'm home!", I want to cry out aloud, remembering the story from a beloved professor of mine of crying out in such a way on her first sight of Florence, Italy. The deep black dirt road in these woods—which may or may not have been the actual road the Choctaws used to trade with the Chickasaws or the actual road the Kaintuck boatmen took north from Natchez *if* the Choctaws *did* trade with the Natchez, and *if* the Kentucky men *did* float boats downstream and walk back north—is the road we remember by. It is our homeplace, our past. The big gold letters on the roadside marker read:

> Preserved here is a portion of a nearly 200-year old road—the Old Natchez Trace. Maintaining this 500-mile long wilderness road in the early 1800's was a difficult if not hopeless task.
>
> As you look down the sunken trench note the large trees growing on the edge of the 10 foot wide strip we clear today. These trees are mute testimony to the endless struggle between man to alter and change, and nature to reclaim, restore, and heal.[20]

The endless struggle between [people] to alter and change, and nature to reclaim, restore, and heal.

The homespun philosopher of the roadside sign, perhaps an employee of the Park Service, has set down the human dilemma as seen from Mississippi or somewhere else, although for my part the words "nature" and "people" are interchangeable: both nature and people struggle, change, alter, heal, restore, and struggle again. Here on this road much of American history is recapitulated. Here is the history of our land and our peoples and our collective national acts. Here as well is the history of our spirit.

As I drive along, I ignore the Lower Choctaw Boundary, one of the parkway markers. I do take a picture of the marker at the "Old Trace and Brashears Stand" and begin to take into account what a "stand" was: a crude inn for food, drink, and lodging for travelers along this road in the early part of the nineteenth century. I note the West Florida Boundary, which the marker said was "drawn in 1763 at the close of the French and Indian War."[21]

Still carrying my sense of joy and connectedness, I stop at the "Upper Choctaw Boundary." So exuberant am I about the tall pine trees along both sides of the road that, just before reaching that point, I had stopped in the middle of the road—the road was little traveled on that Sunday morning, and no other car came along—and took a picture from the median line of the roadway of those pines I so love, green and alive standing high above the road on a February morning. At the "Upper Choctaw" stop, my attention is caught first by the gold and brown announcement, "Southern Pines." A ten-minute nature trail is available to acquaint travelers with this "southern economic mainstay."[22]

Fearing a little to go into the woods as a woman alone, I reluctantly decline to take the nature trail. Then I turn my attention to the sign about the Upper Choctaw Boundary. Here, at the same roadside stop where today we can enjoy learning about the dense forests of southern pines, the economic mainstay of a southernmost swath of the Deep South called by geographers the piney woods, the area which includes my family's land, we are reminded in a parallel parkway sign of the Treaty of Doak's Stand.

In these now-silent woods, in 1820, by the Treaty of Doak's Stand, the Choctaw Indians signed with the United States government the most important cession of their lands. This treaty covered their westerly lands, the best farmland, in Mississippi. In 1805 they had ceded their southernmost lands to the European-Americans by the Treaty of Mount Dexter, and they were to cede their easterly lands in 1830 by the Treaty of Dancing Rabbit Creek, but it was the 1820 treaty, Doak's Stand, in Mississippi, that was decisive. It was after 1820 that, by the cruel process known as "removal," all of the Native Americans across the Southeast were driven off their familiar and fertile land and sent on a perilous, heartbreaking trip to forced settlement on strange and unyielding ground in Oklahoma. By 1731, the Natchez nation had been destroyed by the French. They had successfully captured the French Fort Rosalie (where the city of Natchez is now) in 1729, but in the retaliatory battle the French killed most of the Natchez people. A few survived and went to live with Chickasaws, and a few lived long enough to go to Oklahoma, but they were no longer a nation after 1731. The Chickasaws and Choctaws survived the French and Indian Wars of the eighteenth century and were neutral during the American Revolution. They supported the Americans during the War of 1812 and believed that they would be supported by the American government. The Chickasaws, too, ceded their lands by poorly understood treaties, in 1816 and 1832. And "Doak's Stand" and "Dancing Rabbit Creek" became imprints in our history.[23]

Once a good friend of mine of Irish ancestry who is Roman Catholic said to me, "You realize if you and I were in Northern Ireland, we would be on different sides, don't you?" Startled, I thought it through. Yes, if we were in Ulster, I should parade in orange, she in green. Since then I have been quite silent on St. Patrick's Day.

Likewise, standing at the parallel monuments to Southern Pines and the Treaty of Doak's Stand, I realize a similar historical cleavage between my Native American colleague and me. While I did not know it at the time, my livelihood as a child growing up had come from land ceded at Dancing Rabbit Creek. Yet it had been "our" land as far back as I could remember— our pine trees, our Carson Creek, our fields and pastures, and our Hebron Cemetery. However, if my colleague who stood up for me in the meeting, actually an Ojibwa, had been a Mississippi Choctaw, his people would have been driven from the land before mine came. It was "theirs" just as surely as it is "ours." We would likely feel funny, estranged, conflicted, different, if he were standing beside me at the roadside stop.

(As I write, our daughter is a Peace Corps Volunteer in Botswana, a black-governed, economically developing southern African democracy which shares a long border with the Republic of South Africa. Economically dependent on that country, Botswana is fearful of its politics and government. My daughter writes that she does not think we understand the homelands in South Africa. You see, she lectures to us in her letter, the government of South Africa sent all the black people out of the cities and away from the good lands into areas supposedly of their own, but areas that are the very poorest land for farming, the worst possible land, so that there are not any jobs and the men have to go back to the cities to find work. In another letter she wonders, after her *Newsweek* is detained in Johannesburg because South Africa was featured on the front of it, "What is this world coming to?")

More solemn now, I turn away from the Upper Choctaw Boundary sign, get into my car, and drive on. My next stop is at French Camp.

It is the cane mill by the side of the road that causes me to stop. Uncle John had one when I was a child, and all of the relatives used it to grind their cane and make its juice into molasses. On crisp autumn mornings when I was a small child, I used to ride with my father on the mule-drawn wagon pulling the canestalks the mile up the road to Uncle John's cane mill. Now suddenly, here by my roadside, is a cane mill that is a part of a

Dog Trot House, French Camp, Natchez Trace Parkway.
Photo by Gayle Graham Yates.

museum. The place called French Camp I have never heard of
before. It turns out, quite logically, that it was a French camp
in the French trader times in Mississippi. Then it was a "stand,"
a nineteenth-century inn for travelers on the old road. Now it is
a little town, one of the very few visible from the parkway,
whose main industry seems to be a small fundamentalist Christian boarding school. Flying the American flag, the old un-
painted dog-trot house, the "stand," is intact as part of the living
museum maintained by the federal Park Service. An attendant
sits on the front porch that runs the expanse of the house, and
the two rooms, one on each side of the open central hall, form
an exhibit hall of miscellaneous old domestic items (one being a
sewing machine just like Aunt 'Cile used all her life) and a shop-
room full of locally made needlecraft items. My grandmother
Jones lived in such a house when I was little. Such houses, de-

signed and built by common people untutored in the arts of building, according to the ways of their ancestors and communities, scholars call "vernacular architecture."[24] It is housing in the everyday language of ordinary folks.

The rest of the outdoor part of the museum consists of some old, rusting nineteenth-century farm equipment, the kind that was used clear through my father's era, and the parts of the cane mill, all surrounded by a split-log fence. The emphasis the parkway developers put on this museum is historical agriculture, not French trading or early American frontier innkeeping. As a child of agriculture in Mississippi, I can identify with this emphasis.

The still old cane mill brings long-buried childhood family and farm festivity to life in my memory. It would be harvest-time. Our fathers and the "hands" (farm workers) cut the stalks of sugar cane in the fields and loaded it on wagons bound for the cane mill. At the mill, one worker fed the cane by hand, stalk by stalk, into a grinding mechanism which was powered by two mules harnessed to a single log pole atop the grinder. The mules were made to walk continuously around a circle, the pole turned, and the grinder was powered to crush the cane, squeezing out its juice below. The cane juice was caught at the base of the grinder in a trough and piped down a slight incline, "down the hill," to the outdoor cooker, a large brick wood-heated vat, segmented into a series of troughs, each one for the syrup to be moved into sequentially as it reached increasing levels of doneness. At the end of the process was a spout out of which the cooked syrup was released into buckets, which were sealed on the spot and then opened one by one through the year in our households as the daily-used sweetener for most of our foods.

The making of the syrup was the climax of the harvest. It was a gala time, a ritual as well as an act of farmwork. The women and children would gather, as well as the men, at the end of the day to taste the making syrup, to skim off some of the least bits of the foamy impurity not good enough to go in the buckets, to sneak a last chew of the season on the lengths of cane before they went into the grinder and were all made into syrup, and to celebrate the mounting numbers of buckets that were sealed up against the winter ahead. We all could nod our heads and smile, speak cheerfully and happily with one another, laugh together and feel satisfied. Now, with the syrup made, everything was going to be all right. It had nothing to do with church, with my family's religious life. My adults did not pray over it as the British do at their annual harvest festival in the Church of England, no doubt the ceremonial source of American Thanksgiving. But this feeling was the way I understood "the peace that passeth understanding" that they taught us children to sing about in church: *It is okay now. We have made it again.* The syrup, that is. And one more season of human life.

(Our daughter sends home a postcard from Botswana, where she is teaching science to Batswana children. The postcard shows sorghum-making. It is the women who are the farmers in Botswana. They have tall poles poised above big containers filled with the grain that they call sorghum. In Africa they pound the mealie grain out of their sorghum with human female energy, not that of draft animals, in order to make their food out of it. Remembering my father and Uncle John's mules and their food-producing work, and contrasting the Batswana women's work, I am reminded of the Afro-American saying that I learned from reading *Mules and Men* and *Their Eyes Were Watching God* by Zora Neale Hurston: "Black women are the mules of the world." Yet I think I know the human satisfaction from sorghum-pounding that the Batswana women must know, that I remember knowing as a child—it too, like much of human life, an ambiguous satisfaction.)

Leaving the cane mill at French Camp on the Old Natchez Trace Parkway, I drive on along the two-landed roadway among more tall pine trees in the deep woods, and I begin to remember that my first introduction to this road was through reading Eudora Welty's fiction years ago. My favorite Eudora Welty story, "Livvie," which I have read many times with college students, begins:

Solomon carried Livvie twenty-one miles away from her home when he married her. He carried her away up on the Old Natchez Trace into the deep country to live in his house. She was sixteen— only a girl, then. Once people said he thought nobody would ever come along there. He told her himself that it had been a long time, and a day she did not know about, since that road was a traveled road with *people* coming and going. He was good to her, but he kept her in the house.[25]

Eudora Welty's book, *The Robber Bridegroom,* likewise is set on the Old Natchez Trace. In the total array of her work, this book appears uncharacteristic of Welty's imagination, out of place in the Welty corpus, unless the reader knows Mississippi history and the history of this road. Welty is actually a very careful historian. *The Robber Bridegroom* is a boisterous, satirical short novel set in a fanciful time when the King of Spain ruled the Natchez District and New Orleans, when planters began to grow rich in Spanish gold on crops such as indigo and tobacco sold in New Orleans from plantations in the bottomlands of streams off the Mississippi River, and when flatboatmen and bandits robbed, killed, and raped people on their travels north on the road. There is a little melodrama in Welty's story: naive Clement Musgrove commits his resources and his reputation to villain Jamie Lockhard, the terror of the trace. There is a bit of the grim fairy tale in the story: jealous stepmother Salome plots with the services of an idiot-boy named Goat to destroy the apple of Clement Musgrove's eye, his daughter Rosamond. There is a bit of strong-woman farce in Welty's story: Rosamond, though unwittingly paired off with Jamie Lockhard, the riverboat bandit, survives his scheming as well as her father's and the plots and lies of the legendary Mike Fink and the Harp brothers to become a fine lady and the mother of twins with an upright Jamie Lockhard in New Orleans. Essential to the story is the Natchez Trace and its reputation, from European colonial times into the early nineteenth century, as a place of terror wrought by the "Kaintuck" boatmen and the outlaws out for their gold. In one place, Rosamond is sent out looking for herbs at her stepmother's command, a command given more to endanger the young woman's life than to secure the herbs from "the farthest side of the indigo field." Welty writes of the road: "First Rosamond went through the woods and then she passed along the field of indigo, and finally she came to the very edge, which was by the side of a deep, dark ravine. And at the foot of this ravine ran the Old Natchez Trace, that old buffalo trail where travelers passed along and were set upon by the bandits and the Indians and torn apart by the wild animals."[26]

Reminded of Welty's stories, I am reminded of the dangers to many people passing at many times over this road. Welty suggests it in "Livvie." Old Solomon's Livvie, a young black woman whose name to me suggests "life," was sprung from the old man's house in the springtime just as he was dying by a young black man named Cash, dressed in a zoot suit. But the young man's name and dress suggest that it was not Livvie's liberation he was after but material gain and her youthful vitality.

Farther down the parkway, I pass a mission church, a church built to Christianize the Indians. Then I stop at the first place that looks really familiar: the Jeff Busby rest area. With picnic grounds, a gas station, and a souvenir shop, the place looks much like a thousand other rest stops at a thousand other locations on U.S. government roads, nowadays most of them four-lane interstate highways. The name, of course, honors the Mississippi member of Congress who introduced the legislation that made this a federal parkway. That, too, is common on other American roads and at other rest stops. I buy gas, a Coca-Cola, and some pamphlets and postcards and drive on.

My last stop, after stopping one more time to see what my new brochure calls "a portion of the original road," is at the Bynum Mounds. There is a display building, presumably for artifacts from the mounds, and the rise of the Indian mounds is visible from the car. Again I am alone at the roadside, again I become quite conscious of being vulnerable as a female alone. Seeming almost like a response to my fears, two old beat-up pickup trucks roar up, both fitting exactly a truck-and-man stereotype with which I am very familiar and have learned to

fear. Gunracks across the backs of both trucks, the scruffy white
men inside seem none too kindly and none too sober. I am afraid
to get out of my car. The anticipated intellectually pleasant moment of seeing the artifacts and the mounds close up is spoiled
for me. Reluctantly, I drive on. I only feel safe on the move, on
the road. As soon as I can, I become practical and resolute. I
turn the car toward my destination, Oxford, my day on the Old
Natchez Trace having played out for me.

It has played, however, the full range of the human spirit.

My next, more sociable project, is to talk with people about
what Mississippi has been like in our lifetimes, what it was like
as they were growing up, what it is like now. In these conversations, too, the place itself, the land and its history, kept coming up.

Interviews with Mississippians about Their Mississippi

On my trip South, in addition to many informative informal conversations, I talked as a searching scholar on the record with
twenty-one individuals about their Mississippi, with permission
and tape recordings or full notetaking. As in all my observations, readings, and conversations, my object was to learn the
meaning of Mississippi to Mississippians, to get the spirit of the
place from those it shaped, commingled with, sent away, or
brought back home again.

Some of my interviewees are famous or powerful or both, and
some are ordinary people. Theirs were some of the words by
which I learned and remembered the ways life has been in our
land, in our Mississippi. One of them was my aunt Erma.

Interview with My Aunt Erma

Aunt Erma was the youngest of my father's siblings, he the second youngest child, so the two of them had been companions
growing up. Eight of the children lived to adulthood—in fact all

Erma Gay Mathers.
Photo by Martha Rose James. Used by permission.

lived past seventy years old—out of the twelve born to their mother and father. They grew up in Wayne County at "the Old Place," in the house and on the land that their grandfather had homesteaded. Their father had been born and later died in that house when my father was nineteen. My father was born there and at thirty-two took my mother there as his bride, to live with his mother and two sisters. As they all understood it, as the farmer after his father's death, he had the care of these women. When paved highways were constructed, the new roads were some distance from "the Old Place," so eventually my family built two houses out on the edge of their land on U.S. Highway 45. By that time, Aunt Erma had married and moved to Matherville, a village fifteen miles away. All the other brothers and sisters except one lived in the county. By the time I was born, there was no house standing at "the Old Place," but my father took my brother and me there with rare pleasure, and we enjoyed his pleasure and the huge oak trees standing in the clearing that was still there. When I was ten years old, at "the Old Place" we had a family reunion which I instigated as Aunt 'Cile's fiftieth birthday party. My father set up sawhorses and boards for picnic tables just as they did at Hebron on cemetery-working-day, and the whole extended family came, except for one uncle's wife and their two sons.

When I interviewed Aunt Erma, she and my father were the only sister and brother still alive. She, the most articulate and best educated of the eight, was nearing eighty years old. She had prepared for my visit with photograph albums, her high school memorabilia, a floor plan she had drawn of the house at "the Old Place," and what appeared to be written-out notes for a speech for my tape recorder! After explaining the house plan to me, she started to tell me what she had planned to about our family history and her and her siblings' childhood and youth at "the Old Place." The following is a part of our conversation. What was important for her to tell me, after telling about their lineage, was telling me about the place and the everyday life of her childhood. "The place" is a general term for a specific location in a rural southerner's speech. For such a person, telling about a place, who the family members are, and what people did on the place captures the essence of Mississippi.

Erma Gay Mathers (EGM): Now let's see. Our grandparents, Grandpa and Grandmother Graham, came from Ireland the day they were married and landed in New Orleans, and, I suppose, had to go by boat to Mobile. And then he got a job helping to build the M[obile] and O[hio] railroad up from Mobile. And I guess Grandmother came along with him. And when they got up around Hiwannee they homesteaded the old home place.

Gayle Graham Yates (GGY): And she had several children and then died young?

EGM: Yes, well, she had three children. There was Papa and Uncle Jim and Uncle Tom. And I don't know just when she died. But she must have died real young. They came from Ireland in 1850. And Uncle Jim, I guess, acquired some land some way or other about a half a mile from us. And that's where he lived. And Uncle Tom was in Shubuta, and he had a meat market there. And Papa was the last one to get married but the oldest one, and he lived at the old, old place. And took care of his parents.

GGY: Do you know anything about the parents before they left Ireland? Has anybody been able to find out? I remember seeing on her grave marker, "Came from Ireland in 1850," but there is not a birthdate, so you can't establish her age.

EGM: No, sure can't. Now he had a sister to come over, and she didn't like it in the South, and she went North [to Rock Island, Illinois]. That was Cousin Lizzie's mother. And seems like another brother came over, but maybe he went back to Ireland. And Grandpa kept sending money back to his parents, but he finally stopped because he just knew they were not still living, as old as they would have been. At the time.

GGY: He didn't hear from them?

EGM: No. His other brothers or sisters or whatever he left over there was just getting the money. And not his parents.

And, of course, farming was the occupation. 'Course
Grandpa Graham was in the Civil War. Well, both grandpas
were. In the Civil War. And now I don't know what age Papa
was at that time. Well, the date of his—their births is in the
Bible there at your daddy's. In the old family Bible.

GGY: Your father's?

Erma: Our father and mother's. And, of course, when the boys
grew old enough they worked in the field. And the girls kept
house and did the housework, naturally. And, as we all say, I
went to school some. The school terms were real short. And
we lived about two miles from what you would call county
roads then, one which is the present Highway 45, and then
the other one was the one that goes out by the Lowreys.
You know where that is.

GGY: Now were those roads covered with gravel, or were
they just—?

EGM: No, they were just dirt roads.

GGY: Flat dirt roads.

EGM: Flat dirt roads.

GGY: Were there any kind of bridges? Or how did you get
over waterways?

EGM: Wooden bridges. Just wooden bridges. They were
bridged across. Except for over Mill Creek—Now you see,
we lived off on this road. It was a dead-end road. Nobody
was living on that road but us, so anybody coming, we knew
they were coming to our house. The creek would get up, and
we couldn't go from there to Hiwannee without going around
the road. We had to go out by Uncle Jim's and go out that
road. There would be a highway. There was a bridge out
that way. But that was the only way we could get out.

GGY: When the creek rose!

EGM: When the creek rose. (Laugh.)

GGY: (Laugh) "When the creeks rise" meant something!

EGM: Yes, it sure did. And, well, of course the girls shared
the housework. Bessie mainly did the kitchen, the cooking.
Minnie Lee did the housecleaning. Of course, Lucile being

crippled couldn't do very heavy work but she didn't fall
down on many things. My main job was washing dishes. And
carrying water for the men in the field. And I would go
down and fish in the stream after I would take the water to
them. Down on—in the bottoms on Carson Creek. And I
would fish down there while they were working.

GGY: What did you use for bait?

EGM: Worms!

GGY: Worms. Where did you get the worms?

EGM: (Laughs) Dug them up out of the ground! Back when
you had a barn and fertilize and all—barnyard fertilize—
why, that was just a breeding place for worms. I had no
trouble getting bait.

GGY: Did you take the men food as well as water?

EGM: No, just water.

GGY: They would come home for dinner?

EGM: They would come home to eat.

GGY: And they would eat a big meal at noon? And even then
Aunt Bessie did the cooking?

EGM: Well, Bessie and Mama, and the others helped. Mama
did—you know, helped a lot. And let's see—You know I
mentioned the well on the back porch. It had lime water, and
it couldn't be used for very much. And most of our water
was carried from a spring down the hill,and that's where we
would go to wash. And, as soon [as I could] after breakfast
I'd go down while Bessie and Minnie Lee got through with
the housework and gathered up the dirty clothes. I would go
down to the spring and wash out the washpot, hunt up old
dead broken limbs that had fallen off the trees and make a
fire around it and fill it with water and have the water hot
when they came down with the clothes tied up in a sheet.
With the four corners brought together. Then after we
would wash them, we would use warm water for the wash-
tub—on a scrub board—you've seen that.

GGY: Yes, yes, I have.

EGM: And then rinse water. And then we would carry them
out. There was a pasture or a field out in the open—this was
all down in the woods—and where there was clotheslines,
we hung the clothes out in the field to dry.

GGY: Now how often did you do that? Once a week?

EGM: Yes, 'bout once a week. As well as I can remember.

GGY: And all the women? It would be your sisters and your
mother and you?

EGM: Doing the washing. Let's see now. And, of course, most
of the food was made at home. Papa was a good gardener,
and we always had plenty of vegetables. There was a lot of
the—some of the fruit we dried, just spread out in the sun
to dry, and the vegetables—

GGY: The fruits would be pears—?

EGM: Pears and peaches.

GGY: Did you have any apples?

EGM: Yes, we'd have apples. Apples and peaches and pears.
And we finally got to canning some. About twice a year they
would go to Shubuta to buy the staple things that we
couldn't raise, like flour—buy it by the barrel—sugar and
coffee and things like that. Oh, yes, I meant to [tell you
about] Uncle Jim's family. Well, they were our closest neighbors. We were all time—*I* was all time having to run over
there to borrow something, especially the iron!

GGY: You were the little one!

EGM: I was the little one, and I remember telling them I was
going to change my name. Cause Erma Gay was too easy to
say! It was, Erma Gay, run do this, and Erma Gay, run do
that! And then days were spent ironing the clothes because
we ironed everything. And we used what we called smooth-
ing irons. And they were heated in the fireplace after oak
wood was burned down to coals. You would always have to
have at least three if just one person was ironing, to keep
one hot all the time. So, Minnie Lee was the main ironer, and
Lucile would help some. And, of course, our clothes were all

Jeannie Griffith. Photo published
by courtesy of Jeannie Griffith.

made at home. Mama and Bessie did the sewing until Lucile
got old enough and started into sewing. . . .

A few years before Papa died, he began to plant strawber-
ries, and he had a pretty good-sized patch. They would make
a lot, and we would pick them, and they would be crated up
in crates and shipped to St. Louis. And lots of times we got
big prices for them, and I know that when Papa—I was
home with the flu about a week before Papa died, and I remember him wanting me to go over to see his strawberry
patch because he thought they were so pretty. And I felt
mighty bad, but I did go up there to see them. He would
show me the different places to look and how fine they were
and this, that, and the other. Then he died just a few days
after that. I was always proud that I had pushed myself off
and went up there.

GGY: Yes. Did you know a long time that he was going to die?

EGM: No. Anh-ah. He got sick one night, I believe it was, and
he died—maybe before the morning—the next morning. He

had a cerebral hemorrhage. And Mama was always a great hand to find something to be thankful for, and I remember after he died, I said, "Well, Mama can't be thankful about anything now." And first thing I knew, I heard her say, "Well, I'm thankful he was spared until my children were nearly grown." I was the youngest one. I was about sixteen or seventeen years old.[27]

My Interview with Mrs. Jeannie Griffith

I was introduced by a mutual friend to Mrs. Jeannie Griffith. A black woman of Aunt Erma's generation, she had worked all her life as a maid and school cafeteria worker and had recently retired. I interviewed her in her home on Pecan Boulevard in Jackson. She told me about her early life near Star, Mississippi. Like Aunt Erma, she told me about her home place and details of everyday life there. As Aunt Erma did, she told me about her school.

GGY: I want to know about your life growing up, and especially how it is different now.

Jeannie Griffith (JG): Well, one difference—you could take a dozen eggs and buy your salt (laugh). That's how we bought our salt and sugar and, you know, different stuff [trade eggs for them]. Take fifty cents and buy enough meat to last you a week. We didn't have any money because money was something of the past. You didn't have any money at that time. Now—you have a little. But you can't take a dozen eggs and buy some salt now.

We came up kind of hard. We were working on a plantation [sharecropping], and we didn't have a home then, and he would give you—the man would give you the seeds and the fertilizer. You'd pay for half of it, and when you picked your cotton, he'd get all of it because you'd used the money buying up fertilizer and seeds to plant. We just didn't ever have any money. He would give you the seed money when you would gin the cotton. Then you would get the seed money, but it wasn't very much in it. And that's how we got the few clothes that we got, other than what our relatives were able to give us. And we would pick berries in the summertime and sell them. Papa would sell them. He would bring them up here [Jackson], and we'd buy something. And I can remember when tennis shoes—we called them then, they call them Keds or something now—were thirty-nine cents. That was when my sister would take a flour sack— you know, the sack you buy the flour in?

GGY: Yes.

JG: Five-pound flour sack. She'd made us little white dresses and put ruffles on them and starch them and iron them and tie a ribbon around them, and that was Easter outfits. That was when we were real smart. And when we went to school to Piney Woods, the only thing that helped us was that you had to wear a uniform. And so we just had two uniforms. We'd wear one and wash it and wear the other one. That's how we went through school. With one pair of shoes and one pair of socks. We'd wash them out every night.

GGY: I want to ask you about food. On the plantation, did you cook garden vegetables, did you can foods?

JG: Yeah, we canned peas and beans and okra and jellies and berries, corn, peaches—whatever. Whatever we could find, that's what we ate. We'd dry peas in the winter. When they dry, you know [after drying on the vine]. You'd eat them green in the summer, then in winter they'd dry and we'd eat them. Potatoes, sweet potatoes, syrup, cornbread.

GGY: Always cornbread.

JG: Right. Not much biscuits. Didn't have the money, you know, to buy the flour.

GGY: But you grew the corn and then had the cornmeal?

JG: That's right. And I remember in the summer, during the time when they say you "laid by your crop." Well, the corn

would be getting hard, and we wouldn't have any meal at
that time, so my daddy would get the hard corn that's just
too hard to eat, to cut and cook, you know? And my mama
would have a grater and she would grate it, and make bread
out of it. It wasn't exactly dry, but it wasn't green enough to
eat.

GGY: Well, that's interesting. Did she invent that?

JG: No! *Everybody*, everybody did that. I'll tell you, you'll do a
lot of things when you don't have anything. That's the way
she had of making out. And I remember when she'd plant
her garden in the spring, and the turnips would get ready.
They were real small, and she didn't want to pull all of them
up. She'd pull up a few and put them in the pot and cook'em.
And then she'd take some [corn]meal, and make some meal
dumplings some way or another and drop in the pot.

GGY: That sounds good!

JG: And we ate that. And the same thing with English peas.
She'd make dumplings for them. We wouldn't have but a
few, and she would make dumplings for that, just to make
enough so we'd have something to eat. And we raised geese.
When we were small, my sister and I, we would be playing
and so we would have to watch the geese. We didn't have a
fence to keep them in. You know, if a goose gets out and you
got peas, or whatever you got planted, they eat them when
they first start coming up. So that was our chore—we had to
keep the geese out of the peas. I was laughin' and laughin'
one time: Sometime we'd get to playin', they'd start out in
the watermelon patch and the pea patch and the corn.
They'd just pull up corn, you know, and just eat it. So we
had to keep them out of the field.

GGY: Did you, then, cook geese at some time?

JG: At Christmastime was our time to have geese. And my
mother would take the geese and pick them. They would still
be alive, you know. She would pick the feathers off and make
pillows and bed mattresses. Then my mama liked to piece

quilts. You know, she wasn't able to work in the fields like the other ladies. And so she would piece quilts. . . . She made lots of quilts. For ourselves and different people.

GGY: Did you or your sisters quilt?

JG: We would quilt when we were home. You know, she taught us how, but that's as far as it went. I did sew. Oh, yeah, you were talking about working. While I was working, the children were goin' to school, I would sew on the side. In the evenings, I would come home, and sew until late over in the night. . . .

GGY: Has Jackson changed [since you moved here]?

JG: Oh! Jackson has *changed!* When I first came here, where I lived before I moved to this house, on the other side of Jackson College [Jackson State University]—they had fields there then. And a lot of places. I worked out in Shady Oak, they call it, and it was fields there. It was just a few houses, and they planted cotton and corn there. But it's populated with houses now.

GGY: Do you think people act much different now?

JG: Yeah, it's a city. When I came here, it was kinda like a country town. Everybody knows everybody. You got neighbors. But you don't have neighbors now. You just see people and speak to them, but as far as neighbors, you don't have that anymore. Not here. . . .

GGY: What kind of lives do your daughter and son and their children lead that are different from your generation?

JG: Yes. When I was coming on, black folks didn't—couldn't do the things that they are doing now. I mean, at least if they could, they didn't have the places to work. My daughter is a librarian at Florence Elementary School, and my son is disabled, but before he was disabled, he was in the workplace. He was a job consultant. He had several jobs.

GGY: Is your husband living?

JG: Yes, he's retired, too. He used to cook. He likes to fish and hunt. He fishes in the summer; he fishes year-round, but when it's huntin' season, he hunts.

Martha Bergmark.
Photo by Gayle Graham Yates.

GGY: Do you fish with him?
JG: No, that's too much like work![28]

My Interview with Martha Bergmark

I think of Martha Bergmark as one of the New Mississippians. Mississippi-born and -reared, white, educated at Oberlin and Michigan, now a Hattiesburg lawyer providing federally funded aid mostly to clients who are poor and black, she was in her mid-thirties when I interviewed her. When I went to her office in downtown Hattiesburg, I had one of my Rip-Van-Winkle attacks of cognitive dissonance. The Hattiesburg I had known and loved as a child visiting my Jones cousins now was entirely bereft of business. As in Jackson, the downtown retail district of Hattiesburg has departed entirely, replaced by nationwide-look-alike shopping malls on the outskirts of town. To see the city center abandoned to office buildings and insurance companies

was as startling to my mind as the existence of the law firm
Martha and her Chicago-bred husband successfully had founded
to serve poor and neglected Mississippians. When I bought ice
cream cones and "went to the picture show" on these streets
when I was "spending the week with Aunt Velma and Charlotte
and them," offices with fat law books like Martha's new service
for the poor and black were unavailable. And for such work to
have been organized by a white woman was unthinkable in the
Mississippi I knew as a child. Yet Martha, whom I first knew
when I was a college student and she was a child, finds her work
well received by many Mississippians. She works hard, though,
at being a mother and a regular person, as well as at being a
lawyer. She is passionate and intense about her work. Her
growing-up days were hard work, too. She described them to
me this way.

Martha Bergmark (MB): I guess as I approached adoles-
     cence—I had a sort of schizophrenic existence by the time I
     reached high school, which consisted, one, of a very tradi-
     tional middle-class Jackson upbringing. I aspired to all the
     things everybody else did: to be popular in school and to do
     well and to be involved in extracurricular activities and to
     involved in church activities. And, on the other hand, that
     was occurring in the early sixties, at a time when the whole
     place was in utter upheaval. And my parents were some-
     what involved in that, so at the same time I was doing
     things that nobody I knew was doing. I was going to Touga-
     loo to meetings at night. I had friends that most of my other
     friends would have considered totally unacceptable. I really
     worked for a time to keep those two lives separate. I
     worked—in the summer I was—the first summer there was
     Headstart in Mississippi, I was a volunteer teacher's aide
     and then the following two summers I got in on the very
     ground floor of the Upward Bound program and was a paid
     teacher's aide at Tougaloo for both summers. So I had
     friends from two completely separate worlds at that point.

GGY: Were they Tougaloo students and faculty?

MB: They were high-school students my age.

GGY: Who were both black and white?

MB: Who were black! There weren't any more white ones! And then what happened—at the end of my junior year in high school. They were slowly integrating the schools. They had started with first grade, and I think they had worked up through first, second, and third sequentially by year. And then at the beginning of 1965, they were to integrate the senior class of the high school, and I was to be a senior. And that was really the first occasion on which I had to face a merger of those two worlds and how I was going to handle that was a source of enormous moment to me.

GGY: Yes.

MB: Because I had really, I had done well in high school. I was the incoming editor of the yearbook. You know, I had a life there. So at the beginning of that year, I was asked—I don't remember exactly how this came about—somehow I came to serve as sort of the orientation counselor for the—I think it was eight, eight or nine, black students who were going to be coming to Murrah [High School], and I knew, because you got your schedules in advance, that I was going to have two of—two of the students were going to be in my Monday morning first-period class. I was going to have to face the decision about how to handle that. And I don't think I slept much the night before. It was really, it was enormously traumatic. Because I knew just how much resistance there was. All the previous year in high school, I had teachers who would talk about what they were going to do to the blacks when they got there and, you know, use extremely racially derogatory language, you know, racial jokes, you know, just as part of the class-period situation, so I knew that it was not going to be a pretty scene. You were really going to put yourself on one side or the other, and you couldn't be in the middle.

I made what I thought was the correct decision, which

was to [join the black students]—and by that time I was
friends with these eight kids. You know, we had been to—
we met at the "Y" down on Farish Street [a black business
district in Jackson]—a couple of times—I don't think it was
more than twice. I brought copies of the school newspaper
and copies of the yearbook and told them which bathrooms
to use because they were considered—where tough kids
go—you know, where they were likely to get into trouble.
Of course, none of that was offered by the school system.
Murrah offered no help or no orientation, or none that I
know of. And as far as I knew, [everybody in the school was]
going to be quite hostile about it. The principal I knew
would be very hostile. So I was friendly to [the black stu-
dents] that morning in class. And then the hardest moment
of the day was lunch. And so I did it—I went to eat with
this group. They were way off by themselves with a buffer
zone of several tables. By the time I got to sixth period,
which was gym class, the gym teacher called me aside and
said, "Martha, you're never going to get to be squad leader
again in my class if you keep associating with them." And I
said, "Well, you know that's just—" And that was so humor-
ous to me. That was the one thing funny that happened to
me all day. The teacher thought somehow being a squad
leader in her gym class should be something that should be
so painful for me to give up.

GGY: Yes.

MB: That was, as I think about it, what motivated me to want
to do what I do now. It had a lot to do with that particular
day. Although it had a lot of background to it. And of course
I had the support at home, which was different from a lot of
kids. People I was friends with were not open-minded
people. They were bright, interesting people, who didn't
have a strong feeling one way or another on the civil rights
movement. Some of them were sympathetic. Many of them,
while sympathetic, couldn't possibly have done what I was
allowed to do, couldn't possibly be allowed to go hear Joan

Baez sing easily or hear a [Martin Luther] King speech or
any of that. So I certainly had it easy in that sense, but I did
feel that there was a sense in which I was called upon to,
you know, to make a choice.

GGY: Yes.

MB: To give up some things.

GGY: And you were on your own.

MB: (overlap) Like being a squad leader!

GGY: (laugh) Yes.

MB: But I did give, it did happen eventually that year. I was
yearbook editor, and we had a good yearbook. The position
pretty much [put the editor] in the hall of fame, for example.
It was just that way, you know. That if you had that position
[of editor], you were automatically "in." And I was not "in." I
was told that I had been blackballed by the advisor of the
yearbook, who used to sit down with the yearbook committee and make fun of the black kids in their senior English
class, [talk about] the way they dressed and the way they
talked, and that kind of thing. And I was just—I don't recall
that I was rude about it, but I am quite sure I was very cold
about it. I was not what the yearbook editor is supposed to
be for this advisor, and I know that. And I know exactly how
she would tell it.

And so then my revenge was on our class day—nor did I
get any of the citizenship awards, which was fine, but I got
all the academic awards. There wasn't any way they could
keep me from it. And that very day, then, the telegram arrived at my counselor's office announcing that I had won a
Presidential Scholarship Medal (one of two from each state,
who would go to the White House and be presented the
award by President Johnson). And that was great. That
made it all worthwhile. They somehow couldn't stop that.

So I think I left high school—I think I related to that
whole experience the way I continue to relate to living here
now, which is fairly comfortable to me. I'm sure other people
may feel a great discomfort about it, because they don't

share the same views, but I left Mississippi to go to college
with the view that I would never be back in Mississippi. And
by the time I was a sophomore or junior in college, I had
pretty much decided that I wanted to come back. And I
wanted to come back with some kind of skill or profession or
something that I could use here. And then followed that
through. I think it was a conscious choice, that I could be
comfortable with that certain amount of schizophrenia. Even
today I feel that I can pick and choose from what I like about
Mississippi, you know, the culture here.[28]

Philadelphia, Mississippi: A Prism for Light on the Mystery of Meaning

After some time traveling in Mississippi as an adult returning
long afterward to my childhood home, in Philadelphia, Mississippi, I found a crystal image for the thing that I was searching
for. Its refracted light gave me clues to the meaning I sought,
to the changes that had come to Mississippi in my adult lifetime,
the changes that have come to us all. It is a particular irony of
symbolic meaning to compare Philadelphia with its Pennsylvania namesake, William Penn's "City of Brotherly Love," where
Quaker pacifism was brought to the Americas and where the
United States Constitution was forged to establish democracy.
Both Philadelphias have fallen short of the their founders' aspirations. Mississippi's Philadelphia is a microcosm of the continu-
ing struggles of the American peoples.

On an autumn drive from Oxford, Mississippi, to Meridian,
my friend Cora Jordan and I went through the main street of
Philadelphia, Mississippi. Philadelphia is a typical small Missis-
sippi town. Mississippi's Philadelphia reminds me of St. Mary
Mead in Agatha Christie's Miss Marple murder mysteries. Miss
Marple, the old lady who is the amateur detective, believes that
all the types of human characters are present in her village life.
To solve a mystery of human motivation, she needs to think on

the villager from her home St. Mary Mead who is most like the person from some other setting she is considering in the current plot. Miss Marple has hit upon a profound human truth.

It occurred to me, in my reverie driving through Philadelphia with Cora, that Philadelphia is a St. Mary Mead. In Philadelphia lies the *Nanih Wayia*, the sacred mound of the place of origins of the Choctaw Nation. The Mississippi Band of Choctaws lives near Philadelphia now. These people are descendants of the Indians who did not go to Oklahoma. Today's Choctaws on the Philadelphia Indian Reservation have successfully combined economic independence for their community with preservation of the traditions of their people. It was in Philadelphia, too, in 1964, that the most brutal of the civil-rights-era murders took place. These murders—of Michael Schwerner, Andrew Goodman, and James Chaney—were committed by officers of the law. Philadelphia is the home of the Neshoba County Fair, one of the nation's most splendid rural county fairs and historically the setting for political rallies that have launched, bolstered, or destroyed many a state and local political career. Ronald Reagan threw his hat in the presidential ring there in 1980. Also in Philadelphia was launched the football career of Marcus Dupree. Born within weeks of the civil rights murders in his home town, Dupree, a black, went to school all his life in the newly desegregated Mississippi public schools. As the hottest football recruit nationally in 1979, he was sought by college coaches all over the country. The waterboy on his team, who idolized him, was the son of one of the white deputy sheriffs who had spent four years in prison for the racial murders.

As Cora and I approached this Mississippi small town after our pleasant drive through the browning late autumn leaves, she commented, "I always get a chilled feeling driving through Philadelphia." And, as if on cue, the letters rose before us on the main street of Philadelphia, spray-painted on the side of a store: "KKK," Ku Klux Klan.

It is all here in a little Mississippi town, just as Miss Marple knows—all the human drama, the pieces of its past as well as its present, its dilemmas and its affirmations, its evil and its good, all of them here for the world to see. Give or take a prop, a cosmetic change, or a change of costume, and we solve many mysteries by watching this one, the one that is whichever one we happen to be in. Or we lose—or gain—our lives. To re-remember, to look again in a different light, and never to forget is to know. Philadelphia and its images became the crystal light for my homecoming journey into America's Mississippi and my own. I traveled many weeks and talked to many people and began again to know this state in many ways—to know it as it once was, to know it as it is now, to know it sometimes for the first time. I began to know it sometimes in horror, in hatred and pain, sometimes in joy and love and exultation; to know it sometimes in familiar discord and sometimes in familiar harmony; and to know it sometimes again in a precious fleeting moment of belonging.

2

Race

Yet, deep down, I knew that I could never really leave the
South, for my feelings had already been formed by the
South, for there had been slowly instilled into my personality
and consciousness, Black though I was, the culture of the
South. So, in leaving, I was taking a part of the South to
transplant in alien soil. . .

Richard Wright, *Black Boy*

Why should a Negro be forced to leave such things? Because
of fear? No. Not anymore.

James Meredith

Rachel Peden saw a newspaper headline on the New York sub-
way that March day in 1961, and our fantastic week away from
Mississippi at a national student religion and arts seminar was
ruined. "Gayle, Gayle," she screamed at me in great distress,
"the sit-ins have come to Jackson, and we aren't there!"

We might nor might not have been there if we *had* been in
Jackson in March 1961, when the first black students sat in at
the Jackson Public Library, in the first public civil rights movement protest in that city, but Rachel's immediate sense of history was correct. The New York seminar had been heady—we
had met Jacques Lipchitz, the sculptor; Edward Albee, the
playwright, whose pair of new one-act plays, "The Zoo Story"
and "The American Dream," we had seen Off-Broadway. We had
met Uta Hagen, the actress; and the director, Alan Schneider.
Alfred Barr himself, the distinguished and extraordinarily influ-

ential curator of modern art, had given us our tour of the Museum of Modern Art. We heard lectures by Tom Driver, theologian and theater critic; and by Amos Wilder, biblical scholar, arts and religion theorist, and brother of playwright Thornton Wilder. Meeting these talented leaders and interpreters of the American arts world and having the exhilarating pleasure of being special visitors in New York City with unusual access to its arts institutions had been a fabulous educational experience for Mississippi girls such as we, but there was no doubt in Rachel's mind that we had missed the big event of our generation by being away from our college city when the sit-ins came. She was right.

History of Race Relations

Race, in all my lifetime in Mississippi and probably in the whole history of the state, has been the dominant cultural divider of individuals, groups, and behaviors.[1] This fact is true in many other cultures of the world and in many other American settings, but the division is exaggerated in Mississippi, both internally by Mississippians themselves and outside by people making judgments and forming impressions of Mississippi. The schism is often interpreted in extreme ways and sometimes in absolute terms. Racism has been particularly brutal in Mississippi in the past, and an impression of that racism is often likely to shape one's entire judgment of Mississippi society as a whole, whether as an antagonist, a sympathetic or casual outsider, or an insider.

And Mississippi's history of racist cruelty indeed has been extensive and shameful. Blacks and whites in Mississippi, but particularly blacks, have suffered mightily from this division by race—from white dominance and control of public social power throughout the generations. Blacks have suffered first from slavery, then segregation, and then racial prejudice, each with its own ideology of the rightness of white mastership and the purity and goodness of white exclusivity. The legacy of white oppression of blacks in Mississippi is not spent, but it has changed. Proud white Mississippians have bent a little to the changes that came in their society, largely against their will as they were watched by an international eye at times over the last twenty-five years. Black activists, both women and men, have stood tall and gained much for black people. And some whites have struggled greatly to support black civil rights, to be open to justice and opportunity for black people, and to befriend black people.

Before the Civil War, Mississippi was a slave state dominated by a plantation economy. Plantations were scattered about the state, once covered with a mixture of crops such as indigo and tobacco and grain, and later with large acreages of slave-worked cotton crops. The largest concentration of the oldest plantations was along the Mississippi River and its tributaries, around the cities of Vicksburg and Natchez and south of them; but by 1850, development of the slave-worked cotton plantation system had become established in the rich delta of the Mississippi River, stretching in a narrow band from Vicksburg to the Tennessee border, an area still considered to be among the finest farmland in the world. The white plantation elite was only a minuscule portion of the Mississippi population. These people were quite distant and alien to the black slaves. They were also nearly as foreign-seeming to my white ancestors, who belonged to a class of men, and sometimes women, who plowed and hoed their own small fields and came to be known derisively as "rednecks," for the rusty, leathery color of their sunburned skin. Yet, in the early years of statehood, the planter class thoroughly ruled Mississippi's politics, economy, and social life. Under this rule, an ideology of black human inferiority was developed to rationalize keeping black humans as property in the slave system.

After the Civil War, early Reconstruction was a hopeful period for opportunity and citizenship for black people. While women both black and white were disappointed that the Fourteenth Amendment guarantees of citizenship rights included only men, black men voted and served on juries and held public office in Mississippi, including U.S. Senate seats. A black man named Hiram R. Revels was appointed to the U.S. Senate by the state legislature in 1870, after Mississippi ratified the Fourteenth and Fifteenth Amendments, and another black Mississippi man named Blanche K. Bruce was elected in 1874 and served a full six-year term.

Segregation, the public and social separation of the races, was not so thoroughgoing before the war as it came to be after. Black slaves had shared churches and other public places, even cemeteries, with whites; but after the war, to some extent, both races—as much as blacks had any influence to decide—established more separate institutions. However, after 1875, the political triumph of the white Mississippi conservatives, a coalition of the old planter aristocracy, merchants, bankers, and lawyers, known as the Bourbons, led to the promulgation of laws that enforced the growing customs of rigorous segregation. Such laws were passed across the South in the aftermath of Reconstruction. They were known as "Jim Crow" laws. The Supreme Court of the United States upheld them in the 1890s. An 1890 case called *Louisville, New Orleans, and Texas Railroad Company v. Mississippi* backed a Mississippi law separating the races on the railroads in railway passenger cars and waiting rooms. *Plessy v. Ferguson* in 1896 upheld segregation in public facilities as constitutional.[2]

Violence against blacks returned after the Civil War and Reconstruction, unrestrained by law. Mississippi had more recorded lynchings of blacks than any other state, 534 between 1882 and 1952, according to historian Charles Sallis.[3] Since such actions are not ones that are readily recorded, the numbers of such violent deaths are surely much larger. To understand the import of this violence, it is helpful to be reminded of the historical development of lynching. At first lynching was frontier mob violence done by any group taking the law into its own hands and any mob violence done to a person, including injuries such as beating or tarring and feathering. After the war, lynching became a white violation of blacks by killing. The provocation for lynching could be quite diverse, sometimes even small actions—anything from arson to writing a letter to a white woman to economic competition with whites.

There is a telling poem in a 1929 collection by a socially prominent white Mississippi woman from Brookhaven, Tallulah Ragsdale, titled "The Lynched Man's Mother Prays." Showing how ironclad the social designation of persons as black was, the poem centers on a son with red hair, suggesting a red-haired and thus white father or grandparent. The boy is nicknamed "Red" by the white men who tease him and then lynch him:

Dey made a pet o' him—
De white men did:
De whole town made a pet o' him
An' had him f'r deir fun
Even when he was a little boy—
A little ragged kid
Wid hair like red fire blowin' t'rough brown leaves,
An' skin ez bright ez a new copper cent—
M'lato spud—
Dey called him 'Red,' an' laughed to hear him talk;
Dey gabe him nickles, dimes, to make
Him say de funny t'ings he said. . . .
Dey made him mad to see him blaze like fire;
Dey egged him on, an' laughed, . . .
He t'ought dat Mister Rufus was his friend;
He bought his Car from Mister Rufus Lunn—
. . . An' how he loved dat Car! . . .
And when a-sudden Mister Rufus tuk
His Car back, cause he owed on hit—
'Bout firty dollars all he owed—
. . . He done went crazy, Jesus—crazy, plum!
An' run an' git his gun.
He sholy wuz clean crazy when he shot! . . .
An' den 'twas like a Cyclone in de town;
De whole place stormed, an' roared, an' clapped, an' flashed,
'A nigger's shot a white man!' 'String him up!'

An' yet he only frazed his arm—
T'ank Jesus dat he hadn't kilt no man!

Dey tuk him frum de Sheriff, quick az dat!
Dey had a rope around him fo' he knowed . . .
Dey hanged him to a tree! . . . [4]

And so it was that the social and economic pattern of segregation and lawless violence against blacks brought a racially divided Mississippi into the twentieth century. The ideology of white superiority and black inferiority, of black service to white authority, and of separation into white privilege and black limitation lasted well past World War II. It was not effectively challenged until the civil rights movement. Into this world view I was born when I came onto the Mississippi scene in 1940, a world view which preceded all others for my generation as well as for the one before me.

This world view is well illuminated by the treatment of Chinese-Americans in Mississippi. Recent scholarship on the Mississippi Delta Chinese has also shed light on the social patterns of discrimination between whites and blacks. James W. Loewen, a sociologist, has written a fascinating book titled *The Mississippi Chinese: Between Black and White.*[5] It illuminates segregation better than anything else I have read. Before I read it, I understood very little of the heritage and identities of the Chinese persons in Mississippi settings. After I read it, their presence had been explained, and so had much more than Chinese-Mississippians alone. The epigraph for Loewen's book is from a conversation he had with a white Baptist minister from Clarksdale, Mississippi:

> 'You're either a white man or a nigger, here. Now, that's the whole story. When I first came to the Delta, the Chinese were classed as nigras.'
> ('And now they are called whites?')
> 'That's right!'[6]

Loewen writes that the first Chinese people, single men, came to Mississippi during Reconstruction. Planters brought them to the Delta, hopeful that they would replace slaves as farm laborers. This did not work, but soon the Chinese men began to establish themselves as grocers in the Delta towns, an occupation their descendants still follow. They maintained essential connections with their families back in China, sending money, returning to marry, and usually leaving wives and children in China, strengthening the family commitment back in China. Careful workers, they were very successful as grocers but had no contact with the towns other than their business ones. They served blacks and whites equally. Sons came from China to work with fathers, and occasionally wives and older children came or stayed, but over the generations the Chinese people remained very close to each other, tied to their homeland, and apart from their Mississippi customers both white and black. Loewen points out that for many decades they regarded themselves as sojourners rather than residents.

However, during and after the 1930s and 1940s, the Mississippi Chinese began to want to identify with and to be involved within their communities. It is then, Loewen shows, that the Chinese became a particularly visible showcase for the workings of segregation and racial discrimination. At times accepted by both blacks and whites as more like them and includable into their group for limited purposes, more often the Chinese were placed by one group into the other and so for the most part left out of both.

By the 1930s, settled into the Delta towns as families, the Chinese began to seek community involvement and inclusion in the power structure. Usually an unorganized group, for this purpose they organized tightly and pressed their case. It quickly became obvious in segregated Mississippi that the white power structure identified them with blacks. When no longer detached from the communities as performers of a single service, grocery sales, the Chinese were required to fit on one side or the other of the black-white caste system. At first their place was clearly with the blacks, as the town authorities would have it. However, during the 1930s and 1940s, the Chinese leaders urged their case town by town, in terms of their children going to the white public schools. Before 1954, all of them had succeeded in being classed with the whites in segregated institutions; thus for education, the keystone of social acceptability, the Chinese were "white" rather than "black" in Mississippi society by that time.

The Mississippi Chinese, Loewen's book makes clear to us, show the workings of segregation more powerfully than a parallel-sized small group of either whites or blacks. There was no room for pluralism in segregated Mississippi, no cultural relativism. People were either white or black, no matter what color they were. The Mississippi Chinese were officially black for some decades, and then, by the political skills and no doubt helped by their unthreateningly small numbers, they became white.

As a young person, I used to wonder why we did not grow up in Mississippi self-conscious of being Italian- or French- or Irish- or Ibo-Americans, like other hyphenated Americans. From the sociology of the Mississippi Chinese, I now understand. In our social structure, it was imperative that we be white or black, and there was no room for subtle variation, for "ethnicity" that would make us more or less one or the other. It was by that principle that persons with a small fraction of known black ancestry were defined as "black," (or Negroes or colored people or nigras or niggers, as, in declining order of politeness, they were known to whites before the 1960s).

Perhaps by now, even the Mississippi Chinese exhibit the pluralism that scholars of American society expound. I met a Chinese-American student at Millsaps College on my visit there. A professor told me of her father's funeral the year before in a small Delta town. He had been a grocer. His customers were Chinese, black, and white. At his funeral, they were all there together, people who did not have anything to do with one another from day to day, the professor told me. There were all sitting there side by side in the 1980s, at the funeral of the Chinese grocer in the Mississippi Delta town.

Mississippi has a history of race relations that is particularly bitter. Yet it has a history of familiarity between people, of close contact as a personal level between blacks and whites, that, while it could be put to use as a distancing mechanism for whites who patronized or persecuted blacks, also could be put to use in restructuring tolerance and respect after the agony of the civil rights fighting. In the rural areas and the towns, houses occupied by blacks and whites are often next to each other. During periods of greatest racial antagonism, white people who had had black nurses as infants had to exempt at least one black person if they were to have categorical antagonism toward blacks. Black people who had had white playmates as children had to remember that at least those particular white folks were not all bad. When the force of the new civil rights laws in 1964 and 1965 and thereafter shattered the import of lifelong custom, knowing one another gave good-willed Mississippi blacks and whites a basis on which to build and an advantage over people in other regions where neighbor-anonymity, rather than familiarity, was the norm.

The long history of white supremacy, intolerance, and racial strife built up. In the 1960s, with the civil rights movement, it erupted, in Mississippi most extremely, in what was essentially both racial and internecine warfare on behalf of the whole nation. And that history quieted, when peace came, to a Mississippi purged of a large chunk of its racial hatred. It has its racists still, but most of them know now that they are racists. And if they do not, now the law of the land is against them rather than with them.

When I went to Mississippi in November 1984, a new permanent exhibit on the civil rights movement, developed under the direction of Patti Carr Black, had opened at the Old State Capitol Museum. Seeing it was one of the first of many experiences I had on that journey of being in something like a time warp. Having lived away from Mississippi for nearly two-and-a-half decades, since the very year of the beginning of civil rights protests in Jackson (on flying visits home as a southern expatriate visiting my parents, I had observed very little), I was to be astonished over and over again: at the extent of change; at both black and white pride in the civil rights achievements; at the amount of true integration of the races—clerks in stores, waitresses in restaurants, blacks and whites side by side, sometimes with blacks supervising whites, black and white friends meeting and embracing in public; at school children at play, a mixed sea of black and white bodies; at the friendships and good relations between whites and blacks. The first measure of such change that I saw was the exhibit at the Old Capitol Museum.

In this splendid old restored building—with its carpets and drapes exact reproductions of the originals, its sober portraits of governors and other Mississippi politicians, its memorabilia from Mississippi's part in the Civil War, and its rich treasury of Mississippi history as military, political, white, and male—the first permanent installation in the wing being devoted to the twentieth century is an exhibit titled "The Struggle for Civil Rights." Housed there are blown-up photographs of black students being arrested by white police officers, of hooded Ku Klux Klansmen before a burning cross, of a solid wave of protest marchers. Framed and displayed are papers and artifacts such as protest literature from civil rights groups and events; placards from the White Citizens' Council; an FBI poster seeking the whereabouts of Andrew Goodman, James Earl Chaney, and Michael Henry Schwerner, the civil rights workers murdered in Mississippi in 1964; painted wooden public building signs segregating the "White Waiting Room" and the "Colored Entrance."

I remember the water fountains, I thought as I stood there, marked "White" and "Colored." In my town there was an outdoor public well at the end of the main business street for drinking water, what would have been indoor water fountains in a colder climate or urban setting. It had a steady flow of constantly running water rising from one central pipe, sent in full public view through pipe joints separating the stream east and west to flow at most only two or three feet apart. It overflowed continuously as drinking water at each separate end from a round-cupped upright pipe, unmarked but absolutely designated in the minds of all the town and country marketgoers, "White" to the west and "Colored" to the east.

The exhibit contains a ballot box, voter registration forms, and a copy of the complicated literacy test that, under the old state voter-registration laws, registrars were empowered to give and to use against blacks at their discrimination. An old television set continually plays a silent documentary of jeering whites behind black protesters sitting in, of the violence against blacks being arrested for demonstrating, of the marches and rallies and the dedicated people, and of Mississippi black leaders such as Fannie Lou Hamer, Medgar Evers, Aaron Henry, and Unita Blackwell. It is a powerful and moving exhibit. We can tell the truth now, the exhibit tells us, Mississippi's children, all of us, black and white, Choctaw and Chinese, and the outside world, too, it too being Mississippi's child. We no longer have an awful, poisoning secret, no cancer growing in our body politic. Our people have risen up and made us righteous, fought a just war inside the bowels of our body and catapulted us in the direction of social health. This is its sign for the world to see. We have risen, risen together out of the ashes of hatred and crosses burning. A new Mississippi is rising from the ashes, a chastened one, one less cocky than before, but one that has given moral leadership under moral testing, one that has been both brave and cowardly for all the world to see, for us all, for all its children at home and abroad to see. This is what I saw at the exhibit at the Old Capital Museum when I first went back to Mississippi.

Patti Carr Black's exhibit makes it possible for us to see. Her exhibit makes us remember and acknowledge what has happened and what has changed. It gives us a necessary ritual. It makes us assess where and who we are and how we came to be in those places and as those persons. My drinking fountain is not in Patti Carr Black's exhibit, but the power of the exhibit evokes it in me and with it the recognition of the inhumanity of the rules that totally separated me all through childhood from the nameless, faceless black people who regularly drank the cool, fresh running water the same as I did, piped from one pipe, but we standing the distance of the east and the west apart, that distance close but complete.

Mississippi has changed since the civil rights movement, the exhibit in the Old Capitol Museum tells us. Ritually recognizing the moral struggle and purifying by fire and violence undergone as a society, the exhibit helps us remember that Mississippi is the better for it these years later.

Even if, as Martha Bergmark says, we still have a long way to go. The goal is still too much unachieved, is her way of saying it.

Later in the year, in a fashionable bar in Jackson, six feminist Jacksonian women, five white and one black, had invited me to have a drink before dinner. We were joined spontaneously by a black man who was a friend and colleague of some of the women and who was greeted warmly and invited to have a drink with us before he caught his plane. As he left first, he insisted that he pay the check, and we let him. I don't know how the other women felt—we didn't mention it—but I felt ashamed, like a relapsed, guilty white-liberal-feminist-dogooder. In our dress-for-success suits, we did not deserve such treatment from him, even if he did carry a briefcase and have on a Brooks Brothers suit. It was a kind of reverse patronizing on our parts. And I was even more ashamed when I realized I would not be giving it a second thought if he had been white.

The Civil Rights Movement

What happened in the civil rights movement in Mississippi?

In 1954, with the Supreme Court decision banning segregation in public schools, Mississippi, as southern historian C. Vann Woodward says of our homeland, took "her historic role as leader of reaction in race policy, just as she had in 1875 to over-throw Reconstruction and in 1890 to disfranchise the Negro."[7]

Black people's civil rights were denied systematically with the laws and court decisions that followed Reconstruction. Blacks were not allowed to use the higher-quality schools and colleges; or the public restrooms, swimming pools, hospitals, parks, and playgrounds that were provided for whites. Most white businesses such as restaurants and clothing stores, and most trained professional people such as doctors and dentists, served clienteles of whites only. In the event facilities had to be shared, as in public transportation, sections of cars or waiting rooms were divided, whites in the front, blacks in the back. In small communities, often no public facilities or services were available to blacks, but custom backed by law kept blacks out of the ones maintained for whites. Government officeholding was inaccessible to blacks. The citizen's jury duty, and with it the right to be tried by their peers, was denied to blacks, along with the basic right to vote. Similarly, the less tangible rights—to privacy, to hold property, to freedom from unwarranted search or seizure, to freedom from fear, to the "pursuit of happiness"—that Americans hold as basic norms and defend as "constitutional," guaranteed by the Constitution of the United States, blacks were not allowed to a degree to that enjoyed by their white counterparts or were denied entirely, all across America but particularly in the South, and within the South, certainly in Mississippi. In Mississippi and nationwide, blacks never ceased to yearn for those rights and sometimes to organize to try to gain some of them, but in Mississippi the price of articulating such yearnings, much less taking actions intended to realize them, was beating, job loss, or even death. Therefore, it is no wonder that, out of fear, many blacks were kept in the place assigned to them by the white-instituted state and local laws and customs.

The 1954 Supreme Court school desegregation decision gave some relief from that fear, and some blacks in Mississippi took that occasion to organize and state their case before the governor. It was to no avail. White Mississippi took both official and private action to tighten segregation after 1954. The infamous literacy test was instituted for voting, allowing local voter registrars to administer to blacks but not whites a test interpreting obscure sections of the Mississippi constitution as a prerequisite for voting. A state law was even passed to abolish the public schools, to keep them segregated if it became necessary. Under the ideology that states' rights have priority over federal authority, a state "Interposition Resolution" was passed, claiming power for the state to refuse to enact the Supreme Court decision. In 1956 the state established a State Sovereignty Commission that was intended to maintain segregation and which had power to conduct secret investigations of persons in Mississippi believed to be trying to undermine segregation. This state agency even gave funds to the [White] Citizens Council, a private segregationist organization, even though providing tax money to a private organization was illegal. In the late 1950s, violence against blacks in Mississippi increased. There were several murders of black men who were leaders of their towns' National Association for the Advancement of Colored People (NAACP) chapters. The terrible 1955 Emmett Till case of the murder of a fourteen-year-old boy in Greenwood, Mississippi, ostensibly for whistling at a white woman, is another example. Anne Moody, writing in *Coming of Age in Mississippi*, tells of this event being the pivotal one in her racial consciousness. She herself was fourteen years old at the time. She writes:

> On my way to Mrs. Burke's that evening, Mama's words kept running through my mind. "Just do your work like you don't know nothing." "Why is Mama acting so scared?", I thought, "And what if Mrs. Burke knew we knew? Why must I pretend I don't know? Why are these people killing Negroes? What did Emmett Till do besides whistle at that woman?" . . .
>
> Before Emmett Till's murder, I had known the fear of hunger, hell, and the Devil. But now there was a new fear known to me—the fear of being killed just because I was Black. This was the worst of my fears. I knew once I got food the fear of starving to death

would leave. I also was told that if I were a good girl, I wouldn't
have to fear the Devil or hell. But I didn't know what one had to do
or not do as a Negro not to be killed. Probably just being a Negro
period was enough, I thought.[8]

Till, a northerner, was big for his age, as well as unaccus-
tomed to the ways of the South. The two men who murdered
him thought he was eighteen. They told a journalist, after they
had been acquitted, that the reason they killed him was not the
wolf-whistle but the fact that he defied them when they rebuked
him and showed them a picture in his billfold of a white girl who
he said was his girlfriend. They took a large piece of machinery,
the fan out of the local cotton gin, and tied it around his neck
and threw him in the river.[9]

I too was about fourteen years old when Emmett Till was
murdered. But I was white. In my community, the Devil and
Hell were all I had to fear.

Nationwide, the civil rights movement is dated from the day
Rosa Parks, a black woman, refused to give up her seat in the
back of the bus to a white man in a routinely segregated Montgomery, Alabama, city bus. Her feet were too tired, she later
told the press. She was, however, a seasoned advocate of black
civil rights, a savvy political participant, and a longtime leader
in the Montgomery NAACP. Her action was taken in accord
with a careful, broadbased plan among the city's blacks. The day
Rosa Parks made history was 1 December 1955. A few days
later, the Montgomery Bus Boycott was begun by the black citizens of Montgomery. They chose for leadership an unknown
young Baptist preacher with a Ph.D. from Boston University,
Martin Luther King, Jr. Nearly a year later, the city of Montgomery desegregated its buses, and a national movement had
begun.[10] The movement phase of the civil rights efforts had
come to an end by 1968. The pivotal events that mark the end
of the movement are variously identified as the passage of the
federal Civil Rights Act of 1964, passage of the Voting Rights
Act of 1965, the election of a number of black state and local

officials in 1967, or the assassination of Martin Luther King, Jr., on 4 April 1968.

The student sit-ins began in Greensboro, North Carolina, on 1 February 1960, when four black students claimed seats at a segregated lunch counter at a Woolworth's store and were arrested. This method of protest by students swept the South, and black students with some white cohorts begin to sit in, swim in, and kneel in at all-white businesses, recreational areas, and churches to protest racial segregation in several southern cities and towns. Whites responded quickly with jeers and violence, police with arrests, jailers and jailmates with ridicule or worse; and the conflict became highly visible, highly publicized, and very tense.

In Mississippi, the first action of this sort was an April 1960 walk by forty-five blacks onto the beautiful Gulf Coast beach that had been reserved for white use. There was violence into the evening in Biloxi.

The first sit-in was at the Jackson Public Library, where Tougaloo College students were arrested for sitting in on that March day in 1961 when Rachel and I were in New York. It makes sense that Tougaloo's students were the first brave demonstrators in Mississippi, for that high-quality private black college long had been effective in teaching its students pride in their black heritage and understanding, courage, and strategies to face derogation of their race. In the late 1950s and early 1960s, a few students from my white-segregated college had been invited to participate in "interracial seminars" by Tougaloo sociology professor Ernst Borinski. The greatest "lesson," of course, for all of us was sitting in the same room together as black and white students, as peers. *As human beings.*

The students' demonstration was not the first civil rights action in Mississippi, however. After the 1954 Supreme Court decision on desegregation in education, the NAACP had activated chapters widely in the state. An effort was made by black leaders to persuade the governor to comply with the Supreme Court action, but that failing, leaders of five NAACP groups, those in

Clarksdale, Vicksburg, Natchez, Jackson, and Yazoo City, began a petition effort for the black children of their towns to attend the white schools. That drive was soon quashed by the white power structure, by such means as firing black petition-signers from their jobs with whites.

Equally if not more important in catalyzing results were organized black economic boycotts of downtown city businesses. The economic boycott in Nashville, Tennessee, in 1960, conducted in tandem with the sit-ins, was a model for the rest of the South. In Jackson, Mississippi, a similar boycott in 1962 was effective. After months of loss of profit due to black pressure, white business leaders were persuaded to compromise.

The countermeasure of white antagonists across Mississippi was organization of the Citizens Councils. Founded in Indianola, Mississippi, in 1955, the Citizens Council quickly became the organization whose local white members entrenched themselves in a segregationist position, and blocked or did violence to the blacks and other advocates of black civil rights who did anything to effect change. The councils were bolstered by the more lawless older organization, surviving from the 1920s, the Ku Klux Klan, the secretive white-hooded riders in the night who demonstrated their racist hatred, the platform of their organization, by violence against blacks and other minorities. The signal of the Ku Klux Klan was a burning cross implanted in front of the home, church, site of a threat, or site of the death or mutilation of its victims.

The founding home of the Citizens Council, Indianola, is a town of special complexity in the annals of American race relations. In the 1930s, although the town's identity is disguised in both the books, Indianola was the location of fieldwork for two now-classic studies of race relations, works well known and highly respected nationally, sociologist John Dollard's *Caste and Class in a Southern Town* and anthropologist Hortense Powdermaker's *After Freedom*. Later in the town's history, Indianola was to make national headlines on both sides of the 1960s civil rights struggle. Besides being the birthplace of the Citizens Council, it was the town where black farmworker Fannie Lou Hamer attempted to register to vote on 31 August 1962. She consequently lost her plantation job in nearby Ruleville and quickly became a leader and a national hero within the civil rights movement, appearing at the 1964 Democratic National Convention, a decisive time for both Mississippi and the national movement, in a moving public testimony about the abuses she had suffered.[11]

After the sit-ins came to Jackson in 1961, the Freedom Riders, many of them students, soon came on buses from Washington, D.C., under the sponsorship of the Congress of Racial Equality (CORE). They were making the point with their demonstration that they considered it illegal on interstate transportation to divide the passengers white and black, to make the blacks go to the back of the bus as was the custom. The Freedom Riders were stopped, shoved about, harassed, mobbed, not allowed to meet such needs as use of toilets, and not served food at many stops across the South. When they reached Jackson, Jackson filled its jail to overflowing with them and then turned the state fairgrounds into temporary jails for the rest. Some of them were imprisoned for two months at the state penitentiary at Parchman.

In 1960 and 1961, the organization of these forms of protests was being done in a loose network of mostly young, mostly student groups. Across the South, the umbrella organization of these groups came to be the Student Nonviolent Coordinating Committee (SNCC). In Mississippi as elsewhere, SNCC was aided and supported by the NAACP, whose members typically were older, locally-established community leaders, as well as by other black activists and black rights organizations such as CORE and Martin Luther King's Southern Christian Leadership Conference (SCLC). In addition to desegregation of public schools and businesses, which the NAACP had been working for, the objective of SNCC's demonstrations was desegregation of all public facilities and services. In addition, SNCC workers wanted to teach black citizens about voter registration and a full range of citizenship opportunity for all blacks. They actively organized "Freedom Schools" to teach citizen rights to blacks and voter registration projects to assist blacks in their attempts to become voters. The student demonstrations also were aimed at making education, employment community services, and health, religious, and recreational opportunities as readily available to black people as to whites—in short, the goal was to overturn racism and its instrument, segregation.

The first voter-registration project in Mississippi was in McComb. A young Harlem-born, Harvard-educated black man came to assist in that project; because of his sharp intelligence, his acumen at strategy, his charisma, and his leadership skills, Robert Moses soon became a significant leader of the civil rights movement in Mississippi and was recognized across the country as such a movement leader.

During 1961 and 1962, there were many demonstrations, arrests, and turmoil in voter registration, sit-ins, and protest marches. Northern activists who joined the efforts were seen by many white Mississippians as "outside agitators" and met with sharp hostility. Many activists, many of them whites but a surprising number of blacks, who were from Mississippi experienced excruciatingly painful rejection by and alienation from their families and former friends. People whose families and friends were with them in the movement were the lucky ones. But going to jail together in a moral camaraderie, if a grim one, forged new bonds of affection and loyalty. Singing freedom songs like the theme, "We Shall Overcome," and facing danger together, demonstrating and going to jail for what they believed to be right, at times risking their lives, brought mutuality and friendship. And, as movements often do, this one had its followers who did not understand its purpose or its seriousness, but who joined in to follow the crowd, for the adventure, for the hope of rebellious and forbidden easy sex, for the heady taste of danger, or for some kind of small or personal settling of scores. On both sides, in both crowds, some people flowed with the crowd. Some people turned bitterly and brutally against their own children, and their neighbors went along unthinkingly, approvingly, turning on them, too. Others went along with the movement, not knowing why, not knowing why not—it was the thing to do. The entrenched whites and their dependents. The movement activists and their camp followers. *Human beings, human beings all.*

A riot in 1962 in Oxford on the University of Mississippi campus preceded the first achievement of black entry into formerly whites-only privilege in the state. On 1 October 1962, James Meredith registered as an undergraduate student at the University of Mississippi. He did so out of very deliberate planning on his part to break through segregation and by federal court order that both the governor and lieutenant governor, acting for the state, had each attempted to defy, but in the end, had only stalled. The evening it was learned that Meredith was in the dormitory and prepared to register the next morning under the protection of federal marshals, white opponents, students and otherwise, gathered in the grove on the campus, and in the words of eyewitness history professor, David Sansing, in his Mississippi history textbook, "The crowd on the campus slowly and gradually turned into a mob. By eight p.m. a full scale riot was in progress. Tear gas was fired into the rioters and the sound of gun shots echoed across the campus. At eleven o'clock about sixty Mississippi National Guardsmen were rushed to the campus to quell the riot."[12]

Vassor Joiner, an Oxford resident, recollects the time:

> You have never seen the likes of it. Fifteen thousand troops. [She was washing dishes with her mother at the nearby University United Methodist Church. They heard all of the noise.] Folks were running around out there and we didn't know what was going on, didn't know nothing, didn't know that they was out there on the campus having a riot. Meredith was out there. You know, Ross Barnett had sent them folks up here and they were all acting up, you know, so I never will forget it.[13]

Professor Sansing continues:

> By two p.m. the first detachment of federal troops arrived on the campus just in time to reinforce the guardsmen who were in grave danger because their supply of tear gas was exhausted. At 6:15 am., Monday morning, October 1, 1962, General Charles Billingslea, the

commanding officer, advised President Kennedy that the riot was over and that the campus was secure.

. . . Later that morning James Meredith was escorted by federal marshals to the Lyceum. At eight o'clock Meredith was registered. . . . [T]he color barrier had been broken in Mississippi.[14]

Also, 2 people had been killed by shots in the crowd and 160 others hurt. Armed Mississippians had faced armed Mississippians as President Kennedy's National Guardsmen, many of them Mississippi men, had fought to stop rioting by other Mississippians.

The national movement was moving to a peak in 1963. That was the summer of the nationwide March on Washington, at which thousands of people gathered in the national capital for a show of strength in support of federal civil rights legislation. In Mississippi as elsewhere, some civil rights supporters had become disappointed that the Kennedy administration was moving too slowly and showing too little support. The meeting in Washington was planned to be an exuberant and challenging demonstration to the federal government and a high showing of cooperation among civil rights groups—SNCC, the NAACP, the Urban League, CORE, and the SCLC, groups that had shown some strain among them and differences in strategy in recent months. The climactic March on Washington was an emotional success but a strategic disappointment, in that there was no tangible response from the government. It was, however, the occasion of the SCLC's Martin Luther King's eloquent "I Have a Dream" speech, probably the most famous rhetorical statement of the movement's aims and a composition that has moved into lasting American political literature as meaningful, moving, brilliant, and beautiful, alongside Lincoln's "Gettysburg Address" and Thomas Jefferson's "Declaration of Independence." I missed the March on Washington, just as Rachel and I had missed the first Jackson sit-ins. A black law student named David Dansby; my husband, Wilson Yates; and I directed a voter-registration project with twelve student workers in summer of

1963, in Nashville, Tennessee, and most of the others in the project went to Washington. I was too pregnant, however, my obstetrician insisted, to make the trip safely. I am sorry I obeyed him and stayed behind in Nashville reading my books. Even so, our daughter, born soon after, has something of the spirit of the movement. Right now, as a Peace Corps Volunteer teaching science to black African children in Botswana, across the dangerous border of the apartheid-bound Republic of South Africa, it is as if she has a prenatal memory of the complexities of world affairs as they mix and mingle in the home and in politics, domestically and abroad. The spiritual child of the jailed singers of "We Shall Overcome" and of the black and white listeners to Dr. King's dream, having missed the March on Washington *in utero*, is making up for both of us what we missed.

Well before she was born and before he and I were acquainted, her father had been the first white student jailed in the Nashville sit-ins in 1960. Only later did we identify the sexism as well as the racism in our group's 1963 version of the movement song, in which an improvised additional verse used not David Dansby's name and not mine, but my husband's—not the black man's nor the woman's name, but that of the white man: "Wilson is our leader,/We shall overcome!/Wilson is our leader,/ We shall overcome . . ." In the ambiguity of all our actions as human beings. *Human beings all.*

In Mississippi, in the summer of 1963, Medgar Evers was shot. At the time of his assassination, he was the state field secretary for the NAACP, a position he had held since 1954. Active in the NAACP and on behalf of rights and opportunities for blacks since he was a high school student, Evers, along with his brother Charles, had been a U.S. military draftee in World War II, and he determined to work for desegregation after his experience of discrimination in the Army. Seen as intelligent, honest, and reliable by his friends, he gave his life to civil rights. He was a leader in college at Alcorn State and, with others, attempted to register to vote in that period, meeting near-violent tension in the confrontation that took place at that time. He helped organize or restore chapters of the NAACP across the state, and in 1954, after the U.S. Supreme Court desegregation decision, he made a bid to enroll in law school at the University of Mississippi, a bid that was denied by state officials on a technicality.

After 1954 he was supported by the national NAACP as its state field officer, and he spent full time demonstrating and organizing for civil rights. A mild-mannered man, committed to nonviolence, he did not retaliate against blows he received for sitting on the front seat of a bus, attempting to use the men's restroom in a service station, or the many other demonstrations he led or performed alone for the overthrow of segregation. Rather, he worked doggedly and thoughtfully to change the attitudes of black people themselves when they held themselves inferior, and to change patterns of discrimination by negotiation as well as by the greatly visible demonstrations. Highly respected in the national organization and popular among blacks, Evers was realistic about the danger involved in his work and took philosophically the many threatening telephone calls that he received, though he prepared his children to face danger. When he was killed on 12 June 1963, the nation's attention was once again riveted on Mississippi and the horror of it.[15]

Local Jackson writer Eudora Welty articulated for many people this horror in her story "Where Is the Voice Coming From?" She writes of her experience that night:

That hot August night when Medgar Evans, the local civil rights leader, was shot down from behind in Jackson, I thought, with overwhelming directness: Whoever the murderer is, I know him: not his identity, but his coming about, in this time and place. That is, I ought to have learned by now, from here, what such a man, intent on such a deed, had going on in his mind. I wrote his story—my fiction—in the first person: about this character's point of view, I felt, through my shock and revolt, I could make no mistake. The story pushed its way up through a long novel I was in the middle of writing, and was finished on the same night that the shooting had taken place. . . . [A]t *The New Yorker* . . . the fiction's outward details had to be changed when by chance they had resembled too closely those of actuality.[16]

Movement leader Dave Dennis remembers both the surprise and the foreboding:

> When Medgar was killed, I had his car all day. I had gone to Canton, Mississippi, came back in, met him at the church, gave him his car, and he told me that why don't I come have a drink. I told him, "Naw, you're a bad risk for me to go with you to have a drink." So we laughed about that. I told him I wasn't going with him; we just laughed. He got in his car and went home, and I got a ride with somebody else that took me home. And a little while later, there was a phone call saying Medgar Evans had just been shot.[17]

Black leaders from all over the country came to Evers' funeral to express their respect and admiration, and Jackson's black leaders were galvanized to renewed action to carry out his work in his memory. Byron de la Beckwith, who made a swaggering racist claim of responsibility for the murder, was acquitted. Mississippi did not yet have black jurors or a climate of lawfulness for blacks.[18]

In 1963, in addition to sustaining economic boycotts against white businesses in Jackson and other places, black leaders demonstrated that blacks were eager to vote by fielding a list of candidates for state office. Official voter registration of blacks had crept at a snail's pace, in the face of the obstacles and attacks facing black persons who attempted to register, yet when asked to "register" for an election with a straw ballot led by the Mississippi Freedom Democratic Party, with Aaron Henry, longtime NAACP leader, on the ballot for governor and Ed King for lieutenant governor, eighty-thousand people "voted."

Robert Moses and his associates—some say Moses alone—decided sometime in 1963 that they needed a contingent of summer student workers from all over the country. Thus was born the Mississippi Summer Project of 1964. For the project, civil rights organizations joined together to form the Congress of Federated Organizations (COFO). There was controversy among factions of civil rights workers in Mississippi over whether this was a good idea, with some feeling that local black leadership deserved higher priority, but in the end the project took place. Some say that the guiding reasoning behind the project was the calculation that nationwide public attention and federal protection would be afforded more to northern white students than to local blacks. Students were recruited from all over the country to come and work in voter registration, in Freedom Schools, and in other forms of education.

The students were trained on a college campus in Oxford, Ohio, and came to Mississippi, to be met with severe threats to their safety insinuated from the dug-in white establishment. The summer's events in Mississippi were in the daily news around the world. Very early in the summer, Michael Schwerner, James Chaney, and Andrew Goodman disappeared from Meridian, Mississippi; and the largest search the state had ever seen took place. Weeks later, led by an FBI informant, the FBI found their bodies buried eighteen feet deep in a earthen dam near Philadelphia, Mississippi. Schwerner was a Cornell graduate and a native New Yorker who, with his wife Rita, ran the COFO office in Meridian. Chaney was a young black Meridian man who was attached to COFO and its work. Goodman was one of the student volunteers who had arrived just the night before they were killed. Their murderers were Ku Klux Klansmen, some of whom were also county law officers.

The summer was a turning point. While there was considerable violence and little evidence of tangible success, hundreds of blacks came to believe that their hopes for citizenship could be realized, and some communities of white people decided that they had had enough. Continued resistance could only destroy the whole society. The national attention contributed to getting the civil rights law passed. And the murders early in the summer probably saved the lives of more of the workers. Yet, as it was that summer thirty-seven churches were burned and thirty homes and office buildings bombed. One thousand people were arrested, and eighty reported being beaten. To some in the civil rights movement, it was known as "Freedom Summer." To others it was "the Long, Hot Summer."[19]

In 1964, the Mississippi Freedom Democratic Party challenged the state's regular delegates at the National Democratic Convention. The regulars walked out. During the convention, Fannie Lou Hamer was asked to tell her story, and when she did so, it was broadcast on national television. In 1968, regular Democrats were not allowed the seats at the convention, and by 1971, the Mississippi Democratic Party was integrated.

This was not the end, but it was the turning point in the civil rights battle. A racially instigated shooting occurred at Jackson State University in 1967. With new federal legislation, Head Start and other federal programs that served racially integrated or black groups drew attention away from the movement itself. Then, in 1968, to revive interest, James Meredith began a march from Oxford to Jackson. At first it was lonely, but then he was shot and injured. The march into Jackson was twenty-thousand strong. During that march, Stokely Carmichael cried out, "Black power!" In the Jackson rally following the march, there was much divisive talk. There was a new slogan, "Black Power," but it split the movement.

In the late sixties, some legal changes came. School desegregation plans were made. While many communities created segregated private academies, most put into effect the new law and eventually had children of all races attending one integrated system of public schools.

After the Movement

Many Mississippians white and black have been damaged by their participation in the civil rights movement and its aftermath. As in any war or enmity, the participants did not consider that some individuals or groups invariably suffer a crushing or limiting of the spirit after the action of struggle and fighting

Anne Moody. Photo by Gayle Graham Yates.

have passed. Some people died, and countless numbers were hurt directly in the front lines of the civil rights movement battles; undoubtedly some people grieved themselves to death over their losses, and some choked to death on their rage over civil rights movement events. But when the battles were over, the laws had been changed, and even some political practices and social customs had been altered for the greater freedom and full citizenship of all Mississippians. Other people, however, were surprise casualties of the very process of the struggle itself. They were like the veteran-victims of the Vietnam War or even of those holier wars, World Wars I and II, returning home to find no special glory to equal the "high" of the war itself, coming back to plain everyday life with no special skills and psychic wounds so deep and so foreign that these people became unrecognizable even to themselves. Some such Mississippians fled. Others buried themselves alive in some remote part of Mississippi. Still others tried to go about some normal life. Some succeeded, but others were damaged for life.

Anne Moody was such a soldier.

Anne Moody was a civil rights leader who took twenty years to recover from her battle trauma and to feel safe to return to her native Mississippi. To help to heal herself, she wrote her autobiography, a book which explored her childhood and youthful development in rural, black Mississippi poverty and segregation until its climax in her student days in civil rights movement leadership in the early 1960s. To aid in the healing, she went far away and lived in New York and Europe, Paris and East Berlin. She had to tell over and over again how, burned out from her years of movement organizing, protesting, jailings, aggression, and terror, she left Mississippi. Suddenly, she had had enough and left one night after seeing a young man named McKinley in Canton, Mississippi, "get his brains spattered all over the church grounds. That was just too much."[20]

After a long time in far-distant places, Moody came to find some relief from her Mississippi wounds. At last, in the woods in a special part of the Black Forest in Germany that reminded her of the beauty of Mississippi woodlands that she had loved, she and her husband made love, literally, in the woods; and she felt alive again, felt something for Mississippi. This brought her back to recognition that she could remember and love some parts of Mississippi, and that eased a bit the pain of the shell-shocked memories of Mississippi destructiveness, white hostility, and killing that had filled her for some years and had pushed out the beautiful woodlands and supportive friends that also had been hers in Mississippi. From that lovemaking in the German woods, as she tells it, her son, Sasha, was conceived.

Fifteen years later, she could return triumphant as a hero to Mississippi, with fourteen-year-old Sasha by her side, return as a celebrated world-class literary figure, revered by whites as well as blacks for the very work she had written to make sense out of her civil rights agony, *Coming of Age in Mississippi.*

Invited in 1985 by the University of Mississippi and other formerly all-white colleges to come on a lecture tour, and coming from New York, which is now her home (no longer Paris, as is often rumored), Anne Moody told an audience at Millsaps College:

> In 1963, I was one of the first black students to integrate Millsaps. Eudora Welty was giving a reading. A Tougaloo student group with John Salter and Ed King [both movement leaders and Tougaloo professors at the time, both in the audience that February 1985 day as well] had spoken with Miss Welty, and she said she did not want her readings to be exclusive. I love Eudora Welty. I had read her work. I had the opportunity to come here to hear her as one of the first black students. We came in. Millsaps did not make a fuss. We were very uptight. But there was not an incident. I spoke with Miss Welty. Now I am told you have one hundred black students. [A black student told her after the lecture that that number was more like fifty.]

So, she told her audience, it was very special to come back to Millsaps as a lecturer and with an audience almost equally divided between black and white members: "I think Mississippi is making quite a bit of progress. I'm happy to appear here as not the only black here."

Coming of Age in Mississippi ends in 1964, she reminded us in her audience. In that year she went off to New York after having seen McKinley get his brains spattered out. "I came from Canton," she said, "and I found this bus sitting on the yard there. I didn't have a toothbrush, not a penny, not anything. I got on that bus. I went to Washington, D.C. I went to testify at the COFO hearings. I didn't come back to Mississippi for eleven years."

She said David and Carla Cohen of Common Cause and athlete Jackie Robinson encouraged her most to write the book. She said she had gotten to know them just before she left Mississippi, when Chaney, Goodman, and Schwerner were missing. It was a long time before the bodies were found. She was giving a talk the night she heard they were missing, and she "just knew" they were dead. She talked for three hours at the meeting, which was for raising money for CORE [Congress of Racial Equality]. She raised twenty-thousand on the spot. After that she was assigned to raise money across the country. She was assigned to raise money with Jackie Robinson for a community center in Meridian.

"The man who was sponsoring this fundraising," she said, "wanted me to go to Europe and get over being 'shell-shocked,' but I said no, not this time. I'm in too much pain. I'm too angry. I want to write it where all people can read it and get something out of it."

She took a job working for Cornell University for two years. And then, when she was not hurting so badly, she wrote the book. My edited notes record the rest of her talk at Millsaps; my added comments are in brackets.

I wanted to write about what made me this kind of person, how it came about, how I came to hate racism. We couldn't change so much. We [the movement] were like an angry dog on a leash. The master could tighten up on the leash, could kill. In the North, I was too close to see the implications of what had happened. I had come full of idealism and hope, but I learned quickly. We were too self-absorbed in the Negro problem. Human rights, not just ours, was the problem, the fight of every suppressed person. We have yet a long way to go in Mississippi before black persons and white persons can sit down together and look each other squarely in the face.

In 1967, I married in New York a Jewish guy from Brooklyn. My son was conceived in Germany. We came back to this country just so Sasha could be born in the country [the United States]. In Speissard Nature Park in Germany—this is a place where Germans go. I really didn't know that I loved Mississippi so much. Our tall pine trees. I had been told by doctors everywhere that I couldn't have a baby. But when I got to those woods, I was so happy. These woods re-

minded me of Mississippi. I was reliving Mississippi. My
husband and I made out two or three times a day—literally—in those woods. Mississippi created him [Sasha] in
Germany. He only spoke German when we first came back.
He was being kept by a German family. He was identifying
with the children. "My son!" my husband said. "A Jew living
in Germany, and my son only speaks German."

On a train, we said, "Go over and tell that black guy to
give it to you!"

Which one is the black guy?" Sasha asked.

As soon as my divorce was over, we went back to France
for five years, and Sasha's education has been French. There
will come a day when kids will be so innocent, like Sasha
was, that they will not have black and white matters. My
grandchildren will live to see the day when America—and
Mississippi, too—when it won't matter. There's not much
difference. It's America. Mississippi is a little tougher than
some places.

Things have changed. This Friday the Dan Rather news
hour [CBS Evening News] is doing footage on the civil
rights exhibit at the State Capitol Museum. [In the broadcast Anne Moody was shown visiting the exhibit.] The psychological changes are one of the best results of the movement. We believe black is beautiful. It doesn't matter about
nappy hair. Black women are among the most beautiful there
are.

The questions from Moody's audience came from both black
and white students, who boldly asked her if she didn't think she
were overly optimistic that blacks and whites could get together, could be friends. White students and black students
alike seemed impatient with her on that point. That was the sole
theme of the question period. It revealed a lot about what 1980s
Mississippi students feel. Most of them were enrolled at Millsaps, the college which Moody had told them had no black students in 1963.

Moody struggled patiently with their questions. "Think back to my time," she beseeched them. "Sitting hearing Welty read. Somebody might have split my head open [just for being there]."

In Anne Moody's audience that 1985 day at Millsaps was her white Tougaloo chaplain and fellow leader from the Mississippi civil rights movement days, Ed King, himself a 1958 Millsaps graduate. King is now on the staff of the University of Mississippi Medical School in Jackson, and that winter of 1985 he and his movement cohort, John Salter, were doing research for the ACLU on the papers of the Mississippi Sovereignty Commission, an extralegal antidesegregation state commission formed in the civil rights years.

Ed King and his former wife Jeannette had been my friends when we were students. Jeannette Sylvester was the senior dormitory counselor in Founders Hall when I was a freshman, and we younger women watched eagerly as the romance developed between the two presidents of the non-Greek social clubs at Millsaps. He was "Eddie King" in those days, and Jeannette sometimes called him "Ed-eye," affectionately, humorously, a nickname I thought fit the gangly, serious, big-eyed preministerial student she was about to marry. Later we all spent one of the same years in the Boston area as students, and Jeannette and Eddie had my husband and me over for a home-cooked Chinese meal, something quite unusual to me at that time prior to my own gourmet-cooking phase. The year the Kings returned to Mississippi for him to become chaplain at Tougaloo, a black college, Ed King was refused ordination in our Methodist judicatory, the Mississippi Conference of the Southeastern Jurisdiction, all-white at the time. Black Methodist churches at that time belonged to the Central Jurisdiction of the same national body. The year Ed King was refused ordination because he was going to work on a black college campus, I was the national president of the Methodist Student Movement, and I still have a copy of the blistering letter I wrote on my national official letterhead to our Methodist bishop in Mississippi about Ed's not being ordained clergy in his own church. As hot letters do, I have slowly learned, mine probably did more harm than good.

Ed King dedicated much of his life to the cause of black civil rights, and he has a massive scar covering half of his face to show for it. That scar on Ed King's face is a symbol of the unexpected damage done to some Mississippians by the civil rights movement, damage from which some have never recovered.

King himself wrote about the accident in which his face was irreparably damaged in his foreword to John Salter's book, *Jackson, Mississippi: An American Chronicle of Struggle and Schism*. He wrote of a day on which Jackson's movement leaders were scheduled to have a secret meeting with U.S. Justice Department officials, a day on which he believes he and Salter were attacked with the intention of their being destroyed and, with them, their movement leadership:

> Then, as we drove home, police cars followed us. We never reached home. Several miles out of downtown Jackson a car driven by a white man darted out of a side street toward us. Salter was driving and tried to avoid the collision. The streets were wet from rain. In the maneuvering a third car, driven by a Black woman, was struck by the white man's car and forced to crash into us. Salter was seriously injured and I was almost dead. The white driver (whose brakes failed, according to white police reports) was uninjured and had only minor damage to his car. The Black driver of the other car was also uninjured. Soon Salter and King were in the hospital instead of in the prison—and instead of in the Movement strategy meeting.[21]

The scar that is left on Ed King's face from that accident surely must have been borrowed as a symbol in the novel by Rosellen Brown, *Civil Wars*. The central male character of *Civil Wars*, Teddy Carll, has an enormous, vivid, sometimes vibrating scar on his face: "Under the places where the surgeon had stretched tissue, added skin, stuck on flesh like a baker mending broken pie dough with moist fingers, his body would speak up: pain, real pain, it would say."[22] In middle age, Teddy is a textbook salesman who has a master's degree in sociology but still holds to his past glory as a leader in the Mississippi civil rights movement of the early 1960s as the center of meaning and sustenance for his life. I see in Teddy Carll the sociology education of

John Salter, the traveling sales work of Medgar Evers, and the scarred face of Ed King. Jessie Carll, the female hero and his wife, is equally complex and probably drawn equally from Mississippi movement models. But Jessie, unlike Teddy, has come to terms with life in 1979: "Her children were half grown, and the days of Earnest White Girls for Integration were over."[23]

The novel, set in 1979 in Jackson, Mississippi, deserves its title *Civil Wars* on a rich list of levels. The civil rights movement often was called "the second Civil War." The South historically has been preoccupied with the Civil War to the extent that such preoccupation is one measure of a "true southerner." There are no parallel Union history buffs in the "North": New England, the Mid-Atlantic States, or the Midwest. The period of the civil rights movement was a second period of serious civil upheaval, of violence and death, of racial conflict, and of antagonisms that drew deep and horrible lines of divisions within families. Neither of these periods was very "civil," in the other meaning of the word, courteous.

In addition, at the literal level, Brown's novel is about a domestic relationship, a marriage, about its "civility" and warfare. Teddy and Jessie Carll are a married couple who have been civil rights movement activists. They met in Ohio at the training session for students participating in the 1964 Mississippi Freedom Summer, Teddy as a Mississippi native, a white movement leader instructing the students; Jessie as a politically tough volunteer, the New Yorker child of Communist parents, not overwhelmed by radical politics as so many of the students were. Although they were in the movement together, Teddy, having been at the forefront of everything, trusted by everyone, yearned for by all the women, sought out for advice by the men, jailed more times than he could count, wounded so badly he was said to have come back from the dead, had gotten national and media attention, his style and his speeches becoming "classics." He and Jessie had moved into a black neighborhood next door to a biracial couple also out of the movement, who were also their best friends.

Now it was over. Jessie taught in an alternative school; Teddy sold textbooks. Their son Andy was a teenager, their daughter growing up. Jessie wanted a larger, more convenient home. Teddy harangued her about selling out. He was often empty and listless, brightening only at promised regeneration of movement work. Into this situation come two improbable orphans, Teddy's racist sister's children, and so begins the intricate rich tale of the end of a marriage and of the innocent hope that time will be kind, will stop, and will let humans have it their way. For its heroes and victims alike, by the 1970s the civil rights movement was over. Life goes on, sometimes as cruel and hard in its dailiness as in its crises. With the four children, her teaching, his malaise, and eventually a flood to cope with, Jessie surpasses Teddy emotionally and becomes the decision-maker for them both. Near the end of the book, she ruminates on what form their identities have taken: "But the two of them were too deformed by their pasts, she thought, to be so endlessly malleable; they had to live bent out of shape to fit each other. . . . there was another thing she was going to tell him: that she had one answer, at least, to the question of who he was, who he had become. He was the hunger artist of the seventies. He wanted to perfect his fasting; he would never let himself be satisfied again."[24]

Civil Wars is a fictional account of the social fabric of a post-civil-rights-movement Mississippi family—and of post–civil-rights-movement Mississippi. With a character who is a sociologist, the novel provides a text for social interpretation of Mississippi's recent past that is a beneficial case study for work a sociologist might do to explain society.

One Sociologist's Experience

On one occasion in my Mississippi journey, I had the opportunity to observe a Mississippi sociologist, Vaughan Grisham, at work at the front of his classroom. Though not a Teddy Carll in move-

Vaughan Grisham. Photo by Jack
Cofield. Used by permission.

ment celebrity or interpersonal deterioration, this working sociologist displayed all the agony and the passion remaining
within Mississippi activists these many years later. In a skillful
interdisciplinary lecture combining sociology, literary analysis,
and current history, Grisham also showed himself to be an ex-
periential scholar, engaged and even tortured by the civil rights
past.

On the morning of 19 March 1985, I had tried unsuccessfully
to go to a University of Mississippi Afro-American studies class
on "The Experience of Black Mississippians." However, Professor Ron Bailey had cancelled his "Afro" class that day in order
to be in Washington so at the same hour that it met, I went to
another building where perhaps fifty white students and one
black student were gathered in the interdisciplinary southern
studies class for Vaughan Grisham's lecture. The students' reading assignment had been the novel by Mississippi writer Ellen
Douglas, *The Rock Cried Out*. Douglas' book, like Rosellen
Brown's, is an after-the-movement saga of a longhaired white
1960s Mississippian, Alan McLaurin, who returns to Chickasaw
Ridge in Homochitto County seven years later to recover from

his memories of 1964: racially instigated church burnings, severance from his father over his conscientious-objector draft choice, and the violent death in a car accident of a cousin he loved.[25]

The lecture is on race relations and the civil rights movement in the South, also the topic of the Douglas novel. Before he starts, Grisham announces that Josephine Haxton, the woman who writes using the pseudonym Ellen Douglas, will be in the class on April 2. On April 11, Charles Wilson will lecture on religion in the South.

Grisham begins his lecture. He refers his audience back to the ideas of sociologist John Shelton Reed with whose book, *The Enduring South*,[26] they began the course. He reminds the class that Reed characterizes the South as having especially pronounced measures of localism, religiosity, and violence. These are the features of the "ethnicity" of being southern, Reed believes. While Reed recognizes race relations as a theme important to southern identity, he did not treat it in the questionnaire for his study because of the high emotionalism surrounding it, Grisham tells the class. Reed sought characteristics of the South that helped preserve "southernness," and he believes he found three: localism, religiosity, and violence.

On the first one, localism, "attachment to locale," location, Grisham points out in his lecture, Ellen Douglas does well at showing in her novel, *The Rock Cried out*. She fills in the skeleton Reed provides in his sociology. He quotes from the novel the point at which Miriam, Alan's northern girlfriend, tells Alan what she thinks of his Mississippi:

"How can you stay here? Come away with us."
"Do you think there is someplace in the world that is different from here?"
"Yes, I hate your seafood gumbo and picturesque darkies, your ridiculous cabin."[27]

In order to study such localism, Grisham tells his students, he often takes his sociology classes out to a rural Baptist church. Sometimes it is Methodist, but in the rural South Methodist and

Baptist churches are interchangeable, Grisham claims. (I sit in his audience and disagree silently, but that is a different story.) Sometimes in rural communities they have church one week at the Baptist church and one week at the Methodist church. People's strong tie is to that rural church. "You should visit it before it dies out," Grisham enjoins his students. Grisham himself visited such a church in the 1970s, and he was the only one there with a matched suit of coat and pants. He could tell that the men had coats bought at the end of World War II. They had once been parts of suits. Now the men had newer, different pants, but they had not worn out their coats. The church service was very emotional, Grisham reports. The worshippers worked up into a frenzy. Ushers went out and put ammonia into little vials.

Once in a church near Pontotoc, Mississippi, Grisham says, he heard a sermon on "The Red Line of Hell." Grisham had studied homiletics, had been a theology student, had been with the Billy Graham crusade, but he hadn't before seen anything like what he saw that night near Pontotoc, Mississippi. They put the lights out, the preacher held a red lantern up to his face. It was black dark, hypnotizing. "You'll see the devil like this," the preacher said. "No doubt there were many dirty pairs of underwear before that service was over," Grisham said. "That preacher had those psychological skills to pull on people. Like Dallas [the character captivated by evangelical fundamentalism] in the novel [Ellen Douglas' *The Rock Cried Out*]."

You have to understand the poor poor in Mississippi in the 1940s and 1950s, Grisham continues. Religion gave them hope. "Not much hope, but some hope. You begin to understand their care of the cemetery. You begin to understand 'homecoming' when everybody comes to clean up the cemetery. You see the links between sexuality and religion." Where he pastored, Grisham says, they always invited the same group back to sing. At first he did not understand, until the men said they "saw the sights" of a big-busted woman in the group who would stand by the window in such a way that her underwear showed. The women would take that occasion to go outside and fix the tables, while the men stayed and watched the woman standing by the window singing with her underwear showing.

Reed's third characteristic of the South, violence, is also prominent in the Ellen Douglas novel. Grisham mentions the car wreck in which Alan's cousin was killed and its effect on everyone's lives. As I listen to Grisham, I think of the church burning and its centrality to the novel. Grisham says that John Reed pulled back from race relations because it added too much emotionalism to his questionnaire. Douglas adds race relations, and it permeates her novel, he points out.

Sam Hill, that spring the Eudora Welty Professor of Southern Studies at Millsaps, a sociologist and close friend of Grisham, had frequently told him: "You need to get your book done on race relations in the South."

"I can't. It is too painful," Grisham says. "I had people spit on me. There were sixty-seven threats on my life. Tommy Terrence, a Ku Klux Klan leader, had been my good friend. He told me he personally would kill me. One month the Klan followed me every minute. Going down to Jackson once, they pulled up next to my window, and I saw a shotgun coming through the window. But the guy just flipped me a bird and drove on. For me, to this day, it is very, very painful."

Vaughan Grisham turns away from the present, back to history. He puts dates on the blackboard and sums up events regarding race relations in American, southern, and Mississippi history from the 1870s to the present. Grisham says that he has interviewed hundreds of people white and black about World War II, asking, "Could you see that desegregation would come at the end of the war?" When, after the war, they began to sense the end of segregation, politicians began to be more overtly racist. Grisham has studied Theodore G. Bilbo (the most notoriously bigoted of Mississippi's twentieth-century politicians, who served as both governor and senator) rather carefully. "In 1946, it almost becomes who can be the most racist," Grisham says. Bilbo was so blatant in his racism that the Senate voted to censure him. He died of cancer in 1947. John C. Stennis replaced him. "Bilbo was a very smart, calculating man. A slick little bastard, he regarded himself. He was shrewd, politically astute. He was very careful, then became very foolish. In 1946 he wrote a letter, 'Dear Wop, Keep your goddamned nose out of my business. In Jew York, nobody has any right to interfere in my campaign.' The Italian New York woman to whom he wrote this letter put it in the *Times*. He was so racist in his 1946 campaign that some of his constituents were so embarrassed they sought a nonracist man (Tom Abernathy, who won in 1952)."

The tone during the war was that segregation was going to end, but the South dug in and resisted. In 1945–50, the literature was very emotional, Grisham continued. "A more balanced book of that time is Hodding Carter's *Southern Legacy*. There was a kind of dual mood: 1) Segregation is going to end. 2) But the South is going to make one last effort to maintain segregation, one last exercise to hurl themselves into this racist effort."

There were race-baiters such as Bilbo. But also, behind the scenes, conservative businessmen worked to improve economic conditions in the South. Grisham argues that these businessmen paved the way for desegregation. "If you change your technological base, you also change your ideological base," Grisham says. "So with changes by the 1970s from farming to manufacturing, you can expect change in ideas."

The South is the poorest section of the U.S. In 1970, the very poor in the South were very poor indeed. Twenty percent of the people had 4.5 percent of the wealth. Twenty percent of the people had 43 percent of the wealth. There was a vast difference.

It was in 1954 that Grisham first saw the movement in the literature. The movement centered around church. The countermovement, the Klan, also centered around churches. In 1954, there were five cases regarding race relations and segregation before the Supreme Court. *Brown v. the Board of Education of Topeka* was the decisive one. The Brown decision said that segregated facilities were unequal, unconstitutional. Grisham describes the civil rights movement. In 1955 and 1956 there was the Montgomery Bus Boycott, and the movement spread from schools to public accomodations. In 1963, there was the Birmingham response. In 1965, the Selma march. In 1964 and 1965, the movement culminated in the Civil Rights Acts, 1964 public accomodations, 1965 voting. From 1950 to 1960, there were six deaths from civil rights actions. Between 1963 and 1968, there were ninety-seven deaths. It heated up. The Douglas book is set right in the heat of 1964–71.

The bell rings, and Grisham laments that he has barely started what he prepared for the heart of his lecture.[28] The students gather their books and backpacks and amble out. Another day, another lecture. But I see Grisham and his wife two hours later, after lunch, and he is still keyed up. His wife says he had been practicing before the mirror when he was shaving that morning. I got the feeling that I had heard a terribly important lecture. There were at least two of us for whom it was very significant. What I had heard from Grisham was palpable and alive, painful and unresolved, the living past.

3
Politics

Them Democrats has got theirselves in a heap of trouble.
Overheard in a roadside restaurant
near Philadelphia, Mississippi

Former Gov. Cliff Finch died the day before I interviewed former Gov. William Winter. The Mississippi and Memphis newspapers and the television news were full of tributes to Finch. Finch, a Democrat, had defeated Winter in the Democratic primary in 1975. Winter came to victory in 1979 at least to some extent because of charges of scandal and governmental mismanagement against the Finch administration and federal criminal indictments against some of Finch's key appointees in his administration. Finch was a thoroughgoing populist, Mississippi variety. Born into extreme rural poverty, he worked his way up through early education and law school, the state legislature, and district elective office. Very much an underdog when he announced his candidacy for governor, even ridiculed by some political professionals, he made carrying a lunch pail—a rural "dinner bucket"—and driving a tractor his campaign hallmarks. He captured the imagination of the many rural Mississippians, white and black. Black leader Aaron Henry said that Finch made a coalition of what he called "rednecks and blacknecks," something that had not been done in state government before. His was the first administration to include a mixture of black and white officers.[1]

Winter, an erudite, cosmopolitan, and sophisticated personality and a patient, cautious liberal politician who had had a life-

time career in Mississippi politics and who had supported John
F. Kennedy for the presidency in 1960, seemed more likely to
have been the first-of-his-kind Mississippi governor to head a
black-and-white, liberal administration. However, by losing to
Finch, he lost the timely initiative that 1975 could have given.
It was not until the mid-1970s that the racial conflict of the civil
rights movement era cooled in Mississippi, 1971 before blacks
voted in large numbers without hindrance or obstacles set up by
state and local officers themselves. In 1971 also, several black
individuals were elected to public office, including the state legislature.

In Winter's 1979 primary campaign, his leadership was as-
sailed by charges not so much of racism as of sexism. Gender
was introduced into the race by the presence of Evelyn Gandy
on the ballot. Winter defeated Gandy in the Democratic primary
for governor in 1979, but some voters perceived his campaign
against her to be "antiwoman."

It was a complex issue. Gandy was the first "electable" female
gubernatorial candidate of a major party in Mississippi. She had
been elected lieutenant governor in 1975. Although in Mississippi the lieutenant governor and the governor do not run as a
team but are elected separately, Gandy had served with Finch.
Also, her political history, like Winter's, included a lifetime of
public officeholding. She had been a staff associate and ally to
both the extreme segregationist governor and senator, Theodore G. Bilbo, and the archconservative Sen. James Eastland.
Some of her supporters wanted to argue for her election on the
basis of her gender. This desire reflected a national phenomenon
of women uniting to press for political leadership for women,
women in office, and for women as candidates. To appear qualified to many voters, especially in a state as socially conservative
as Mississippi, a woman candidate necessarily had to have credentials and experience similar to those of the male candidates.
She must appear to be like the men against whom she is running
and to have done the kinds of things in office or in government
service that the men have done. But most women have not had
opportunities to gain such experience.

This is the dilemma of a woman-*qua*-woman candidate, who might not be as well qualified as men in traditional male-dominated ways, compared with a politically experienced female candidate who, while being a woman, might be representative of an old order. It is that old order that is often being rejected as one tenet of a program that includes woman-consciousness. In Gandy's case, she could be seen as belonging to the old regime because of her Bilbo and Eastland associations and even her service with Finch.

This gender dilemma is one of our generation's critical questions. It was first posed in elective politics in Mississippi in the Gandy-Winter primary of 1979, as it was on the national scene throughout the 1970s and 1980s, including Geraldine Ferraro's 1984 candidacy for vice president of the national Democratic Party. I am glad we are as far along with it as we are. I should like to see a woman as governor of Mississippi. But I like William Winter. I am glad he defeated Evelyn Gandy, and I am glad he was governor of Mississippi. Yet I would like the day to come when two out of every four candidates for every government office would be women.

Now that we have identified it, the gender question raises its head every day of our lives, in each arena in which we find ourselves. In the informal politics of how we organize ourselves into groups and form alliances or betray them, gender habits and gender assertions or gender antagonisms make or break us, over and over again.

On the day Gov. Cliff Finch died, I observed a woman journalist do a disservice to all those women and friendly men who want to see more equity for women, as they say in Mississippi, "serving the public." A television reporter and a photographer came to a library reading room in the Mississippi Department of Archives and History, where I was working quietly and several scholars and genealogists were studying silently. The woman reporter was a young, pretty, petite blonde. The photographer was an attractive and serious black man. He seemed to know what he was doing, but neither of them seemed especially to know how to use the library. While the reporter was a take-charge sort of person, she not only was not informed about how to use the library, she did not expect to have to do her research for herself. Impatient with the receptionist's insistence that she apply for an entrance card, she snapped that they were just coming in to "get some pictures of Mr. Finch." She did not have any identification and was annoyed that she was asked to produce some. She said she had left her driver's license in the car, but she went back to get it when the receptionist quietly insisted that she had to have it. She was impatient with the reference guidebooks to which she was directed. She spoke loudly, ordering the librarians about, albeit ineffectually, regarding her need to have "pictures of Mr. Finch" and some information about him. Finally, standing exasperated at the reference notebook for special collections, she yelled out in the quiet library reading room, "Will somebody tell me how to use this book to find what I want?"

As she started to leave, the guard asked to search her purse. "Y'all are the strictest people I have ever seen?" she said curtly. As long as I was there, I did not see her put her hands on any actual research source materials either visual or print or manuscript. Hers was the kind of behavior that gives journalists a bad name, and women a bad name, and especially pretty, young southern women a bad name. I felt badly for all of us. That night I watched her television station's coverage of Finch's death: there was one still picture of Governor Finch and then perhaps two minutes worth of old footage of television tapes, a brief picture of the pretty, young blonde reporter and already-familiar commentary of facts about Finch's life and public service, much the same as the morning paper had carried.

The next day I went to visit William Winter.

William Winter: A Political Life

Former Gov. William Winter himself came for me as I waited in the tasteful reception room of Watkins Ludlam & Stennis on the twentieth floor of the Deposit Guaranty Bank Building on Jack-

William Winter.
Photo courtesy of Mississippi Department of Archives and
History. Used by permission.

son's East Capitol Street.[2] I had been a little nervous. He instantly put me at ease. We wound through a maze of halls of filing cabinets and panelled offices back to the sanctum of his corner office, comfortable, elegant, understated. He offered me a Pepsi-Cola. I thought of telling him that that drink was Republican, that he and I, Democrats, should drink Coke. I had recently seen a public broadcasting television report about the war between the cola companies that told how Pepsi's makers were Republican contributors and Coca-Cola's Democratic and how the White House served Pepsi during all the Republican administrations and Coke during the Democratic ones. However, I thought better of starting my interview with this esoteric information and accepted the Pepsi. His choice was then Dr Pepper, even more locally southern than Atlanta-based Coca-Cola, and I remained silent on our drink choices.

William Winter was elected governor of Mississippi in 1979,[3] and, since Mississippi governors can serve only one term at the time, was governor from 1980 through 1984. He had been born in Grenada County in northern Mississippi in 1923. He studied at the University of Mississippi, earning a B.A. in history in 1943. In World War II, he served in the Army in the Philippines. He returned to the University of Mississippi Law School and in 1949 graduated first in his class. Before finishing law school, he was elected to the state legislature, where he served six years, 1948–54. He returned to the Army and rose to the rank of major in the infantry in the Korean War. He was state tax collector from 1956 through 1963, at which time the state abolished the office at his urging. In 1963 he was elected state treasurer. In 1967, he first ran for governor, losing to John Bell Williams in the primary in a bitter segregationist campaign, the last totally acrimonious campaign holding onto the old racial order in Mississippi. In 1971 Winter was elected lieutenant governor. He advocated "opening the government to the public and to the press." For that he won the Margaret Dickson Freedom of Information Award from the Mississippi-Louisiana Associated Press. In 1975, he ran again for governor, this time against Cliff

Finch, and lost. From 1975–79, he was again in fulltime law practice in the office where I visited him. In 1979 he was elected governor. He has been president of the Mississippi Association for Mental Health and vice president of the national Mental Health Association. At other times, he has been president of the Board of Trustees of the Mississippi Department of Archives and History, president of the Mississippi Historical Society, a trustee of Belhaven College, and active in the Presbyterian Church. He has served as president of the University of Mississippi Alumni Association and was University of Mississippi Outstanding Alumnus of 1975. His wife is named Elise Varner Winter. They have three daughters. One of them, Lele Gillespie, was the curator of the James Silver Papers at the University of Mississippi library, and I had met her when I studied in those papers in the weeks preceding my interview. At the state Department of Archives and History library, I found a term paper of hers on "The Civil Rights Movement in Grenada, Mississippi, in 1966," in which she quotes her father proudly, though not admitting that he is her father: "'We must not only condemn acts of violence after they've taken place but we must create a climate in which they will not be attempted in the first place,' were the forceful words of State Treasurer William Winter, a native Grenadian himself."[4]

The phone rang soon after we were settled in Winter's office. "Hey, Charles," he said into it in that wonderfully southern colloquial greeting, "how are you?" Without asking me to leave, he talked business with Charles for a short time, then hung up and gave me his full attention.

I told him that I actually less wanted information from him than I wanted his views of Mississippi, his sense of and feel for Mississippi, past, present, and future. I wanted his understanding of Mississippi arts and education, business and natural resources, as well as politics. I asked him: "As a public official, what have you most enjoyed doing for the people of Mississippi?"

As governor, he told me, he had had two prime objectives: 1) to raise the quality of education, with particular emphasis on early childhood education; and 2) to improve the relationship of Mississippi with the rest of the country.

"I spent a lot of time trying to interpret Mississippi in a favorable light, to eliminate some of the old stereotypes. One of the great strengths of the state has been the role of writers from the state who have been for a long time unappreciated in Mississippi—Welty, Faulkner, William Alexander Percy, Shelby Foote—folks like that. We have not utilized these cultural resources we had either inside or outside the state." So, Winter continued, "When I was [inaugurated] governor, we had a symposium, utilizing some of this literary talent. We had Leontyne Price come down to participate. We continued [spotlighting] these [talented Mississippians for] four years. We invited many of them to the Governor's Mansion to have dinner with people from all over the state." That is to say, he matched economic leaders, state and national, with eminent Mississippi artists and writers at social and cultural events.

I asked him when he started reading Mississippi writers and made the mistake of inquiring when he first read William Faulkner. Only after he got to Ole Miss, he said. It seems that when he was a boy, many Mississippians didn't think it proper to read Faulkner. I remember that myself from my upbringing in Wayne County; although I had been taught Faulkner's works in college, that was just before Faulkner's death.

He said, "I started reading Mississippi writers as a young boy. Stark Young's *So Red the Rose*, lots of James Street's books. One of Street's books, *By Valour and Arms*, was about my great-uncle, Captain Isaac Brown. I read *Taproots* about Jones County, read more biography and history than I read novels. I read some of the Dunbar Rowland books on Mississippi history."

"What was your introduction to politics?" I asked him.

He said that in 1932 his father had been in the Mississippi State Senate. "I used to come down to Jackson to the Senate and sit on his knee. I remember visits to Jackson, spending time at the Capitol, listening to political stories, being involved.

My family was active politically. Politics was discussed in our home many times a day. My father was something of a local historian. . . .

"Then as soon as I came back from World War II, I was elected to the legislature."

I asked about his World War II experience. He said it gave him a much broader perspective on the world. Before the war, he had spent literally all of his life in Mississippi, with the exception of one or two trips, one to New York to the World's Fair in 1939. Out of his service in the Army came association with people all over the country and service in an all-black infantry training regiment of the Army. The officer corps of the regiment "was integrated about the time I came in. I came to know black people in 1945 in a desegregated relationship. And then in the Philippines I served with people literally from all over the world. I came back with the view that the old social order that had isolated Mississippi was going to change, not quickly or radically, but change. We had to start getting ready for it and take steps to improve educational opportunity for both black and white people."

He reminded me of some of the facts of his political officeholding and campaigns. Just back from the war and while still a law student, he was elected to the legislature and served for three terms. As a part of a young veterans group in the legislature, he had run for Speaker of the House against incumbent Walter Sillers, the very powerful established figure who had stood for many years as the very bulwark of archconservatism, racial segregation, and white supremacy as the Mississippi way of life.

I asked him if that challenge was a part of the idealism of a young returning veteran.

"Naiveté might be a better word," he said wryly. But then the politician in him added quickly, "It was a closer race than the final tally shows. I counted at least fifty-five potential votes out of seventy needed to elect. Forty votes was what we actually got, but that was a fairly good showing."

I mentioned former Gov. J.P. Coleman. I wanted to know if

the two of them had had a special political alliance and asked if
Coleman had been his mentor in politics. "Judge Coleman and I
were always friends," he said. "He was a little older. I was his
political supporter in those years when he ran for district attorney and circuit judge. Later, of course, I supported him in his
two races for governor. We were compatible politically and ide-
ologically, and I admired him. It would probably be inaccurate,
however, to claim him as my mentor."

As Winter recalled it, "I was working for reform, as a legislator. In that group of GIs that came back, there were several
of us who were trying to make government more responsive,
more efficient, trying to eliminate some of the holdovers from
an outmoded era. Later, when I became a tax collector, I tried
to dramatize the need for change by advocating the abolition of
the office. The legislature responded by consolidating the office
into the Tax Commission."

Knowing that his administration was recognized as one of reform of the mechanisms and agencies of state government, I
asked him whether, when he became governor, he set out to
make institutional change in state government.

"I've always thought government a fluid sort of thing," he
replied. "Just because we had been doing something a certain
way [does not mean that it should be that] way always. I was
motivated to make the changes I did make because of ineffi-
ciency in some agencies. [There had been] charges of improper
administration [in the previous administration]. We set out to
put [government] in a better light. [We made changes in the]
Tax Commission, Banking Department, Office of Federal-State
Programs that resulted in a better program and at the same
time reduced the number of employees."

Winter commented on the Educational Reform Act: "In all of
my races for governor, education was a top priority. If Mississippi is to make progress economically, we have to be strong
educationally. We had lost some industries to other states because it was not perceived that we had skilled labor. I called
business groups together. They saw this need. Got them to-

gether with the legislature. Mississippi was the first state—in the fall of 1982—the first state to pass a comprehensive Educational Reform Act." That bill provided universal kindergarten education for the first time in Mississippi, established curricular and institutional reforms in K-12 schooling, and consolidated higher education into one system. "It served as a model for other states. The next year [the report of the] President's Commission [on Education, which] came out under the leadership of Secretary of Education Bell, publicly cited Mississippi as an example for the rest of the country."

When I was a child in Mississippi, I told him, I thought we had a collective inferiority feeling in Mississippi, a kind of statewide cultural defensiveness, based perhaps on racism, poverty, and isolation. After the civil rights laws and related social change, did he think that had changed? I quoted Ray Mabus, one of his "Boys of Spring," the group of young, well-educated, political innovators whom Winter had appointed to his administration staff. They were dubbed "Boys of Spring" in the legislature, at first in derision at their persistence and early-bird consistency in having advance information. I quoted Mabus, who had been elected governor in 1987 but at the time of this interview was the state auditor: "Integration has set us free: it let us get on with the business of improving our economy and improving our schools."

Do you share that opinion?" I asked Winter. "Or maybe he learned that viewpoint from you?"

He said yes. "Once we got through the trauma. We went through a decade and a half after the Brown decision trying to avoid it. Then we went through another decade adjusting to it. In the eighties, about the time I became governor, we were looking for a way to make the system work. Strengthening public education had its real beginning in the early eighties."

I had another question, a loaded one. Didn't he think this gradual employment took a lot of patience from a politician? He did. "The life of a politician is one long roller-coaster ride. The exhilaration from the achievements is great, but the frustration and disappointment are also extremely great. You have to develop an outlook that you are not to expect too much too quickly. Persistence and tenacity are necessary qualities. You have to have patient friends and supporters. The people who stayed with me recognized that sooner or later [we would realize our objectives]." After the 1975 race, said Winter, "When Finch defeated me, and by the largest margin anybody had ever been defeated [for governor of Mississippi], I came back to this law office and said I'd never run again. I thought I had missed that once-in-a-lifetime opportunity. Four years later, though, things fell into place in an adverse public reaction to the Finch administration. I probably would not have been elected in 1979 if lots of folks hadn't felt they had made a mistake in 1975. That shows you the ups and downs."

"Now let me ask you a personal question," I said. "How do you *feel* about Mississippi? What is your Mississippi like emotionally?"

"Let me answer by telling you a story. I was in Chattanooga recently to make a speech. There was a black man there, a public official, who wanted to meet me. I found that he had grown up in the same rural community in Mississippi where I did. His grandfather was born a slave on my great-grandfather's farm. As a boy I had played and hunted with this man's cousins in Mississippi. Now there we were in Chattanooga discussing our roots—one of us white, the other black."

He continued, "My great-grandfather in 1834 settled this farm on which I grew up and which I still own. There is a part of that past buried in my own psyche and in my memories. I can't imagine being removed from that. I have tried to use that identification with this state to eliminate many of those ills of the past and to realize that almost unique opportunity we have here."

In sum, Winter said, "Having grown up in rural North Mississippi when life was not unlike it was one-hundred years before, on a Mississippi cotton farm in a segregated society and having seen almost a quantum leap forward in educational and economic opportunity, [I have found] it a very fascinating and exciting and constructive period in which to live."

He stood up and took down from the office wall a small oil painting of a one-room country school. "This is where I went to school. This is where my mother taught. I feel as if in my own lifetime I have seen the most incredible changes take place and yet find that they have not resulted in great violence or great dislocation in people's lives. Most people now cannot believe we would have fought so hard to resist the changes. My own children cannot."

He had told me what I wanted to know. I rose to say goodbye and thanked him for his time and for his full discussion with me. Amiably, with the easy courtesy of his class and gender, he *thanked me* and told me that if I would be seeing Lele the next day up at Ole Miss to tell her hello for him. He saw me back out through the maze of hallways filled with filing cabinets and paneled offices. In the reception room he told me, "I'll be going up your way this summer. I shall be attending the General Assembly of the national Presbyterian Church in Minneapolis."

Cora Norman and the Mississippi Committee for the Humanities

Another Mississippian in government service whom I interviewed was Cora Norman, the executive director of the Mississippi Committee for the Humanities.[5] Since her job is a federal government one, it is appropriate to turn next to her after my visit with the former governor of the state.

In Cora Norman's office in the Education and Research Center in Jackson, she has a needlepoint piece which has the words worked into it, "When you get to the end of your rope . . . tie a knot in it and hang on!"

She told me, "Update: it should read 'and swing!'" She knows whereof she speaks. Norman has been one to improvise and to swing with what comes as the administrator for the state coun-

Cora Norman. Photo courtesy of
Mississippi Department of
Archives and History. Photo by
Dr. William H. Norman. Used by
permission of Dr. Cora Norman.

cil, the Mississippi Committee for the Humanities, of a federal
program, the National Endowment for the Humanities, for
more than a decade and a half, a period that has seen great
changes in both her work and her society.

Cora Norman was the chief staff officer for the state administration of the national humanities agency from the latter's creation in 1972. The first state-based programs, as they were
called then, of the National Endowment for the Humanities had
begun in 1971, and Mississippi was not far behind in the establishment of its state advisory body the following year. That first
year, each state organization was given $100,000 to develop in
its state public programs that would bring scholars in the humanities into interaction with members of the public. Federal
funding increased in subsequent years, but the objective was
always to place responsible citizens of each state in charge of
both the allocation of funds and the assessment of program proposals from within their state. Mississippi's state council was
particularly effective, winning one of the five National Endowment Chairman's Awards for Excellence.[6]

The leadership of Cora Norman was behind much of that suc-

cess. At the tenth anniversary conference which the Mississippi
Committee for the Humanities held in Jackson in 1982, many of
the speakers and the participants praised Norman's work, but
Dr. Sarah Rouse of Mississippi College expressed gratitude and
appreciation most fully. She said:

> I remember so well when the committee of five came back from
> Washington. Cora Norman called me and she said, "Would you come
> and have dinner with me? I'd like to talk with you about something."
> And so there sat two women at LeFleur's Restaurant one evening,
> and she told me what she had been asked to do in the state of Mis-
> sissippi. One woman with five wonderful people standing behind
> her. She started with absolutely nothing except her wonderful
> mind, her wonderful personality, and determination to do what she
> had been asked to do for our state. . . .
> So the committee has done a good job, but back of all of this has
> been Cora Norman. I know all of you realize that, and I just feel
> like every time we have a meeting like this we ought to just stand
> up and say, "We know that you started with nothing, and you have
> come to this." She's done it with our help and with her determina-
> tion to make it go for our state. She cared. Her values were high,
> and she saw to it that we did the same thing, that we kept ours
> high.[7]

A very beautiful and stylish woman, Cora Norman is a legend
among her national colleagues in the National Endowment for
the Humanities and in the National Federation of State-Based
Programs. Before I met her, one of them told me, "At the meetings, people are always waiting to see what Cora Norman is
going to wear. She lives up to that southern-lady image of being
glamorous and gorgeous and charming, and then she opens her
mouth in a meeting and those all-business men are totally dis-
armed. It takes about two seconds to realize that she has a mind
like a vise!" She is also a person of compassion and vision. Her
job was far from easy in 1972, administering a federal program
in Mississippi in the years of the last throes of civil rights antagonisms that had sometimes pitted the state and reacting whites
against the federal government and blacks. She knew well what
she was doing when she engaged her womanliness as well as her

intellect and organizational skills in actions of conciliation that her office made possible for Mississippi society.

An incident I observed in her company makes the point of this feature of her achievement and its part in social change in Mississippi. On my 1980s Mississippi visits, I was still bearing the memories that in my growing-up time blacks and whites did not eat together or interact socially in any way, that blacks went to the back door of white people's houses, and that, above all, white women would be restrained or ostracized and black men severely punished for any social contact between the two. In those days, racially mixed social contact was against state law, as well as thoroughly disapproved by custom. Once, going into a hotel in Jackson as Cora's guest, I was to see in Cora's actions how much all that has changed.

The two of us entered the large hotel lobby on one side, beautiful, stunningly dressed white Cora and me. In the far distance at the opposite lobby entrance, a well-dressed black man came in, and the two of them hailed one another. Then, before my astonished eyes, the black man and my white blonde female companion, arms outstretched, rushed to meet each other in the middle of the busy Jackson hotel lobby, and hugged and kissed right there under the twinkling chandelier in the middle of the carpeted hotel lobby. Though I was bug-eyed, nobody else paused or looked twice.

The man turned out to be Dr. Matthew Page, a medical doctor from Greenville, Mississippi, who, from its beginning and for ten years, served on the Mississippi Committee for the Humanities. Among his interests in humanities subjects, he told me, was the study of distinctiveness of particular heritages of black Americans. He wants more people to be able to know about the diversity of their African origins. His own people were Ibo, he told me, from what is now Nigeria in western Africa.

In her pleasant office in the Education and Research Center, I formally interviewed Cora Norman about the Mississippi Committee for the Humanities (MCH) and her work as its executive director.

When the MCH started in 1972, she told me, it was mandated that the group deal with public policy issues. Mississippi elected to deal with education—with the low status of education for the most part, but also with financial issues. Science people could get money from government, Cora felt, while humanities scholars and intellectuals had much more difficulty; the low status of education was a humanities question. What follows is an edited version of my notes recording Cora Norman's words that day, which she later approved for publication. My comments are in brackets.

Those first three years, we tried to attack the problem of desegregation in the classroom—linguistics [the words people used about race]—attitudes born in us—get it out on the table and deal with it.

Some of our best programs were, from a humanities point of view, around the committee table (the state board meetings.) There were twenty members, approximately six or seven blacks on the committee—we never tried to keep it half-female, though I wanted to. Walter Washington [a patrician black patriarch, the long-time president of Alcorn State University, originally an all-black school] said, "Cora, you want 'em all female!"

"No," I said, "I just want my part!"

Some very open discussions took place around that table—we never used a tape recorder—had some confrontations—if we funded a proposal, it was funded by the committee, if not, not by the committee. They have always been members of a team. There was one episode that I thought was going to break up the committee completely. A militant black woman and an older conservative male had a confrontation. She had had enough. He took it, and then he said he was not going to do that. He shredded his committee papers, and he left the meeting. She called to resign. I asked her not to resign. She left a few meetings, but she came back. She went into statewide public office. The man called and congratulated her on [her election]. After four years she called him for a reference for a man from his town seeking employment with her.

At other times on the committee, blacks around the table said they had to speak up, to bring up sensitivity. Out of that came some good, strong friendship ties that connected Jackson State (formerly all-black) and Mississippi State (formerly all-white); Mississippi College (white, Baptist, near Jackson) and Jackson State.

The programs were well received by blacks. And I have always tried to have a black on the staff. When we got full-time money, I hired a black secretary, an Alcorn graduate, Sadie Schaeffer Clark. I had a friend, Mrs. Vivian Tellis, through AAUW, from Alcorn. The office was at Ole Miss at that time, and Chancellor [Porter] Fortune [of the University of Mississippi] was chair. Chancellor Fortune was chair for the first five years. Then they elected Estus Smith from Jackson State and had a black chair for five years.

For the first five years, if we had any success at all, looking back, it was the first time professors had gone into communities and met people, talking person-to-person at tables. People said, "This is the first time I have ever talked to university professors." They were looking at subjects through a sociological point of view, through literature.

One of the reasons we had such a problem launching the program in Mississippi was the difficulty over confrontations. (Desegregation was so recent and so centrally focused in education.) We were supposed to have public meetings. After the 1969–70 desegregation, we had to have so many public meetings. Attention turned to school superintendents. Some retired early, there were probably some mental illnesses produced by the tension. At first there was no response to public meetings. I remember Troy Holliday from Ripley in Tippah County sent me a one-sentence letter: he asked for information about the program. He later got four county superintendents of education in the north corner of the state to show some interest—Tishamingo, Alcorn, Prentiss, and Tippah counties. That was the first proposal from the people we wanted to serve. They submitted a proposal and got some support.

The coolest reception I ever had: I went to the statewide superintendents' association on the Gulf Coast. They wanted none of [a federal program on education in Mississippi].

"Peggy Prenshaw has been involved from the beginning. [Peggy Prenshaw is a university professor and dean at Mississippi Southern University, a longtime member of the Mississippi Committee for the Humanities, and later, in 1987, was to become an officer in the national federation of these state committees.] She has gone all over the state. She tells a story of going up in Holmes County. There were less than a dozen white children left in the school. They had just pulled out. David Jones was assistant superintendent in Holmes County, a black superintendent. Jones wrote a proposal that professors come to a Holmes County radio station in Lexington, Mississippi. He pointed out that there was no place in the county where blacks and whites could sit down together. He drew professors for the radio show from every institution of higher education in the state. For a year. Nobody ever called in while the show was on. The next year there was a proposal for the schools. Peggy Prenshaw went up there [to speak on the radio program and in the public school as a professor from the MCH]. Her father went with her. They were from Mendenhall. They stopped in Lexington, her father was getting directions. He was directed to the white school, the academy (the white private segregated school opened as a reaction to integration). Peggy said, "No, I want to go to the attendance center [the public school with mostly black students]." They couldn't believe her.

Lucy Howorth up in Cleveland says, "You just have to keep plowing. Peggy is just making that old horse work." Lucy Howorth is a lawyer, then ninety years old, a former Mississippi state legislator, as was her mother before her, and a former commissioner of Federal District Court. She spent her young adulthood years, between 1916 and 1918, being politically active in New York City.

The League of Women Voters, the AAUW, black organizations, a few church groups, and librarians were top-notch groups to work with. The Mississippi Library Commission in 1976 was looking at the Bicentennial, particularly at issues at the beginning of our country that are still with us.

Joe Stockwell and Bob Phillips, English professors at Mississippi State, working with the library commission, also wrote some proposals to us. One [was] to go into libraries of the state and discuss issues connected with the state. Topics like: Are Libraries Worth What They Cost?

Bill Russell, from Tunica, a creative-writing teacher at a community college in Memphis, did library talks on letting views be known by writing to editors about values in the United States that have been with us from the start.

On another program, Peggy Prenshaw [from Mississippi Southern University] and Betty Hearn and Sarah Rouse from Mississippi College went into libraries and made recommendations for books.

In the summer of 1978, Joe Stockwell went down to Waynesboro [under this libraries-and-the-humanities project] as a scholar-in-residence for one month. He was housed at the library. Dr. Dennis Mitchell, assistant director of MCH, paved the way—he talked with the newspaper publisher and the board of supervisors and the librarian, who was cool to the proposal. Dennis met with the board of supervisors and sold them on the idea. A member of the board of supervisors said, "We fund the library. We'll see that the library provides space for the scholar."

Joe Stockwell went down there, and he sat there in the library. [Apparently he got very little business, the Waynesboro people being mystified about what they were to do with a humanities scholar.] He spent one summer month there. The librarian was very nice to Joe. Joe wrote newspaper articles every week. One day he saw a little boy bring in a wagon and take home a whole wagonload of books. That was

the highlight of his summer. There was no civic activity in
Waynesboro. In the fall, Dennis Mitchell returned to
Waynesboro to conduct an evaluation. The chief of police
[who grew up a mile down the road from me] said, "How can
you measure an intangible?"

By contrast, Dr. White, the other scholar in a parallel
scholar-in-residence position, had a ball in Greenville. In
Waynesboro, someone today would surely remember Joe
Stockwell [because he was such a novelty]. No-one would remember Dr. White in Greenville.

I got Joe Duffy [the chair of the National Endowment for
the Humanities] to write a letter to the president of Mississippi State to commend Joe Stockwell for his work in
Waynesboro. But it didn't count for tenure or points toward
promotion. Professors need some rewards for this work, but
it didn't help at Mississippi State University at that time.

One project we have now was copied from New Mexico—
a newspaper project. After our program on "Making the Self
Heard" on writing letters to the editor. New Mexico had
funded professors writing for newspaper consumption. They
had been into that for three years. With the Mississippi
Press Association, with Wayne Wiedie heading the program.
He is from Ocean Springs. We have a board made up of
newspaper editors and humanities professors. If an article is
selected for a newspaper, we pay $125.

We have also funded projects to examine the status of
women: Do We Need the ERA?", "ERA and the Family." We
got a lot of guff from some committee members, but they
went ahead and funded them.

About 1980, we funded fewer proposals dealing with public policy issues and got into local history. There were two or
three funded here in Jackson in the black community. Leila
Rhodes involved Dr. Margaret Walker Alexander for a program on "Gowdy"—a cottonseed mill town outside of Jackson at one time, now within the city—in the Harmony community. Blacks owned their land there and had provided

haven for the civil rights movement, but they also gave
money for legal battles.

The next scholar-in-residence program after [Stockwell
and White went to] Greenville and Waynesboro was a folk-
lorist in Yazoo City. Then one in Neshoba County. That got
some attention because it was Neshoba County, Mississippi
[where Philadelphia is located]—a socioanthropologist. She
was there nine months or a year. Worked on Choctaw, black,
and white. Courtney Tannehill, the librarian there, became
very good friends with Seena Cohen, the anthropologist. She
also collected photographs, showed pictures at the Choctaw
Fair.

Madison County had someone—a historian—look at rural
and urban issues. A $75,000 Chairman Excellence Award
went to Picayune, DeSoto County, for a historian looking at
the impact of urbanization in Picayune. An anthropologist in
Biloxi looked at different ethnic groups there. She got a lot
of publicity on her articles in the newspaper. She would seek
out a shipbuilder, another worker—they wanted to develop
a seafood museum. We did not want to fund a museum, but
looking at the impact of ethnic groups on the seafood industry was funded. They were up in arms about the Vietnamese
[immigrants arriving], but, looking back, these groups—
Hungarian, Lebanese, a few Chinese, most European mi-
grants—realized how they had not been "accepted" when
they first arrived on the Mississippi coast. There was an interesting article in the Picayune paper after the historian
left. "It was good you made us look at ourselves," it said.

The scholar-in-residence at Vicksburg wanted to consider
how the river had been a part of the town.

There has been a Eudora Welty scholar at the Mississippi
State Department of Archives and History.

Cora had given me a full impression of her work and of the
interests of the Mississippi Committee for the Humanities. Now
I asked her to tell me something about herself.

She told me that she went to college during World War II. She did a pre-med program in two years and a summer at the University of Arkansas. In 1945 she went to medical school. She met a lot of difficulty there because of being a woman and withdrew after one semester. After that, she married and had a baby. In 1949, with a baby at home, she went out to work. In 1961, as a "reentry woman" with two children and a professor husband, she went back to the university to do work that eventually led to a doctoral program at the University of Mississippi. She received one of three College Faculty Awards in Mississippi from the AAUW. In 1975, in a month, she drafted her dissertation, "The Status of the Humanities at Mississippi's Public Junior Colleges." She was very interested in the women's movement from the start. She served as the first chairperson of the Mississippi Women's Political Caucus. In 1977, International Women's Year, the Mississippi program for its celebration was a fiasco, she claims, but "the network of women was birthed then." For the meeting, though "we had three hundred women, but seven hundred antis came and swamped us."[8]

I asked Norman if she had a role model. Without hesitation, she answered "Lucy Howorth. She has just won a Radcliffe award for distinguished women. She is ninety years old. Her mother was a suffragist [whose portrait now hangs in the Old Capitol Museum]. She is in the Ole Miss Hall of Fame. She is going to England in May. She gave an address at Delta State this year. I told her she was my first feminist," Cora Norman said.

For many a Mississippian, like her female role model, that is who Cora Norman is as well.

A Meeting of the Mississippi NAACP

The Mississippi National Association for the Advancement of Colored People (NAACP) held its annual convention in Oxford, Mississippi, in November 1984, just twenty-two years after Oxford had been the scene of a race riot over the admission of a black, James Meredith, to the University of Mississippi there, and twenty-two years after the night that Gov. Ross Barnett, in that town, had tried to face down the federal government with his states' rights doctrine of "interposition," placing the governor's authority in the state between the people and the federal government. There, for the first time, he lost one of his battles over the maintenance of racial segregation and white supremacy in Mississippi. Meredith's admission to the university was the first legal downfall of what, in the decade to come, was to be the complete collapse of the state law and the official practice of discrimination against black people.

When the NAACP met in Oxford in 1984, its president of twenty-four years, Dr. Aaron Henry, was a member of the state legislature. The group met in a motel, the Rodeway Inn, that was the kind of public accommodation that in 1962 would have served only whites. With the theme "NAACP Long-Distance Runners (Personalities and Ideas)," the convention program contained leadership and speakers, both black and white, from the highest levels of leadership in government, education, labor, health care, religion, arts, culture, and athletics. Gov. Bill Allain, Lt. Gov. Brad Dye, and three other state officials, all of whom were white, attended. A program on politics included the chairman of the state Democratic party, Steve Patterson; two members of Congress, Jamie Whitten and Wayne Dowdy; and black State Rep. Robert Clark and Gunnison Mayor Violet Leggett. The new chancellor of the University of Mississippi, Gerald Turner, spoke at a luncheon which was attended by the former chancellor, Porter Fortune, and a number of white university faculty members. The coaches of predominantly black Mississippi Valley State University and Jackson State University, Archie Cooley and W.C. Gorden, were joined on a panel by Ole Miss coach Billy Brewer, whose players now are as frequently black as they are white. Successful black Mississippi athletes Willie Richardson, formerly of the NFL's Baltimore Colts, and the USFL's New Orleans Breakers players Marcus Dupree and Buford Jordan were on the program.

There was entertainment by black Mississippi artists, includ-

Aaron Henry. Photo courtesy of Mississippi Department of Archives and History. Used by permission.

ing gospel singers the Amazing Strong Family of Memphis, the Lane Chapel Quintet of Tupelo, the Redmond Brothers of Oxford, and the Rust College A Capella Choir of Holly Springs. A panel of presidents or representatives of all the black colleges in the state presented a "Black Educational Summit" program, which closed with a moving and poetic statement by the famous writer and professor Dr. Margaret Walker Alexander.[9]

The convention was presided over by Dr. Aaron Henry. The membership did not fully agree on the progress of the organization, and Henry's reelection that year was challenged informally by an influential group of local leaders, including the president of the Oxford chapter. Some members were concerned that the membership of the state organization, about thirteen-thousand, was only half what it had been in the 1960s. Some members lamented that the emphasis of the organization was still on civil rights, while the civil rights battles themselves were over and won. They felt that issues such as continued discrimination and segregation in housing, employment, educational opportunity, and economic advancement; support for election of blacks to public office; and black family stability and support should be addressed. Some members, like pugnacious and outspoken State Sen. Henry Kirksey, thought that the NAACP should be more actively involved in black-initiated lawsuits such as the one he had sponsored—and won—to shift the City of Jackson's mayor-commissioner form of government to a ward-elected council with an at-large elected mayor.

In the challenge to his reelection, Aaron Henry was accused of "wearing too many hats," to which he replied unperturbed that he probably did. Suggesting that he would serve for only one more term, he was reelected handily. At the time of the convention, Henry was one of seventeen black members of the state legislature. He had been elected in 1979, joining his colleague, former state NAACP field director Robert Clark, the first black person in the Mississippi legislature, who had been elected in 1967.

A veteran of years of civil rights battles and leadership, Henry had been a leader of the Mississippi Freedom Democratic Party when it was formed and as it gained national attention in 1964. In the summer of 1964, too, he had been the presiding officer of the four organizations that merged to form COFO for the "Mississippi Freedom Summer." He had served, beginning in 1965, as a national board member of the NAACP. During the civil rights movement years, he had suffered much abuse and had served a movement-related-six-month period in jail. Active on the national as well as the state and local political scenes, Henry was a registered lobbyist in the U.S. Congress and was influential in securing passage of the Office of Economic Opportunity Act. In his campaign for the state legislature, he urged the election of blacks, in order to gain responsiveness from whites as well as to secure membership for blacks. He claimed that a large black presence in public office in Mississippi would "make a [liberal New York Senator] Javits of an Eastland [the archconservative Mississippi senator]."[10]

Henry's colleague Robert Clark had taken a strong educational, rather than a combative, approach to officeholding. A teacher before becoming the state field secretary for the NAACP, Clark sought to influence education, health, and welfare issues in the four terms he served in the state legislature. Clark was the author of the Vocational-Technical Education Act of 1982, a bill which he said would give the state "a system of education that will offer young people of Mississippi an opportunity to become productive citizens of the skill-oriented society of today."[11]

Clark ran for Congress and lost twice in the Second District of Mississippi, an area in the Mississippi Delta where 53 percent of the population is black. As an up-through-the-ranks black politician who had exercised strong leadership and gained the respect of some white liberal leaders and some white farm voters as well as the black constituents, Clark had felt that he had a good chance of winning in both 1980 and 1984. In the end, however, it was widely believed, whites voted for the white candidate, blacks voted for Clark, and the election turned on racism. One Greenville voter was reported as saying, "Race? That's not an issue. The whites are going to vote for the white guy, and the blacks are going to vote for the black guy."[12]

In attendance at the 1984 Mississippi NAACP convention, largely unknown and not especially noticed by the leadership, was a nattily dressed young California-educated assistant attorney general named Michael Espy.[13] In 1986, in a campaign in which he emphasized the Reagan government's farm policy and agricultural and economic issues; personally visited every contributor to the last Democratic campaign; and shook an estimated 900 to 1,200 hands a day, purposely downplaying race as a factor, this political unknown Mike Espy was elected to Congress from the Second District and became the first black elected to Congress from Mississippi since Reconstruction.[14]

At the convention Aaron Henry presided over in 1984, however, that was in the future. This convention was a rather modulated one in which gains were acknowledged and people recognized for their long-term contributions to black people's advancement in Mississippi. People who had died for their cause were remembered and honored, and living people who had achieved excellence in individual fields of endeavor were recognized and listened to. Realities of government, school, and church were acknowledged.

During the convention it was rumored that Jesse Jackson was coming to be the final banquet speaker, but he did not come. Instead, the speaker was the Reverend Julius Caesar Hope, the executive director of the NAACP from a neighboring state. While Hope did not provide the convention with the excitement that presidential candidate Jackson's presence could have brought, what he did do was much the same as that which Jesse Jackson could have done: he provided familiar rhetorical inspiration for a sense of togetherness and solidarity. It was the culminating event, the community-building pinnacle.

Everyone dressed up for the banquet evening at the Rodeway Inn, women in their taffeta and sequined silk and shiny-silver dresses, men in Sunday-best coats and ties or an occasional tuxedo. The motel's dinner service for its NAACP guests was shabby. Motel personnel, many of them white, sometimes were insolent or even rude to the guests seeking drinks before dinner. The dinner itself was served cafeteria-style, and the tables, as they were originally set up, were too few for the ticket-holders, causing confusion and frustration at the absence of graceful and efficient hospitality. Even so, the overwhelmingly black crowd responded with patience and tolerance.

After the meal, a number of awards were made. President Henry was thanked for his service and congratulated on his election to his twenty-fifth one-year term. The Reverend Julius Caesar Hope was introduced and began to speak.

And then it was that the convention came to its climax. Then it was that the gathered people were brought to know who they were, and those in the audience who were white understood that we were onlookers onto a community, welcome guests, it was clear, but not members. Then it was that the heart and soul of a people were made manifest, and one could see what it was that made them strong and patient, firm and durable. For somebody white or Catholic or Jewish or northern, it was an experience in otherness. For black Mississippians and many another American who is black, it was a tangible exhibit of the rich core of their humanity, the soul of black folks where it is wholly religious and political, artistic and physical, where it is singular and communal, individual and connected. It showed me what was meant by the black Yale University doctoral student who told me, "To all black folks, Mississippi is our spiritual home."

Hope spoke to the assembled listeners of their religiousness, and he spoke to them of their politics. He told them that they were brave and good and that the Reagan administration was evil. His words or even his themes were not so important to his audience as his voice, with its rhythms and its cadences, not so important as his movement and his energy and his tone. Familiar Biblical references to Moses and Jesus were laced with political references to Jesse Jackson and Fannie Lou Hamer. The Devil was invoked and made an apparent agent of Ronald Reagan. Hope's rhetoric began quietly, with scholarly intonation, but soon he began to punctuate his sentences with a staccato cry, "Are you with me?," in a tone no white man could copy.

"Amen," one woman would say from the audience, and then another: "We're with you."

"Amen, Sister, are you with me?" His voice boomed out, quick, sharp, direct, and dramatic.

"We are with you," came back the reply.

His words came fast now, fast and loud, regular and rhythmic. His voice rose. It rose and fell in a repeating chant. Words of his making merged with Bible words. His voice reached a higher strong pitch. The sharp staccato sounds he made increased in power. His breath worked for him as a bellows to fire his sustained, pulsating sound.

"Are you with me?" he would intone in quick, separate words. His audience was with him. Their eyes bright, some called out in response their familiar church sounds.

Hope began to sweat. He worked up to a greater drumming,

Margaret Walker. Photo by Gayle Graham Yates.

strumming vibration with the instrument of his voice. He held the tension at that peak with masterful control of his art. For several minutes he went on and on, breathing only with the production of the powerful sound. "Are you with me?" he would sing out, unbroken with the vocal drumbeat of his impassioned chant. Their reply would feed his beat, as he spoke on and on, on and on, now more musical and exact, now words in a flow more rushing, and always the steady beat toward his oral crescendo as it mounted and soared. Sweat poured down his face, and his body jerked as he made his verbal music. Transformed together, his audience and he were one in spirit as he came to the might close of his performance. He quieted. He mopped his face with his handkerchief. And he sat down. All together now, he with them, they with him, belonged. They were a people who knew who they were.

On another occasion at that convention, author and intellectual Margaret Walker spoke. Her lecture sounded like a quiet philosophical poem. She articulated an interpretation of black people's union of spirituality and politics not unlike the demonstration of that union in Rev. Julius Caesar Hope's lecture-sermon, but hers was spoken in her scholarly poet's voice. Here are my notes recording what she said.

We survived everything, the Middle Passage. Phillis Wheatley survived slavery. We survived. People like Sojourner Truth and Harriet Tubman survived. We survived that second slavery, segregation. Ida B. Wells and Mary McCloud Bethune fought lynching and poll tax, and we survived.

Now some say we are in a fascist system. All education has failed, they say. I could see that, but I could see that in another way we have survived. We have survived the Middle Passage, slavery and segregation, and we will survive this, too.

The Einsteinian revolution [of relativism in both the physical universe and spirituality] is not in American education. We are still living in a Newtonian system [of mechanical logic]. In our technological society, black people have a "feeling tone" over against a European process. We African people, we know medicine came out of witchcraft, magic. As teachers, our bit of business is to stimulate the student to think. If you have a genius like Michael Jackson, we have to guide that, too. Most black people are creative. We have had to be to survive.

There are three big problems for blacks: money, race, politics. We must deal with all of them. We are still the greatest victims of that system: money—understanding the system, racism, politics. Part of our education for survival, for our own children, is to combat this [victimization]. Twenty years ago Aaron Henry, Medgar Evers, Fannie Lou Hamer, and the Freedom Democratic Party worked to change that. Today we see reaction to those changes. We have to start all over. That's what we have to do.

America is racist to the core.

We have to have faith in the Almighty because we were

born with divinity in our souls. We teach in the black college who you are. We are a people of spirit, of soul. The answer to technology, to racism, to high-finance capitalism, is humanism, not fascism, not Communism. We must apply the whole concept that Einstein gave us, this whole concept of technology and spirituality. Jesse Jackson in the convention worked on feeling tone, because he is a black Baptist preacher. We are a feeling people, a people of soul, numinous.[15]

Mississippi in the Two-Party South

On our drive between the Mississippi towns of Oxford and Philadelphia, my friend Cora Jordan and I stopped at her favorite roadside "pie shop" not far from Philadelphia on the two-laned state highway we were traveling. Eating our pie at the bare linoleum-topped table, we eavesdropped on the conversation of the tableful of men nearby. They were the kind of white men who have tobacco juice in the wrinkles of their chins and who wear their tractor-advertising caps at the table.

"Them Democrats has got theirselves in a heap of trouble," one of them said.

"Yeah," another replied, and they all chuckled. "It's them niggers they got sittin' up in Jackson [in the state legislature]. They got theirselves a nigger party."

"Well, that sho' is the way it is," another said.

University of Mississippi political scientist Alexander P. Lamis has written an illuminating book entitled *The Two-Party South*. Lamis shows how, in the period immediately following the civil rights movement, the Republican party has gained votes, influence, and offices in the traditionally Democratic "Solid South." In his book, arranged state by state, the Mississippi chapter is subtitled, "It's All Black and White." He begins his chapter:

Mississippi's entry into the era of two-party competition exhibited in an extreme manner many of the political tendencies observed throughout the region. The outstanding feature was the difficulty that Black and white Democrats had in bringing about the biracial coalition that became so important for the Southern Democracy in the post-civil rights era. The situation can only be understood in the context of the state's heavy preoccupation with race.

The successes of Republican presidential candidates in Mississippi are easily linked to the national Democratic party's advocacy of civil rights for Blacks. As early as 1960 an unpledged slate of presidential electors, supported by Gov. Ross Barnett and other Democratic segregationists, carried the state with 39.0 percent of the vote to continue the protest that had begun in the 1948 Dixiecrat revolt, when Mississippi's Gov. Fielding Wright was Strom Thurmond's running mate.[16]

In a footnote, Lamis quotes his predecessor, scholar of southern party politics V.O. Key, Jr., who wrote about Mississippi in *Southern Politics* in 1949:

Mississippi adds another variant to the politics of the South. Northerners, provincials that they are, regard the South as one large Mississippi. Southerners, with their eye for distinction, place Mississippi in a class by itself. North Carolinians, with their faith that the future holds hope, consider Mississippi to be the last vestige of a dead and despairing civilization. Virginia, with its comparatively dignified politics, would, if it deigned to notice, rank Mississippi as a backward culture, with a ruling class both unskilled and neglectful of its duties. And every other southern state finds some reason to fall back on the soul-satisfying exclamation, "Thank God for Mississippi!" Yet Mississippi only manifests in accentuated form the darker political strains that run throughout the South.[17]

Lamis shows in his study the development in Mississippi of an active Republican strain, almost entirely white and almost entirely conservative, like southern Democrats used to be, alongside a new, tenuously merged, and sometimes factionalized biracial Democratic party, made up of old-line Democrats converted to new ways and a coalition of blacks, liberals, and labor.

After the 1964 Democratic convention, when the all-white regular Mississippi delegation walked out, the national party recognized the black-white loyalist coalition as the official delegation for the 1968 convention. Charles Evers, brother of murdered civil rights leader Medgar Evers, was named Democratic National Committee member from Mississippi.

In Mississippi, the 1960s saw considerable political turmoil around elections and party politics as well as around rights. After Mississippi went Republican in several presidential elections, Republican candidates began entering the field for statewide office, largely vying with Democrats over who was most segregationist. In the 1963 gubernatorial contest, self-proclaimed "staunch segregationist" Republican Rubel Phillips tried to associate fellow-segregationist Democrat Paul B. Johnson, Jr., with the Kennedy administration and federal government civil rights policy efforts. Johnson won. When Phillips ran for governor again in 1967, he ran against Democratic-primary-winner John Bell Williams, the right-wing member of Congress who was very active in the [White] Citizens Council and who had publicly supported Goldwater in 1964, a stance which his fellow Democrats in Congress had punished by taking away his seniority. The Mississippi Freedom Democratic party, black-dominated, endorsed Phillips, to his horror and dismay. Phillips' repudiation of his black supporters was tangible evidence that his Mississippi Republican sympathy for black voters was rhetorical only. Williams won.

In 1971, many blacks were ready to support a black candidate, and Charles Evers was eager to be a Democratic candidate for governor. The state Democrats split around the primary campaign into the loyalist faction, the black-and-white coalition that was recognized by the national party, which supported Evers; and the old-timer Mississippi Democrats, who ran William Waller, a man who previously had been a segregationist and now called himself a populist. Waller won the primary and the governorship.

In 1972, a Republican "moderate," Gil Carmichael, a car

dealer from Meridian, ran against U.S. Sen. James O. Eastland, charging that Eastland and his kind of entrenched Democratic conservatives in the Senate were the cause of economic, educational, and social backwardness of Mississippi and other southern states. Eastland, as expected, was reelected handily.

With the victory of Cliff Finch for governor, the year 1975 saw the first fruits in state government of the Democratic racial coalition. Finch had been a segregationist in the early 1960s and had supported Gov. Ross Barnett in his all-out efforts to maintain racial separation; but when Finch won the primary in 1975, he made a successful effort to bring the embattled factions of the Democratic Party in Mississippi back together again in one party. Lamis quotes the *New York Times* as saying that Finch ended up having "the support of almost all of the state's leading Democrats from Senator James O. Eastland, who is backing him heartily, to Aaron Henry, the Black chairman of the liberal loyalist faction, who endorsed him with obvious reluctance. . . . Observers attributed Mr. Finch's Black support to his workingman theme, which apparently elicited blue-collar sympathy across racial lines."[18] Since Finch's Republican opponent in the general election was the moderate Gil Carmichael, the campaign shifted more to the left than Mississippi had seen in the twentieth century (while still remaining considerably right of center on a national scale).

The Finch administration was a turning point for both the Mississippi parties, shaping new identities and changing the alignment of Mississippi's participation in national elections. Lamis writes:

At the 1976 [state Democratic] convention, cochairmen for the unified [Mississippi Democratic] party were chosen: Aaron Henry, the loyalist Black leader, became one cochairman; Tom Riddell, a white representative of the regulars, the other. The unified party leadership worked enthusiastically for the election of fellow Southerner Jimmy Carter. And in 1976 the Democratic party's presidential nominee carried Mississippi for the first time since 1956; Carter received 49.6 percent of the votes cast to Gerald Ford's 47.7 percent.[19]

The next serious challenge to the Democrats, and the event that most firmly established the Republicans in Mississippi officeholding, was the 1976 Senate campaign, when Senator Eastland had decided to retire. Black Democrat Charles Evers decided to run as an independent and captured a large black vote from the Democratic nominee Maurice Dantin, so that both of them lost the Senate seat to the Republican candidate, former U.S. Rep. Thad Cochran. Lamis writes of that win, "Cochran acknowledged the obvious: the Black-white Democratic split was the cause of his good fortune. A month before the election he told a *Washington Post* reporter, 'It's a fluke, a most unusual set of circumstances that happen to benefit me. If I had to write a script, I couldn't have done a better job.'"[20]

Evers' candidacy angered some black political leaders, as well as the establishment white Democrats. Aaron Henry wrote to him that such independent candidacy "put a section of the Black community outside the political world—outside the decision-making processes of the real political world. . . . The Black political structure is as much or more involved with the decision-making in this state's Democratic Party as they are in any place else in the country. And we tell everyone that when you lay down with Independents, you wake up with Republicans."[21]

The Democratic party came back together to elect William Winter governor in 1979 and worked for President Jimmy Carter in 1980, although Carter lost the state's electoral votes to Ronald Reagan that year. The Democrats worked for the reelection of eighty-one-year-old Sen. John C. Stennis, the irony of whose reelection with a heavy black vote could not have escaped many people, for although Stennis is soft-spoken and intelligent and gracious, he was for many years as diehard a segregationist as Eastland.

With the Republican administration in the White House came some conservative Mississippi Republican influence in Washington. Larry Speakes from Merigold, Mississippi, became President Reagan's press secretary. And U.S. Rep. Trent Lott from the Gulf Coast district became the minority whip in the House of Representatives. It was Republican Lott who in an interview summarized for Lamis the dilemma of Mississippi Democrats in this time:

> They're in a bind with the national Democrat party. If they subscribe to the national Democrat party's principles, platform, they are clearly going to alienate the overwhelming majority of the white people in Mississippi. If they don't do it, they are going to offend the Black folk in Mississippi. . . .
>
> So, if they go with the typical national Democrat base, they wind up with Blacks and labor and your more liberal, social-oriented Democrats, white people. Put those groups together and they are a minority in Mississippi. . . .
>
> So, they [statewide Democratic candidates] have got to have some of these old redneck George Wallace white voters. If they have these other groups, they alienate that group.[22]

Lott's prediction proved correct, for the next election, anyway. (Lott himself won the U.S. Senate seat vacated by John Stennis in 1988, in a campaign waged against a Democratic member of Congress, Wayne Dowdy.) In the 1984 election, conducted after Lamis had finished his book, former Gov. William Winter was the Democratic nominee for the Senate seat held by Republican Thad Cochran. In the Second Congressional District in the Mississippi Delta, where blacks formed a larger portion of the population, black State Rep. Robert Clark faced white Republican Webb Franklin. And as the Mondale-Ferraro ticket went down before Ronald Reagan, the Republicans won Mississippi, too, sending Thad Cochran and Webb Franklin to Washington with a resounding partisan vote drawn along the new lines.

In 1986, however, black Michael Espy was elected to Congress as a Democrat from the Second District, basing his campaign on economic, agricultural, and local issues. At thirty-two, Espy was one of a new generation of black politicians, educated outside the South, cosmopolitan and national in outlook. He rightly, it turned out, thought he had no need to emphasize racial matters.

And in 1987, Ray Mabus, then the state auditor, a Harvard Law School graduate and one of former Gov. William Winter's "Boys of Spring," was elected governor as a Democrat. As state auditor, Mabus had distinguished himself as the honest-and-above-board advocate of both economy and accountability in collecting and distributing the state's funds. He achieved massive reforms in practice merely by enforcing laws already in place, from small matters such as denying state employees the use of state funds to buy food, drink, or even coffee for lobbyists or reporters, to large matters such as collecting school taxes from property that had been identified by law but in practice not collected in the past. Most notably of all, he had identified the practice of graft and other corruption by many rural country supervisors, the local country "treasurers" of public funds and overseers of public works, who for generations, as if by rights, had pocketed some of the money collected and served their friends and relatives, as well as themselves, at the public expense as if the business they were in was their own. Some of these backwoods bosses, in fact, believed that it actually was the case that they were the owners of county government and could do with its funds and favors what they pleased. The *New York Times* wrote of the Mississippi supervisors, "Autonomous and freewheeling, with salaries ranging from $15,000 to $24,000 annually, they roam their districts in four-wheel-drive vehicles as the embodiment of instantly responsive local government. They will dig a grave or grade a driveway for a constituent with public funds as readily as they will fill a pothole."[23]

Mabus identified such widespread practices and catalyzed an FBI investigation which resulted in forty-five arrests and a number of indictments of the county officials in federal court. My brother and I laughed together over the report of the indictment of a fellow we had known in high school. And then, a little more soberly, we wondered where the gravel came from for our own farm road when we were children.

When Mabus was elected, the *New York Times* reported it. He won the black vote, it reported, but lost the whites three to two.

The *Times* pointed out that Mabus was a national Democrat, "the sort of young Democratic leader who might as easily be found appealing to voters in California or Massachusetts as to those of the Deep South." The *Times* went on to say that Steve Patterson, the Democratic state chairman in Mississippi, said:

> that the voting patterns diverged from normal in parts of the state, including some of the well-to-do precincts in northern Jackson. There, he said, Mr. Mabus won significant support from "yuppie voters."
>
> Those white professionals, he said, helped Mr. Mabus make up for losses suffered among some rural white Democrats who had ties with the local political organizations that Mr. Mabus, the State Auditor, had assailed as being corrupt.[24]

The election was on Tuesday, 3 November 1987. At 5:30 p.m. on Friday of that week, 6 November 1987, former Gov. Ross R. Barnett died. The obituary in the *New York Times* began, "Former Gov. Ross Robert Barnett, whose advocacy of segregation helped make Mississippi a civil rights battlefield 25 years ago, died Friday, his son said. He was 89 years old."[25]

4

Knowledge, Arts, and Education

[The] honest power of [Eudora Welty's] book [*Delta Wedding*]
lies . . . in the large meaning itself. I take this meaning to
reside in the efforts of three people outside the Fairchild
family to become a portion of it. In a sense, the meaning is
one of the great questions of this century, the struggle of the
individual to attach himself to a group, to acquire the
knowledge of belonging.

Paul Engle on *Delta Wedding*[1]

Being in Oxford, Mississippi, is being somewhere. The air there
is rarefied for an outsider, who finds walking the beautiful
streets of the town of Oxford a breathtaking, heart-pounding,
soul-stirring experience. Yet University of Mississippi students—Rebels, daughters and sons of Ole Miss as the vernacular tradition has named them—sun themselves there on the
grass outside their dormitories and tease one another with their
hot bodies just like students anywhere. To the students, most
of them, Oxford has plain air, real dirt, parties, classes, professors assigning work, too few beer joints, and too frequent visiting parents; and in general life carries on there much as it does
in many another small American university town.

The other Oxford, the one of the outsider-visitor, the current
Ole Miss students scarcely know. Immortalized by its most famous son as Jefferson, the county seat of Yoknapatawpha in William Faulkner's novels, Oxford's past, its Civil War memory, its
beauty, its stormy history in the civil rights period, and even its
everyday life in this era have mythological magnitude all over

the world, if not much in Mississippi—given the stature of prophets in their own country, perhaps in Mississippi least of all. Mr. Faulkner died in 1962, only months before James Meredith's admission desegregated the University of Mississippi and in that idyllic university town, rioters stormed in violent protest and members of the National Guard defended racial desegregation of the university, both sides of them Mississippians.

The Oxford Courthouse Square, the Human Spirit, and Benjy Compson

When I come to Oxford, Mississippi, I am an outsider-visitor. To my South-starved soul in March, the flowering trees and blossoming bulb plants provide a desperately needed earthy resurrection. The stories from that immortal son of Oxford have provided me spiritual nourishment; and I, along with the curious and famous, come to Oxford to honor him. But it is the earthbound country with its fresh growing things, the native soil that he and I shared, that gives my soul renewal. That ground is the means by which I am ready to understand what he knew. Sometime in my young adulthood I found myself no longer in need of a Heaven, as I discovered had been the case for some decades with many of my compatriots, though not for all of them—the latter a discovery that itself demanded difficult recognition of profound and honest human differences. My "scientific" discovery that, as Bertrand Russell is said to have put it, "When I die, I shall rot" made the earth, however, cosmically more significant for me. The Japanese magnolias in the Grove at Ole Miss, the flowering crabapple and pear trees, the redbud and dogwood blooming in the woods, the shrubs my mother called "red-tip," the camelias, and the azaleas are sun-drenched and living holy roods for me in today's Oxford.

Once, with a tour group of Faulkner enthusiasts in Oxford, I sat at dinner in the university cafeteria beside a distinguished middle-aged man named Ernest Sandeen, who was dying. He

Oxford Courthouse.
Photo by Gayle Graham Yates.

Statue of Confederate Soldier, Oxford Courthouse Square.
Photo by Gayle Graham Yates.

told me happily that he had searched all over on this trip south for an authentic country ham and had found one just off the square in Oxford at the Jitney Jungle. He died in his northern home soon after that. Every time I am in Oxford, as I walk from the Holiday Inn by the Jitney Jungle, facing that mythico-historical courthouse in the center of the square, I do my version of a prayer, post–Heavenly, post–camp-meeting-Jesus-saves-us-sinners-all, post–liberal-Methodist-student-leadership, post–Christologically-incarnationally-theologically-educated, post–radical-feminist-advocate-of the-Goddess, a prayer: open-eyed and sense-alert, I remember Ernest Sandeen, whom I knew only casually, and imagine and have hope for him, happy and nourished in the last days of his life by his success at finding a real southern country ham in a junky little supermarket off the square in Oxford, Mississippi. Remembering Ernest Sandeen— an actual man who, as I imagine him, actually walked out of that Jitney Jungle store satisfied, with his country ham in his arms, and satisfied faced the stately old courthouse building that I now am facing, in beautiful mythico-real Oxford—my soul too is nourished, and at long last I am at peace with my Mississippi and in the center of my self.

The Oxford courthouse and the town square in the center of which it sits appear in one of the most famous passages of American fiction. It is a passage associated with a mute idiot, Benjy Compson, whom Faulkner created in his novel that bears the title taken from William Shakespeare, *The Sound and the Fury*. Shakespeare's line goes: "Life is a tale told by an idiot,/ Full of sound and fury,/ Signifying nothing."

The first scene in which the white neoclassical courthouse and its marble obelisk topped with a Confederate soldier, appear is set in the fictional Jefferson that Faulkner make out of Oxford. Benjy's own internal voice narrates as the family makes its usual trip to the cemetery through the town and around the square in the surrey drawn by Queenie and driven by the black servant, T.P. The shadows change as they go right at the Confederate statue with the shops, the dry goods store, the drugstore, the city hall, the bank, and the law offices circling the square to their right, while the courthouse looms alone, solid and graceful in the square's center on their left. These customary shadows provide order and security for Benjy. Faulkner writes in the early passage in Benjy's voice:

> "You, T.P." Mother said, clutching me. I could hear Queenie's feet and the bright shapes went smooth and steady on both sides, the shadows of them flowing across Queenie's back. They went on like the bright tops of wheels. Then those on one side stopped at the tall white post where the soldier was. But on the other side they went on smooth and steady, but a little slower.[2]

In the final scene of the book, though the next day in fictional time, Dilsey, the black nurse and housekeeper who has cared for the Compson children all of Benjy's thirty-three years, against her better judgment allows her own adolescent son, Luster, to take Benjy out for a ride in the surrey, an activity that always quiets Benjy's bellowing. Benjy's grown-man uproar is typical of his daily life and also representative of all his family's disasters—drunkenness, dishonesty, emotional abandonment, incest, suicide, sexual profligacy, narcissism—and his mourning for them. Dilsey tries to comfort him: "'Hush, now,' she said, stroking his head, 'Hush, Dilsey got you.' But he bellowed slowly, abjectly, without tears; the grave hopeless sound of voiceless misery under the sun."[3]

Before Benjy and Luster leave in the surrey, the two black caretakers know to give Benjy a flower, know that he can be made content with a flower in his hand. Luster brings him the one remaining narcissus in their garden. It is broken. When Benjy cries, Luster repairs the narcissus with a splint made of a stick and two pieces of string. Dilsey, fearing Luster's rambunctiousness, says:

> "You know de way now?" she said, "Up de street, round de square, to de graveyard, den straight back home."
> "Yessum," Luster said, "Hum up, Queenie."
> "You gwine be careful, now?"
> "Yessum." Dilsey released the bridle.

But Luster was not careful. As they near the square, he whips his horse into a run. Benjy remains tranquil. But at the courthouse square, Luster makes the major error of turning left instead of right. These are Faulkner's words:

> They approached the square, where the Confederate soldier gazed with empty eyes beneath his marble hand into wind and weather. Luster took still another notch in himself and gave the impervious Queenie a cut with the switch, casting his glance about the square. "Dar Mr Jason's car," he said. Then he spied another group of negroes. "Les show dem niggers how quality does, Benjy," he said, "Whut you say?" He looked back. Ben sat, holding the flower in his fist, his gaze empty and untroubled. Luster hit Queenie again and swung her to the left at the monument.
>
> For an instant Ben sat in an utter hiatus. Then he bellowed. Bellow on bellow, his voice mounted, with scarce interval for breath. There was more than astonishment in it, it was horror; shock; agony eyeless, tongueless; just sound, and Luster's eyes backrolling for a white instant. "Gret God," he said, "Hush! Hush! Gret God!" He whirled again and struck Queenie with the switch. It broke and he cast it away and with Ben's voice mounting toward its unbelievable crescendo Luster caught up the end of the reins and leaned forward as Jason came jumping across the square and onto the step.[4]

Benjy's brother, Jason, stopped the surrey, trounced Luster, and sent them back on their way, slowly and decorously—to the right of the statue in the courthouse square. The story finishes:

> "Ben's voice roared and roared. Queenie moved again, her feet began to clop-clop steadily again, and at once Ben hushed. Luster looked quickly back over his shoulder, then he drove on. The broken flower drooped over Ben's fist and his eyes were empty and blue and serene again as cornice and facade flowed smoothly once more from left to right; post and tree, window and doorway, and signboard, each in its ordered place."[5]

In Faulkner's novel, Benjy's narcissus indicates that it is early spring. Given the classical and psychological associations of the narcissus with self-preoccupation, the lone flower suggests the last "puny inexhaustible" but indestructible voice of the human individual turned in upon itself, as Faulkner spoke about it in his Nobel Prize Speech. But Benjy, according to Dilsey, is "the Lawd's child": being helpless as a mentally retarded person, he paradoxically is the family member who is cared for and who survives the others' tendencies toward self-destructiveness. Since he is unable to care for himself, other people, however unwillingly, take care of him. Yet his bellowing is as dictatorial as the orders of any tyrant. He is accustomed to driving left to right around the square. Luster, puffed up with self-importance at driving the surrey, whips the horse and takes him right to left. When Jason forces him to return to the familiar order, left to right, the book ends with Benjy serene at the world being in order, with the cornices and facades where they are supposed to be in the square, with his homeplace intact.

His faith in the human spirit coupled with his realism about the shortchanging of that spirit that humans can make, Faulkner articulated in the speech he made in Stockholm on 10 December 1950, as he received the Nobel Prize for Literature. One can remember that he learned these lofty lessons perhaps on the Oxford square, perhaps going on foot back and forth from his home to his town square every day of his working life. He told the world:

Our tragedy today is a general and universal physical fear so long sustained by now that we can even bear it. There are no longer problems of the spirit. There is only the question: when will I be blown up? Because of this, the young man or woman writing today has forgotten the problems of the human heart in conflict with itself which alone can make good writing . . .

. . . He [and she] must learn them again. . . . Until [they] do so [they] labor under a curse. [They] write not of love but of lust, of defeats in which nobody loses anything of value . . . [Their] griefs grieve on no universal bones, leaving no scars. [They] write not of the heart but of the glands. . . .

. . . It is easy enough to say that [people are] immortal simply because [they] will endure; that when the last ding-dong of doom has clanged and faded from the last worthless rock hanging tideless in the last red and dying evening, that even then there will still be one more sound; that of [a human's] puny inexhaustible voice, still talking. I refuse to accept this. I believe that [hu]man[kind] will not merely endure: [we] will prevail . . . because [we each have] a soul, a spirit capable of compassion and sacrifice and endurance. . . . The poet's voice need not merely be the record of [the hu]man, it can be one of the props, the pillars to help h[unamity] endure and prevail.[6]

Already when William Faulkner was giving the Nobel Prize Speech affirming the human spirit, nurtured by the Mississippi soil, his female literary counterpart was forty years old and well established as a writer who, like Faulkner, peopled her stories with fictional Mississippians, made up places that were Mississippi towns, and gave her readers a new Mississippi mythology. On my Mississippi journey, I got to spend an afternoon with Eudora Welty.

My Visit with Eudora Welty

Eudora Welty's picture and name are everywhere in Jackson. The city public library in the old Sears building is named the Eudora Welty Library. The portrait of Eudora Welty painted by prominent Jackson artist Karl Wolfe can be seen at night from the street, spotlighted on the second floor of the Millsaps College library near North State Street. At the state Department of Archives and History, a photograph of her in dark-rimmed glasses, pen in hand, bent over her writing desk, is placed over the reception desk in the entry. The display case in the state Department of Archives and History, during the year it had a Welty scholar-in-residence, showed pictures of her and photocopies of precious letters to and from her. A 1936 letter from John Rood at *Manuscript* accepts "Death of a Traveling Salesman" and asks to see more, telling her "various publishers will be interested." One letter from Robert Penn Warren, at the *Southern Review,* dated 13 January 1937, speaks of "Flowers for Marjorie" and "The Petrified Man" and says of his editors' response to her stories that they "have been on the verge of pub-

Eudora Welty. Photo by Gayle Graham Yates.

lishing two of them." Displayed there, too, was a much-revised page of the *Losing Battles* manuscript stuck together with safety pins.

Eudora Welty is much admired and loved in her home city and in the world. I am one of those admirers and joined the fortunate few of them who have been able to meet and interview her. While there exist a number in the hundreds of interviews with her in print and on tape, in recent years, because of the fame that came after her best-selling memoir *One Writer's Beginnings*, there have been thousands more hopeful interviewers who have wanted to meet and talk to her. Long admired by writers and readers of serious fiction, she now holds celebrity status with a much wider audience. I was invited to visit her only through the intercession of my greatly revered college history professor and her friend, Ross Moore.

The jonquils were blooming in Jackson that February morning. The blossoming fruit trees were beginning to bud. Tulips were up and lifting their heads to the sunlight. And I was happy, excited, full of joyful anticipation all morning long. In the afternoon I was going to see Eudora Welty!

I had prepared as if I were a doctoral student about to take examinations. I read *The Golden Apples, The Robber Bridegroom, The Eye of the Story*, selected short stories from her short-story collection. I worried about what to call her: Miss Welty? Welty? Eudora Welty? Not Eudora, wrongly familiar. Not Ms. Welty, not sure about her attraction to its feminist connotation. Miss Welty, I decided, as I had been taught as a child to call unmarried women of my mother's age in cases where we were simply acquaintances. That fits like "Miss Turpie," my graduate school professor who is also my mother's age and who eventually invited me to call her "Mary," though she remains "Miss Turpie" in my affectionate heart of hearts. This goes on long after I have endorsed "Ms." on principle as the proper title for any adult woman without reference to marital status. I am getting this straight. I am going to see one of my intellectual and artistic mother-women, and the strains of what to call her come in a child's voice from a childhood time as well as a childhood place.

I wrote out questions and notes on what I had read of Miss Welty's work in the past. I went to the library at the Department of Archives and History and looked up all the Welty material. The manuscript sources were restricted, and I could have found the general periodicals and literary magazines with works by and about Miss Welty in any good library, but it felt better to be reading about her in her "official" library, the repository library to which *she* had chosen to give her materials. I was glad to have found the article about her by her friend Charlotte Capers, the long-time director of this archive in which I was working and herself a talented writer and Jackson personality. I was glad to study the Welty book-length bibliography assembled by another of her friends, my fondly remembered college librarian, Bethany Sweringen. I mulled over and meditated upon the Welty works and what people had said about them. I well knew that she had been interviewed many times, knew that she regarded public presentation of herself, even in interview form, as something of a trial, knew that there was already a fine collection of Welty interviews, *Conversations with Eudora Welty*, edited by Peggy Whitman Prenshaw. So what was I *doing*, I asked myself in some agony, going to see this famous, wonderful woman and putting her through yet one more interview? I couldn't possibly ask her something that hadn't been asked of her before. I couldn't possibly get her to say something to me and before my tape recorder that she herself would not feel that she could say better in writing. Why was I doing this to both of us? Because I wanted to see her, of course. As fans do, I wanted to talk with her. But, oh, somehow I wanted to be more dignified than a mere fan!

Reassure yourself, Gayle, I told myself, you are a grownup university professor now. With a full case of the jitters. I talked to myself some more. You were just barely twenty years old when you met her before, I said to myself, and she smiled at you and handed you her manuscript and, with her characteristic modesty, invited you to quote from it "if I said anything worth quoting." You are well aware that she is a gracious, generous person, I said to myself, working up my courage.

I was going to see Miss Welty on this sunny, spring-heralding February day, and my spirit of anticipation matched the day's brilliance with eagerness and pleasure mixed with apprehension. On the phone she gave me the directions to her house off North State Street on Pinehurst Street across from Belhaven College. "There is a big old oak tree in the front yard," she told me. I was punctual for my appointment. She drove up a minute or so after I did. Warm and wonderful, she led me into her living room. Instantly I loved her. This would be easy. What follows is my interview with her.

GGY: When we first met, I was an undergraduate at Millsaps, and you read a paper at Millsaps ["How I Write"], which was published as the first item in the Peggy Prenshaw volume, *Conversations with Eudora Welty*. I was present at the paper-reading [in 1961] and the forum that followed. I enjoyed so much meeting you then, and I have been a reader of yours all of these years since then. What I have come back to you for, besides the pleasure of getting to see you again, is to talk with you about your Mississippi. I know that place is an essential category for you as you work in fiction. Is the place that you invent in your mind grounded in Mississippi, nourished by Mississippi?

EUDORA WELTY (EW): Yes, it is. But I feel it really comes from the fact that I am a fiction writer and that wherever I happened to be I would do the same thing. I think it didn't start out because of Mississippi, but because of my wish to write. I don't want to claim that I am a spokesman for the state in itself. It's just that it happened that I was born here.

And I love it. And it has taught me a great deal. But it is for the selfish reason that I realize that I needed that to write my stories within to make them reflect life as I saw it. I nearly always write from the point of view of the stranger or the traveler because that is the only way I could vouch for what I say.

[I recognize the authority of the outsider voice in the narration of Miss Welty's fiction. The stories and novels are peopled by an array of keenly understood extraordinary human beings, women and men, children and adults, whites and blacks, people from town and rural folk. Theirs is an interior psychological, familial, and community reality, rather than a political one; and nearly all of them are placed in Mississippi. Not a single county like Faulkner's Yoknapatawpha, Welty's more indirect mythology makes regions of the state of Mississippi into metaphors for human social and economic meaning. *Delta Wedding* is set in the rich river delta region. *The Robber Bridegroom* is set on the historic Natchez Trace. I ask about *Losing Battles*, which she tells me takes place in the contrasting poorer northeastern part of the state.]

GGY: Let's talk about some specific places that you invented. For example, in the town of Banner in *Losing Battles*, you brought your outsider voice, or brought in a narrator who is an outsider, to create the place. You actually have several regions of Mississippi in your writing. Banner is what?

EW: North Mississippi. Near the Tennessee line. That was chosen for specific reasons. I like to try something new for all my books, though probably the outside world does not think there is any difference between one and the other, but to me they are always different. I wanted to see if I could write a story, as I thought it was going to be, without introspection being described in it, that is, going inside the characters' minds. I felt I had been doing that maybe overly, that I had gotten too contemplative and slow-moving, so I thought I would see if I could do something altogether in action and conversation and still show the same thing, still show what was going on, but to do it in the way a playwright does, by action and voice.

And, so to do that I needed a place where the action could be rather in primary colors, that is, a place where whatever people do normally shows things, so that is action. And I also wanted to write about what the poorest people in the world would probably always have to depend on, which is the family and subsisting on their own devices. And, so [for the time period in *Losing Battles*], I got the epitome of that in the Depression when people didn't have anything, wouldn't have, anyway. In the Depression and that section of the state which never had any riches, never did. And where the family would just be starkly out there. And I was so aware that life can be very rambunctious. People living as the family did in Banner where everything is overt. I did it through a family reunion so everybody would talk. I couldn't have ever laid that story in the Delta or the Mississippi Gulf Coast.

GGY: Because the people in the Delta and on the Gulf Coast are more affluent?

EW: Yes, they are just brought up differently, too. They had more and they expected more and they were more aware of the rest of the world.

And in *Delta Wedding*, it was to be my impression of the Delta. I don't know too much about either section of the state except as a visitor or as somebody driving through it, but I know many Delta people. You are from Wayne County?

GGY: [Yes,] Wayne County.

EW: That's south.

GGY: Southeast.

EW: Southeast.

GGY: About a hundred miles from the Gulf Coast.

EW: Just the opposite from the Delta. That is what I was about to say, but I wanted to be sure. (Laugh) Anyway, I wanted to set that novel at a time when there was nothing except the family again that you have to deal with. And all the men had to be home, so there couldn't be a wartime, any war. It couldn't be a floodtime, for that is another crisis. So I set it in the 1920s—1927 was the terrible flood—I couldn't have it that year. It just sort of came down to the fact that I had to set it in this time in the 1920s when I wasn't really very old myself. So I had a little girl enter the story on the train and everything was revealed to her.

GGY: The little girl is the outsider that you can bring the knowledge to. In your discussion of those two novels and their locations and the need for those locations because of the story you had, you talked about the value of the family in each one, of your wanting to show family values. It seems to me that in *One Writer's Beginnings*, you talk about your own social values and their origins as a basis for your literary values, one of them being respect for the family and joy

in the family. And another being cherishing friendships. And
another being—well—tolerating eccentricities or diversity
among people. But abhoring or rejecting cruelty or human
unkindness. You suggest in *One Writer's Beginnings* that the
origin of those values is in your own family, in where you
were brought up or how you were brought up. Though, even
in *One Writer's Beginnings*, your own voice is the center. You
are not the outsider.

I was interested especially in your attention to values as
you focused that book or that set of three lectures [that comprise *One Writer's Beginnings*]. Was [attention to family val-
ues] at all central to your creation of that book, *One Writer's
Beginnings*?

EW: I think so. It is like the opposite of your question about
place because I chose the place to fit what I wanted to say.
In my case, it was the family life and the way I was brought
up that taught me what I wanted. I am interested in human
relationships. That is my true core. That is what I try to
write about. Certainly it begins in the family and extends
out and out. Of course, all these things are hindsight. I
never thought of anything like this when I was writing the
the stories. Not in an analytical way. I was aware of what I
was doing, but not analytically. What I had undertaken to
do was to try to see what in my life produced certain
things.

GGY: Yes. I understand from Ross Moore [her friend, the
Millsaps College historian] that you were reluctant to under-
take that assignment.

EW: I was. If it hadn't been for Ross I probably wouldn't have
done it, because he had called me on behalf of David Donald
[the Harvard professor who commissioned the lectures]. All
he asked was that I would talk to David Donald.

GGY: Talk to David Donald?

EW: Talk to David Donald. Which, of course, I was delighted
to do. But I don't know if I ever would have undertaken lectures at Harvard. Still it seems to me amazing that I had the
temerity to do that. If it hadn't been—well, I met him [Da-

vid Donald] after Daniel Aaron who was already a friend of
mine had really suggested where I might catch onto a handle
to it. I said I don't know anything to tell graduate students
at Harvard—you know, I am not a scholar, I am not anything like that. He said, well, there is one thing you know
that they don't, and that is you know about what in your life
made you into a writer. And that *is* the one thing that I
could have talked about. So between the two of them they
were very receptive and helpful. I am very grateful to Ross
for setting the ball rolling for me.

GGY: You enjoyed it when you got started?

EW: I didn't enjoy it until I had done the first lecture. I was
petrified—I enjoyed the *writing* of it. But *delivering* it in the
form of three lectures was very frightening because I
couldn't imagine whether or not anything I had written
would communicate itself to the audience I was reading to.
Also, it was a different time, a different place, a different
everything. But they were receptive [in the audience for the
first lecture], and after that I drew a deep breath for the
first time! After the first one.

GGY: And then it [the book from the lectures, *One Writer's Beginnings*] has been number one on the bestseller list [for] just
weeks and weeks and weeks and weeks.

EW: Isn't that amazing?

GGY: I think that's marvelous.

EW: Harvard was as staggered as I was!

GGY: I understand that it is their first bestseller. Harvard
University Press hasn't had another one.

EW: That's what they say. Isn't that funny? I mean, it is
amusing. As if that were what they strove for. Or me,
either.

GGY: Well, if I might move to a short story. My all-time favorite story of yours is "Livvie." I have read it with students
again and again. And I am curious [about its source]. Do you
remember where any of those people came from in that
story? How they came to you. Livvie or Cash or Solomon or
Miss Baby Marie?

EW: Not as a story. In a very limited way—it was the place
  really. And it was the bottle tree that made me write it.
GGY: Ahhh! I love that image. Tell me about that.
EW: Well, there used to be—you have no doubt seen them—I
  don't know whether they have them in Wayne County
GGY: I haven't seen them. I have seen pictures of them.
EW: Well, there are hardly any anymore because of the highways. You know, the interstates have come through. I have
  tried to find some of the old bottle trees down on Highway
  49 where they used to be and where the old houses used to
  be that had them. They have vanished now. Access roads to
  the interstates have just come in and just plowed them up.
  So there probably still are some away back in somewhere.
  But there used to be a number of them that I could get to
  very quickly from Jackson. You know, drive down there.
    None of the people—characters that I invented for my
  story—were people that were where the bottle trees were.
  In fact, I almost never saw any. I saw one. An old man. The
  one that lived with the best bottle trees. The ones that I
  really used. There was an enormous avenue of them. And
  the little peach tree that I put in the story was blooming at
  the time with these beautiful blue Milk of Magnesia bottles,
  you know—
GGY: Oh, my goodness.
EW: —and the peach tree was blooming. So, this old black
  gentleman came out one of the times I passed there to look
  at it. And I asked him if I might take a picture of his beautiful bottle trees and he said that was fine. I wasn't using color
  film. I didn't know how at that time. I am sorry I didn't get
  that. So then I said—I don't remember how I asked him—
  but one of the things that had puzzled me was that he had an
  altar built in there. It looked more like a speaker's podium
  with a slanted desk top—like a dictionary stand or something was standing there. That did puzzle me. I did ask in a
  polite way if the bottle trees were anything besides beautiful. Are they here for beauty or for what? Because somewhere I got the idea that they were sometimes built to con-

tain the spirits of unfriendly or evil spirits that might try to
get into the house. I may have put that into the story.

GGY: I think that is in there.

EW: He said he didn't want to talk about that, though. I was
trespassing. When I asked him, I realized. But I figured that
it had to be an old house—and a very dignified person that
would live there. He was dignified, but he wasn't my man,
wasn't Solomon. When I pictured a spring story, I had to
have a young man come down to Trace, the Old Trace, I used
to call it, deep down. But I saw a man in a zoot suit on Farish Street in Jackson that I copied, that I put on Cash. That
was a real outfit. I couldn't have made it up. Those were the
times of the zoot suit. Nobody now knows what they are.
Your students would—

GGY: —have to look it up.

EW: I have to tell them. When I read that story. Be prepared
for something called a zoot suit. It is a very simple story. It
is about old and young, spring and winter, changes.

GGY: I remember as an undergraduate being taught to look
for symbols in a story. And in a lecture that you gave—it
was a marking point in my literary education—you talked
about how items in a story that could be interpreted as symbols just came. You didn't think, "I'll put in a symbol."

EW: No.

GGY: But in that story there is so much that can be interpreted symbolically.

EW: And, correctly. Yes.

GGY: Cash.

EW: But, also what I would always like to say if I say anything about symbols is that they have to occur organically or
they don't mean anything. You know, they have to be a part
of the story. But, there are people in the [news]paper whose
names are Cash. Of course when I saw it I was galvanized
and stored it away so that when I needed it it came. But I
wouldn't have made up that name Cash if I had never seen it
used anywhere.

GGY: And similarly Livvie?

EW: Yeah. There was a girl that went to camp with me when I was thirteen years old whose name was Livvie. And it never occurred to me that it was probably for Olivia. I just thought they named her Livvie. That's all I know about her. That was intriguing. And there are lots of old people, as you know, old black people, whose names are Biblical and Greek. And Solomon could be—So all these things have precedents in real life.

GGY: The names fit organically.

EW: The people were more than the names.

[I turned our attention to *The Golden Apples*. *The Golden Apples* is a story cycle that some readers have called a novel, since the action in all the stories is related and the characters are all the same. The stories are set in the imaginary Mississippi town of Morgana. Morgana's inhabitants exhibit the full spectrum of human behavior and motivation.]

GGY: You have several times mentioned people, or life, being your inspiration. I interpret your work as saying a lot about society. I think your fictional truth corresponds to what a lot of good sociologists write about society.

EW: Is that so?

GGY: And the society that you have created that I think is most complex is Morgana in *The Golden Apples*. I came late to *The Golden Apples*. I hadn't read *The Golden Apples* until recently. And it was as if someone had given me a new classic.

EW: Oh, how wonderful!

GGY: I was just amazed. And loved it. And I have appreciated all the things of yours that I have read, but I think it rose to the top. Or the near-top!

EW: That gives me a lot of pleasure because I most loved writing that book.

GGY: Oh, did you?

EW: I just *loved* writing it. And it was opening up to me as I wrote. I didn't realize the stories were going to be connected. You probably read my comments on this if you have been reading some of these because a lot of people ask me, Isn't it really a novel? Which it isn't.

GGY: Yes.

EW: But I just *loved* it! And I don't know any time in my life I ever felt so embedded and so carried away by the story. I just loved writing it.

GGY: That shows. You loved the story. And you loved the people. And you loved the language. I think I could read it without paying attention to the story one time around and just pay attention to how lyrical and marvelous the language is, but the story is—the stories are—quite profound. But, how did you make up Morgana? I am thinking of my earlier question about society.

EW: It evolved, too. Because I didn't even realize when I began writing the stories that they were connected. And I think Morgana came to me in one of the stories. I saw it was right because all the characters, as you know, were living under dreams or illusions or even obsessions. I wanted to get a name that would unite all of them. And then I chose Morgana because [of] "back to Morgana" and all those things that you have read about the illusion of the genie on the ocean.

GGY: No, I don't know.

EW: You don't know that? Well, it's in stories and things, fairy tales—maybe it's true that there is an illusion from the fog or something at sea. But it has fooled sailors. But I thought again that it was organically right. Because you know how the Delta has so many place names named after people?

GGY: Yes.

EW: And so, it was named after the Morgans. It was Morgana. So that fit it and everything came together. I thought it helped unite all the stories.

GGY: Yes. And the people's lives all overlap and they interact with each other. They have a mythic connectedness with each other as well.

EW: Of course, I had all this thing about the Greek myths at

the time. Had I foreseen how critics talked! [Laugh.] I just
made free with it! Because I just did whatever came to my
mind. Not only Greek, but Irish and every other kind of
myth. And people have written me all these abstruse questions about what I was trying to do and what the—. I'm glad
I didn't take it too [seriously].

GGY: I love hearing you talk about the liberties you took—
you took with the myths!

EW: That's the only way to write, anyway.

GGY: Yes. Yes.

EW: There are a lot of things. I realized it when I was reading
proof on the *Collected Stories*. I hadn't read most of those
things since I wrote them. I just read the ones I use when I
give readings in colleges, a small handful. And I thought,
Heavens, when I think of the questions people have asked
me on some of those stories! It would have made me self-
conscious. I would have hesitated before I did some of the
things I did. [Laugh]

GGY: Yes.

EW: I don't intend ever to hesitate, but I didn't realize what I
was stepping into.

GGY: Well, it is a good thing you didn't have those critics'
questions!

EW: It sure is! It sure is!

GGY: [Let's] return to my interest in Eudora Welty's Mississippi. I read a quotation from a review of *The Golden Apples*
by Hamilton Basso. He wrote, "I doubt that a better book
about the south has ever been written."

EW: Bless his heart!

GGY: Do you think it [*The Golden Apples*] is *importantly* about
the South?

EW: I think it is important in that if you are not true to the
place you are writing about, it won't be true for life. And I
think it follows that if you are very true to what you might
try to get, things really revealing of human beings in relation to where they live and their time, then it will apply to
anywhere.

GGY: It has to be both/and. It is both about the South and about life.

EW: That's all right. But I was proud of that little Hamilton Basso. He died young. But he was from New Orleans, and he wrote some good novels. One was called *The View from Pompey's Head*. And he reviewed books for the *New Yorker*. I was proud of his saying that because he knew what he was speaking of.

GGY: You also celebrate relationships, friendships, family. Maybe we could talk about one more work [considering] relationships, *The Optimist's Daughter*. That novel has an inside-outsider, an outsider coming back. Laurel has lived away and comes back for the death of her father. In the character of Laurel, in her having her roots in Mississippi but having to go away and come back for a kind of mature self-realization—Is there something different or unusual about that set of relationships in that story from your other stories?

EW: It occurs to me that it penetrates in ways I had not tried before. And it would take another facet. You know the facet of law. And yet the other characters have fully as much value as she [Laurel] has if not more.

GGY: Yes.

EW: And she knows it. I mean, she takes that secondary place, both by my wish and hers—it wasn't just what Laurel thought that mattered—I mean, that is the way it comes through. The point of view that I used. But I think more is shown of all the other characters through the scenes in the book than she. I tried a sort of multiple thing. [Laurel's mother, Becky, had died; and Laurel's judge-father was married again to Fay, a coarse, manipulative younger woman of a lower social class. Around the funeral of her father, Laurel deals with Fay and her ubiquitous ill-mannered relatives.]

GGY: What was that?

EW: I tried to show many of the characters in more depth than I usually try. Nearly the whole thing is introspective, except for one or two rather garish scenes [laugh]—which were necessary. The whole thing. I hoped to see the interiors of nearly all the people in it, like—well, everybody. I was just interested in all the people. I wanted to show how much there was to them.

GGY: They are different in that they come from different social backgrounds, different experiences.

EW: Yes. And yet they all were worth knowing. Even Fay. [Voice changes to lower, confiding tone] I must say I really did hate her.

GGY: You really did hate Fay? [Both laugh]

EW: I really hated her. I couldn't help it. I tried to be fair to her by bringing her family. [Both laugh again] I really did! I thought they would explain her! But, anyway, I hate what she stood for.

GGY: Yes.

EW: I don't mean she was a symbolic character, but the one who doesn't understand what experience means. And doesn't learn anything from it. You could scratch the skin and there wouldn't be anything under it, the way she would see things. And to me, that is horrifying and even evil, almost sinful. And I may have gone overboard in that case. I have been accused of it. But the point was I did want to show—in a quiet way, I wanted to show more of life than I had been able to with some of the others. It was a smaller cast and a direr situation.

GGY: Yes.

EW: Well, I wrote it at a time when I was feeling rather dire. It was soon after my own mother's death. It is not about my own family, but the character of Becky is a little like that of my own mother. She has her background, West Virginia; but I was not writing my mother. You know. But the judge is totally made up. I wanted a man who was—you know that kind of Mississippian, I am sure, like Judge McKelva. And you know there are many like him. I've known many. I mean of his background and substance and so on.

GGY: Yes.

EW: It was necessary for each one to have what—to have the weight they have. What I tried to do was to give it to them. I don't know whether I succeeded, but that is what I tried to do.

GGY: I liked it. And I am glad that Laurel left the bread-board.

EW: Me, too.

GGY: Let me ask you a few last questions about other interests and influences, other than the novels and stories of your own. What about other art forms? You write wonderfully about music, but say you are not a musician.

EW: No, I am not. An extra benefit by Belhaven being over here [the college with a good music program, across the street from her house where we were talking]. In the days before air conditioning, everything came through the window. Right over here to me at my window!

I love music. I love painting. I know more about painting than I do about music just because it is easier to. It has been more accessible to me. When I went to college in the Middle West where you are, in Madison [at the University of Wisconsin], I used to go down to Chicago and go to the Art Institute. It was wonderful to get acquainted with the French Impressionists that were early. So I had more opportunity to [learn about painting]. I minored in art, as a matter of fact. I took art history and things like that. I was better educated in it.

GGY: Do you suppose that your wonderful visual imagery has been influenced by your art education? Your enjoyment of art?

EW: It could well be. I am a visual person. I mean, I don't know whether that got me interested in painting or painting got me interested in it. Who knows? That is, I feel I have learned more through my eyes than my ears. I love photography, and it taught me a lot, too.

GGY: It was a combination of the historical moment—and the job that you had.

EW: Right. That's what it came out of. But when I went to
write this book about—*One Writer's Beginnings*—I suddenly
realized what a good photographer my father had been. You
know. All these pictures turned up, pictures he had taken
before he had ever married my mother. When he was traveling on his—I don't know how he ever managed to do that—
up in *Canada* and out West and everywhere. Wonderful pictures! And just the mass of them simply staggered me. I
didn't know he had done all of that. He and Mother used to
print them at home. So I grew up with picture taking going
on all the time, but I didn't even realize it.

GGY: Yes. Well, as a final kind of question: Who would you say
of people—teachers or family or whoever—most influenced
you? You don't have to pick one.

EW: To be a writer?

GGY: To be a writer and to develop the kind of life that you
developed. Which is one and the same, isn't it?

EW: Yeah. Well, my mother was always very much for my
being a writer. But my father died when I was only—
twenty—and I had not written anything then except school
things. Let's see, he died the year after I had been at Columbia. I was twenty-two when I came home. So he never
knew if or what I could write. But together they made, as
you know from my book they made such a home with respect
to [literature]—I mean, they loved the arts and they loved
reading and they loved things like that. I am sure it put the
mainsprings of my imagination working which is what it is.
And I always had good teachers. I have been so *lucky* all my
life. Teachers and literary agents and editors. I didn't know
that everybody didn't have all these things. Until I hear of
the other kind. I have been very much blessed. And I know
it. I don't think you can put it on any one thing. Just the
combination of wonderful people. They have encouraged me
and understood my work.

And Jackson is just wonderful to me. You know, they're
almost too wonderful!

GGY: What Jackson times have you most enjoyed? I mean the ceremonial ones like speaking at the William Winter inauguration or the Seventy-fifth Birthday Party for you at Millsaps?

EW: I deeply felt the honor. But I also felt on the spot! [Laughter.] To produce. It is hard for me to do anything in public. It really is. I am basically pretty shy. I can talk about work or something that I care about, especially to a friend, but it is *hard* for me to do things in public.

GGY: Well, thank you for letting me come to your home and for talking with me.

EW: I have enjoyed it. I knew I would enjoy it.[7]

I too enjoyed it. I enjoyed it very much. At that point I turned off my tape recorder, and she offered me a drink, and we two sat and talked like old friends for another hour. It was a lovely afternoon.

I left her only reluctantly, and my next stop, when I settled again intellectually, was with a scholar and writer my own age. I did not visit with him. I have never met him. But James Curtis has struggled, much as I have, with literature and life and learning outside Mississippi and the South.

James Curtis, Modernism, Postmodernism, and Elvis Presley

Mississippi-born James Curtis, the age of Anne Moody and me and also the age Emmett Till would be if he had not been murdered in 1954, has written an erudite book entitled *Culture as Polyphony*. He dedicated it:

To three people from Tupelo:
My parents, Malcolm and Earsel Curtis,
and Elvis Presley, *in memoriam*.[8]

This book is an essay in culture theory, an explanation of the difference between modernism and postmodernism in Western arts, literature, and intellectual life. The scholarly "school" to which the book belongs is the most sophisticated and widely followed of current approaches to studies in comparative literature and culture. This theory originated in France and Germany with such scholars as Jacques Derrida, Michel Foucault, and Claude Levi-Strauss, and made its way into American intellectual circles through prominent eastern universities such as Yale and Columbia. According to the theory, modernism is the explanatory idea for literature, arts, and conceptualizations from the early part of the twentieth century, an idea which relied upon understanding boundaries of space and time. Critical theory or explanatory theory for inventive items or systems implies a metaphor. The metaphor that is relied upon for an interpretive vehicle for a literary piece, a made object, or an idea necessarily implied a physics, and the physics of modernism required spatial and temporal limits, boundaries, delineations. Hence, metaphors for modernism required things set in space and time.

Postmodernism, the present-day successor to modernism, relies upon process. Fluidity rather than establishment is the metaphor. Process itself, rather than boundaries or sharp edges of time or space, is the source of interpretation. Modernism separated culture into high culture and primitive culture. Postmodernism, while maintaining a tension between mass culture and high culture, emphasizes "binarism" or belonging to the same system. That is, mass culture and high culture are two expressions of the same impulses. Modernism expounded and exhibited the culture of an economic and educational elite. Postmodernism relies heavily upon popular culture for the central clues to intellectual expression of human behavior. This is a summary of such culture theory from Curtis's advancement of it.[9]

James Curtis is a scholar of Russian literature who has been influenced by theories and methodologies of European comparative literature and culture. He earned his Ph.D. at Columbia University. Of the source of his book he writes:

> *Culture as Polyphony* really had its origins in Tupelo, Mississippi, where I grew up, and where Elvis Presley also grew up. In a way,

I wrote it to resolve the tensions that I came to feel between the culture of Tupelo and the culture of New York City, where I got a Ph.D. in Russian literature at Columbia University. In artistic terms, the tension stretches between Elvis Presley's "Don't Be Cruel," which evokes in me a memory of a particular afternoon in Tupelo, and Foyodor Dostoyevsky's *Crime and Punishment* . . . I have found myself unable to choose between them. . . . [T]his book expresses my own need to use a paradigm that excludes neither songs like "Don't Be Cruel," nor novels like *Crime and Punishment*. I hope that in what I say here I can serve as a cultural mediator for others who feel similar tensions and contradictions.

. . . In my classes at Columbia I often felt frustrated at what I considered the stupidity of the Russians' belief in the specialness and uniqueness of their country because it all sounded so familiar— it sounded like what Southerners have always said about the South. I began to realize that I perceived Russia, and Russians, differently from my fellow students and my teachers. The beauty and repulsiveness of Russian culture had a personal resonance for me—they always reminded me of the beauty and repulsiveness of Southern culture. That which I had sought to escape proved a great source of strength and meaning.

Stubbornly at first and then with increasing fascination and even pride, I began to sense the many similarities between the American South and Russia. Both have existed primarily as agrarian societies in which modernization has proceeded at a dizzying and often destructive pace. Both have responded to this change by trying to deny its existence and effects, and both have compensated for an obsessive sense of cultural inferiority by a fervent regionalism. Regionalism often gives rise to demagoguery, and both cultures have a history of violence and racism in which a decadent aristocracy has played a major role. Finally, much creativity has come from both, especially in the twentieth century.[10]

Curtis explains that his insight about the similarity between the American South and Russia came to him suddenly, when he read Marshall McLuhan's view in *Understanding Media* that present-day global society is moving away from being primarily literate and is becoming more centrally oral. Historically, in McLuhan's terms, following an ancient tribal norm of orality, literacy became the norm for modern societies. When the world moved from tribal to modern times, explanations in the form of reading were linear and literate. In postmodern times, with worldwide electronic communication, the new global society can be explained only as oral and in nonlinear fashion.

In James Curtis's flash of insight, he reports, "I had found a way of making the vital connections between specific facts in various cultures and the general principles of a unified system. To my delight, the system gave me a way of understanding both Elvis Presley and Foyodor Dostoyevsky. But as a line from one of Elvis's songs has it, that's when my troubles really began."[11]

In Curtis's scheme, Elvis Presley's work of originating and popularizing rock 'n' roll music was one of the great arts achievements of postmodernism. Post-1960s, post-Vietnam-War cultural disenchantment and malaise simultaneously provide both an explanation of the popularity and importance of Elvis's music and an understanding of Elvis's premature death as a self-abusive, disillusioned forty-two-year-old.

His book's dedication, linking his parents and hence his own origin in Tupelo, Mississippi, and Elvis Presley, born also in Tupelo, Mississippi, forecasts how the scholarly, adult James Curtis makes sense out of what happened in American culture in the 1950s and 1960s.

Certainly it was not just the words, and not even just the music of his performance that made Elvis great, Curtis believes. It was the total performance, the total phenomenon, the energy and power of Presley's pelvis-rocking movement-and-song events on stage and in media that made him into the biggest, richest, and most famous entertainer of his time. Thereby, Curtis suggests, he was also made into a commodity; and, as a commodity, at the end of his life he had nothing of his person to provide meaning or significance. What he did as a rock 'n' roll singer changed music and changed the way American culture was understood, but he himself was not changed and was left to seek his hedonistic death.

The explanation is in Mississippi. Tupelo is in the poor hill country where Eudora Welty set her novel of a poor family's struggles, *Losing Battles*, and not far from the part of northern

Alabama where James Agee and Walker Evans took the photographs of very poor southerners for *Let Us Now Praise Famous Men.* This region's red dirt is little good for growth, and the people who have tried to farm it have been desperately poor, its townspeople in the country towns little better off. Comparing them to the people in Agee and Evans's book, Curtis describes a photograph of the small boy Elvis and his parents in front of their house in Tupelo, citing the "vacant" faces and the "shapeless" dress of the parents in contrast to the energy and the life in the boy's face. The parents, he says, are the hopeless inheritors of that countryside's "poor, protestant, and puritan" values. In contrast, life is straining to come forth in the boy.

Curtis recalls attending a 1956 concert of Elvis's in Tupelo when Curtis was sixteen, right after Presley had finished making the movie, *Love Me Tender.* The most remarkable part of the memory is not the sound, he recounts, but the fact that the National Guard were called to duty complete with rifles and bayonets:

> They anticipated the soldiers who would integrate Central High School in Little Rock the next fall. For the agitation Elvis evoked manifested the same energy of social change as that of the other upheavals in the South that coincided with his career.
>
> The very orality that Elvis embodied was being fragmented by the process whose energy made him famous; as the rest of the country became more oral, the South became more literate. During his campaign, Jimmy Carter accurately commented that he could never have become a candidate for president if it had not been for Martin Luther King. King's work gave great impetus to the fragmentation of local power structures in the South. The fragmentation of those power structures necessarily preceded the merger of Southern politics into national politics. (Incidentally, King used the rhythms of Southern protestantism for political purposes as Elvis used them for artistic purposes. Somehow, Southern protestantism becomes communicable outside the South only in nonreligious forms.)
>
> Elvis changed the way people dressed and sang and felt about their bodies, and he could do so because of the extraordinary openness and permeability that literacy has produced in American society. . . . Once Elvis had gotten out of Tupelo—metaphorically

speaking—and had become rich and famous as few people have ever been, he became great and irrelevant in equal measure. Elvis agreed to become a product, and products do not confront pain and despair. His movies expressed the mindless optimism which his life, and voice, and body, negated at every instant.[12]

With this application of contemporary culture theory, using his own Mississippi boyhood town and that of Elvis, James Curtis is able to draw meaning simultaneously for his own life and for the processes that have moved us culturally, collectively, in the United States. His analysis suggests that the life that was straining to come forth in the child Elvis in Tupelo, Mississippi, did indeed emerge, only to be packaged and sold as the sight-and-sound show of a new era. However, this Elvis-as-product came at a cost: the return of the "vacant" and "shapeless" look of his parents to the face of the man who made that sight and sound. *A man lost to himself but made into a world property through the objectification of his work. A human being lost through the objectification of self.*

Curtis has provided one plausible explanation for why Elvis, he, and we have been and are the way we are. Artistic, political, religious, and social events are all part of the same cultural fabric in our lives. Personally and collectively, we Mississippians joined the twentieth century and the rest of the United States with the social change, the moral revolutions, the music, and the politics in which we participated in the 1950s and 1960s—just in time to watch the rest of the country head off into the twenty-first century.

The Arts and Education in Mississippi

One night when I arrived in Oxford, Mississippi, in 1984, national public television on Mississippi ETV was showing "Live From the Met" with the internationally acclaimed black Mississippian, opera soprano Leontyne Price, singing the leading role of Leonora in Verdi's opera "La Forza del Destino." During that opera season, Price chose to end her spectacular Metropolitan career with a performance of another Verdi character whom she called "the glorious Ethiopian, Aïda." The *New York Times*, the week of that performance, reported, "In the soprano's box Thursday night will be her brother and his wife, Georgianna; her 'heart's sister,' Peggy Chisholm, her closest and oldest white friend, a playmate from Mississippi days and the daughter of Elizabeth Chisholm, one of Miss Price's earliest and most important sponsors; and other intimates."[13]

On the same night that I watched Leontyne Price sing Leonora on television, it was reported on the Tupelo station's national network news that Tunica County, Mississippi, is the poorest county in the nation, having nine thousand people, 73 percent of whom are black. The news broadcast showed a black extended family of seventeen, with four mothers and their children, living in a dilapidated six-room house with no running water.

The paradox juxtaposed in the coincidence of those two broadcasts is a frequent one for Mississippi, for such a contrast of wealth and talent in arts and literary accomplishments and poverty and deficiency in economic terms is common in Mississippi.

Mississippi is home to a great many achievers in the fine arts like Leontyne Price. Actor James Earl Jones, winner of a number of awards, including a Tony for his Broadway role in August Wilson's *Fences*, calls Mississippi home. So did Alvin Childress, who played Amos in radio's *Amos 'n' Andy*. Movie and television actress Mary Ann Mobley was Mississippi's Miss America. Painters Marie Hull and Karl and Mildred Wolfe were from Mississippi. Composer Lehman Engel was from Jackson. Talk-show star Oprah Winfrey, who came to prominence acting the role of Sophia in the movie *The Color Purple* and who also starred in the 1989 television movie *The Women of Brewster Place*, is from Kosciusko, Mississippi.

Mississippi's literary artists of this century, in addition to William Faulkner, include Stark Young, Hodding Carter, and playwright Tennessee Williams. In addition to Eudora Welty, older living writers include novelist and poet Margaret Walker, Shelby Foote, Walker Percy, journalist Turner Catledge of the *New York Times*, and fiction writer Elizabeth Spencer. Well-known younger writers from Mississippi include Ellen Douglas, Barry Hannah, James Whitehead, Ellen Gilchrist, Willie Morris, and playwright Beth Henley. Asked to name the four best-known twentieth-century writers from Mississippi, most people would probably list William Faulkner, Eudora Welty, Richard Wright, and Tennessee Williams.

Literary artists probably have been most plentiful. Some commentators attribute the abundance of excellent Mississippi literature to Mississippi's history of storytelling, to the oral and folk traditions of the yarn, the tale, the folktale of both black and white people. They believe that Mississippians love a good story, whether an embellished factual account of fishing or hunting, or true stories of relationships—of love and rebuff and tricks and trading, or the spinning of fictive explanations of the mysteries of everyday life or those of the cosmos. Stories are what Mississippians have thrived upon. Mississippians have not been much for abstractions, so theories and philosophy typically have not gone over well in Mississippi, but good stories have.[14]

Mississippi has been home to original music, though much of its original music has been music of the people, music of the folks, folk music, not the classical music brought to America from Europe or created and played first by Europeans and European-Americans. Mississippians have played and performed European-style music but seldom invented it. While orchestra music, music for the ballet and opera, and other works in the classical European musical idiom have thrived in the cities, in town churches,and at the piano benches and in the school band rooms of music teachers in Mississippi, the original made-in-Mississippi music has been blues and jazz from black people's creativity and, among Mississippi whites, "country music."[15]

Dividing people musically, in Mississippi as elsewhere, there is a class difference at least as powerful as the racial one. Solidly middle-class and well-to-do whites, but also middle-class blacks and both whites and blacks who aspire to the middle class, try to learn the dominant culture's music and despise the music of the underclass, even when it is their own. I remember as a child covering my head with pillows on Saturday nights when my brother played the Grand Ole Opry on the radio. It was as if I, who took piano lessons for many years and played hymns at church, could be contaminated merely by hearing the sounds of Little Jimmy Dickens and Hank Williams and their fellows. And blues and jazz were even further from admission to my experience. Nice people did not even know about that kind of music. According to the standard deeply impressed on my mind, that music was vulgar, crude, bad; and ignorance of it was a virtue. The source of that standard seemed something vaguely to do with evil, sexuality, violence, drunkenness, and sin. I have no memory of even wanting to know about it until very late in life. Honky-tonk music, believed to be enjoyed only by drinking, brawling white-trash men, was bad enough, even in the sanitized version played on the radio's Grand Old Opry. Blues added race, the unthinkable ingredient which, along with sex, passion, drink, and a syncopated beat, might stain the soul of a pure upright white girl even by listening to it.

Therefore, all that I have learned about the blues even to date is very elementary. I have read books about it, and I have also learned that reading books about some subjects is a poor substitute for hearing or seeing or having hands-on experience. My imperfect knowledge of the blues reminds me of two books on my shelves, *Automobile Mechanics for Dummies* and *A Woman's Guide to Spectator Sports*, both useful efforts in compensatory education for women. Neither book is fully adequate to make up for the lack of all that time under the hood of a car or behind a baseball bat. Nor can either provide the sure confidence that many men had all through boyhood that such activities were something they were supposed to be doing. My knowledge of the blues is analogous to my knowledge of automobile mechanics or my knowledge of football, baseball, or hockey. My class and racial deprivation of first-hand, immediate knowledge from experience of blues is like my gender deprivation.

A major scholar of the blues is white Mississippian William Ferris. He began his work with a doctoral dissertation in folklore at the University of Pennsylvania; published it as a book, *Blues from the Delta;* and subsequently, through recordings and film, he has made many contributions to better understanding and appreciation of the blues, by both other scholars and the public. His work combines sensitivity, respect for blues musicians as people and performers on their own terms, and careful regard for maintaining the integrity of the music. The following are some of the elementary facts I have learned as an adult book-learner from work such as Ferris's.

Home for the blues is the Mississippi Delta. Bo Diddley, B. B. King, Muddy Waters, Ma Rainey II, to name a few of the most widely recognized blues artists, started playing their music in the Mississippi Delta. Blacks sang Gospel music in church. They also made up or adapted work songs to accompany their labors in the fields, on construction crews, and on railroad lines. But blues was to Gospel the other side of their most intimate music. Gospel expressed their spirituality and longing for community. Blues was its obverse, singing their sensuality and longing for love. Blues was played in private settings where black people could gather in a party atmosphere, drink and dance, or just listen to the music. Juke joints they were called.

Blues was sung in the Mississippi Delta, moved south with black migration to New Orleans, north to cities such as Detroit and Saint Louis and Chicago, and just across the Mississippi line to Memphis, where "Beale Street" became synonymous with blues. W. C. Handy, early in the twentieth century, took note of the blues and popularized it in the songs he wrote, "Memphis Blues" and"Saint Louis Blues." Blues is defined in the words of the song "The Birth of the Blues," by B. G. DeSylva and Lew Brown, as including "the breeze in the trees," "the wail . . . from a jail," and also "a new note . . . from a whippoorwill." These sounds "pushed through a horn" were "nursed" and "rehearsed" and "the Southland" by that means "gave birth to the blues."[16]

On the history of the blues in Mississippi's Delta, William Ferris writes:

> No one really knows where the blues began, though probably they are rooted in the spirituals and work songs which were a part of the nineteenth century black folk music. The blues were first "discovered" by W. C. Handy in 1903 in the Mississippi Delta community of Tutwiler. Handy overheard a guitarist singing "Goin' Where the Southern Crosses the Dog" and was deeply moved by the power of the blues. He later developed this line in his famous "Yellow Dog Blues," so popularizing the music that he became known as the "father of the blues."
>
> Since Handy's discovery of blues in the Mississippi Delta in 1903, an unending stream of outstanding blues musicians has emerged from the area. During the twenties and thirties a series of 78 r.p.m. blues records were issued which were called "race records" because they were made by black musicians and sold to an exclusively black market. Many of the most famous musicians during this period were from the Delta, including Big Bill Broonzy, Mississippi John Hurt, and Skip James.[17]

One of the blues musicians William Ferris recorded in the Mississippi Delta in the 1970s, James "Son" Thomas, defines the blues condition out of which the music comes in this way: "Now it's more than one way you can have the blues. I would say this. If it wasn't for women, it wouldn't be as many blues. That's where the blues first begin. Second you can get blues. You get broke. You got no job. Well you hungry and got the blues, that make you have double blues. It's two or three different ways you can get the blues."[18]

In his front matter for the book *Blues from the Delta*, Ferris gives the dictionary definition for the blues: "A type of song written in a characteristic key with melancholy words and syncopated rhythms." He also quotes a blues player, Arthur Lee Williams, who says, "Blues actually is around you every day. That's just a feeling within a person, you know. You have a hard time and things happen. Hardships between you and your wife, or maybe you and your girlfriend. Downheartedness, that's all it is, hardship. You express it through your song."[19]

Ma Rainey II is a blues singer. This second Ma Rainey was born in Nashville, but she spent some years in Mississippi in the 1920s. She sang for a time with Mississippian B. B. King. When she died in 1985, Ma Rainey II was hailed as the "mother of Beale Street" in her obituary, which said she "starting singing the blues in 1920 and regularly graced Blues Alley until last summer." She was quoted as saying of her start, "I wanted to sing the blues, but my father was a pastor, and the blues were looked on in those days as dirty music. And for me to stay in Nashville then and sing the blues would have been a disgrace for my family. The obituary reports, "'I was the mother of Beale Street,' she said, 'I ruled that street between Fourth and Hernando. I sang at the Chicago House and on Mondays we would have Blue Mondays where the boys would boil.'" Reporting that Rainey and B. B. King sang for fifteen cents a night at a place called Hamburger Heaven, the obituary quotes her as saying, "B. B. once told me, 'Ma, I ain't never gonna make no money singing the blues. I think I'm gonna try something else.' But I told B.B. to stick with it, that someday he would make it."

The newspaper notice continues: "A traditional Beale Street funeral will be held Sunday starting at 3:30 p.m. at Beale and Fourth streets. The procession will be led by Prince Gabe and the Millionaires. A service will follow at W. C. Handy Park, where the All Stars will perform. Musician Ray Glover, no relation, will sing one of Ma's favorite hymns, 'Swing Low, Sweet Chariot.'"

The conclusion says, "Ma Rainey will be buried directly across from the grave of E. H. Crump [racist Memphis political boss], and her tombstone will have this epitaph: 'I don't care what Mr. Crump don't allow, I'm gonna barrelhouse anyhow.'"[20]

There is a lovely film version of a reconciliation between black people's church music and black people's juke joint music, the blues in the movie *The Color Purple*, which Stephen Spielberg created with author Alice Walker's permission. The gospel mu-

sic of the black church and the music of the juke joint meet on a
bridge between the two, meet in the character and through the
singing of the church-alienated daughter, Shug, who has been
confident and celebratory of her sexuality and sensuality and
has insisted in the book that "God love all them feelings."

> Celie elaborates on Shug's theology:
> Here's the thing, say Shug. The thing I believe. God is inside you
> and inside everybody else. You come into the world with God. . . .
> She say, My first step from the old white man was trees. Then
> air. Then birds. Then other people. But one day when I was sitting
> quiet and feeling like a motherless child, which I was, it come to
> me: that feeling of being a part of everything, not separate at all. I
> knew that if I cut a tree my arm would bleed. And I laughed and I
> cried and I run all around the house. I knew just what it was. In
> fact when it happen, you can't miss it. It sort of like you know what,
> she say, grinning and rubbing high up on my thigh.
> SHUG, I say.
> Oh, she say, God love all them feelings. That's some of the best
> stuff God did. . . .
> God don't think it dirty? I ast.
> Naw, she said, God made it. . . . Yes, Celie, she say. Everything
> want to be loved. Us sing and dance, make faces and give flower
> bouquets, trying to be loved. You ever notice that trees do every-
> thing to git attention we do, except walk?[21]

In the movie, Spielberg orchestrates this with music, and reunion comes between alienated characters and within Shug by
means of the music blending across the bridge, the gospel song
of the church's choir meeting and the blues song that comes out
of the juke joint and meets the choir music halfway across the
bridge in a glorious merging of sensuality and spirituality.

During the 1970s and the 1980s, a new public recognition has
come to blues and its home in Mississippi's Delta region. A new
museum of blues has opened in Clarksdale, Mississippi. A blues
archive has opened at the University of Mississippi. The peri-
odical *Living Blues* has moved to Mississippi. A more positive
attitude toward black people's culture on the part of both blacks
and whites in the aftermath of the civil rights movement, a

greater interest in popular and folk types of music, and scholarly works such as those of Bill Ferris all have contributed to a greater public acknowledgment of the blues.

Like blues, country music got its start in the splitting of the sacred from the secular among rural white southerners. Traditional church music for southern Protestants included white spirituals. Whites, too, added work songs. And in the country in the South there was folk music about work and love and mourning, about everyday moaning and groaning and defeat, that was different from the rural white people's church songs.

Meridian, Mississippi, native Jimmie Rodgers is recognized as the father of country music. Yodeling and "hollering" on his records, he was known as the "blue yodeler," and he put his own particular country stamp on the music he sang and wrote. A railroad worker, he sang of working on the railroad. Sick with tuberculosis, he also sang about being sick.[22] One of his most famous songs gives a flavor of his music. It is called "Hobo's Meditation":

> Tonight as I lay on a box car,
> Just waiting for a train to pass by,
> What will become of the hobo,
> Whenever their time comes to die?
> Will the master up yonder in heaven,
> Have a place that we might call our home?
> Will we have to work for a living.
> Or can we continue to roam?
> Will there be any freight trains in heaven,
> Any box cars in which we might hide?
> Will there by any tough cops and brakemen?
> Will they tell us that we cannot ride?
> Will the hobo chum with the rich man?
> Will they always have money to spare?
> Will they have respect for the hobo,
> In the land that lies hidden up there?[23]

In 1933, Jimmie Rodgers died on the road on a performance trip. His body was sent home to Meridian on a train. Loewen and Sallis in their history book describe the sad homecoming using an often-quoted statement by Rodgers's widow telling of the train's arrival: "Then—like a part of the night itself, a low mellow train whistle. Not the usual whoo-whoo—oo, but a whistle that was not a whistle. A long continuous moaning that grew in volume as the train crept toward me along the silver rails." Loewen and Sallis continue, "The train crew had remembered how Jimmie Rodgers loved train whistles." They summarize, "He has not been forgotten. He was the first person to be honored in the Country Music Hall of Fame. His records are still popular all over the world. And his mixture of cowboy music and blues styles has lived on to influence folk singers and bluesmen as well as country music itself."[24]

Today there is a Jimmie Rodgers Memorial Museum in Meridian. On its grounds stands a statue of him holding his banjo, the beloved instrument he called "Lucille." Appropriately, the statue stands next to a locomotive.

Into this Mississippi musical environment came Elvis Presley. It is no wonder that he played his large part in giving the world rock 'n' roll.

Opera soprano Leontyne Price did not leave her Mississippi roots entirely behind, either, as she traveled the world singing on opera and concert stages. A trademark of her solo programs in recitals anywhere in the world is her inclusion of some songs of black Americans. At a Founders' Day ceremony at Rust College in Mississippi, when she was granted an honorary doctorate and was asked her advice to young students, Leontyne Price sang her answer, not from opera but from a spiritual, "This little light of mine, gonna let it shine."[25]

Emerging simultaneously with a new cultural appreciation of blues, jazz, and country music, which has been brought about by the change in social, racial, and political attitudes and by serious and respectful work on these arts by academic folklorists, has been a heightened awareness of domestic arts in recent years. Folklorists and feminist scholars alike have cast new light on women's work of cooking and needlecraft arts. The postmodernist insistence that there is a dynamic interplay across classes, races, gender, and place is nowhere more obvious, once we think about it, than in the matters of foods and clothing. The domestic arts that have the most significance for me are food and quilting.

My Aunt Bessie was an expert cook, my Aunt 'Cile an expert seamstress. Both of them could cook and sew extremely well. Neither thought of herself as at all talented in any artistic sense. To themselves and to all of us around them in my childhood, they were just the folks, and that was what folks did—or what they did was what *women*folks did. Folks grew food on their farms and in their gardens, and women preserved it, canned it, stored it, cooked it, and served it. Folks needed clothes and table linens and bedclothes, and women made them. That was the way it was. Some women were "good" cooks and others poor ones. Some women also made good quilts. But almost all women made food and clothing, table linens and bedclothes of some kind. That was just what you did before the arrival of commercially manufactured household items or if money was not available to buy such goods commercially. Well-to-do women employed poor women to do some of these tasks for them, but *knowledge* of food and clothing, their making and care, was expected of all women, wealthy or poor. It was expected no less by women themselves than by their men. It was the way it was, work it was, but art it was not, in such women's minds. They would have been astonished at—indeed, would have ridiculed as "highfalutin"—the people who today would call them artists.

I know now that my aunts were artists of foodstuffs and artists with their needles. That work was inseparable from the artistry of their love.

One example of the transcendence of their understanding has followed me all my life in appreciative memory. After making nearly all my clothes all my life—school dresses and wool skirts, Easter suits with coats, starched crocheted hats for Sundays, evening gowns for me to wear to the prom or to ride on the homecoming float—my aunts paid their scarce cash to buy me a "ready-made" outfit to wear on my first trip to New York. They wanted to please me but admonished me at the time, as they did repeatedly, "Remember who you are." I feared that my pattern-book clothes in their fine stitchery would show me up in New York as one of the folks from down home. I shouldn't have worried. As soon as I opened my mouth, the New Yorkers knew who I was.

Like many another expatriated child, I came to discover the value of the knowledge of my original adults only when I myself became an adult. In my case, as always for me, I learned from books what Aunt Bessie and Aunt 'Cile already knew. But my midlife learning of it was not *as* they knew it, effective, immediate, useful, complete. My learning was objectified, comparative, fascinated, inquisitive, and relative. I learned *about* it, whatever it was, from my books along with many other possibilities and texts and contexts. My aunts learned *it*, and that was it. In learning from my books, I learned about myself and them, as well as about the books themselves and other books, other aunts and other food and clothes. This was something foreign to people like my original family, people with a system of foodstuffs and clothing so established and sure, complete and closed. It was the same with our food and clothes as with our religion, our politics, our education, our sex lives, and our dreams. They were set, sure, and established, and we did not have to worry about alternative ways of knowing. It was only worried book-learners like I was to become who saw all those alternatives.

As a teenager and young adult, and as a college philosophy major, I deliberately did not learn to cook. But as a newlywed right out of college, I accepted unreflectively the gender-role assignment that I was supposed to cook for the marriage. Going to Aunt Bessie with pen and paper in hand at that point, I left exasperated with a blank sheet after she had struggled to tell me how to make rolls and cornbread dressing:

"How much flour?"

"About two handfuls."

"How much salt is a pinch?"

"Butter about the size of a hen's egg."

"How big is a hen's egg?"

"Cook it till it's done."

"How will I know when it's done?"

In all the college-educated wisdom of a twenty-one-year-old, I turned to my more familiar territory, books. And by my book-learning I became a very good cook, strictly scientific, urbane, and cosmopolitan, according to the *Joy of Cooking*, the *Better Homes and Gardens Cookbook*, Julia Child's *Mastering the Art of French Cooking*, and Craig Claiborne's food columns in the *New York Times*.

Living in Cambridge, Massachusetts, I had a gourmet cooking phase, and I started a cookbook collection. My friend Katie and I bought meat from the same butcher that Julia Child used, and sometimes we saw her in person in the shop, as well as on "The French Chef" on TV. We made sukiyaki, boeuf à la Bourguignonne, shrimp Meringo, lasagne, bouillabaisse, beef Stroganoff, wild rice casserole, chocolate mousse—nothing I had ever eaten as a child. But at Thanksgiving and Christmastime, I would sometimes long for familiar tastes and find myself making cornbread dressing for the turkey (albeit translated into cups and tablespoon measures in a book) and spending hours peeling the membrane off orange sections and grating fresh coconut to make ambrosia like Aunt 'Cile and Aunt Bessie made for Christmas. Craig Claiborne, food editor of the *New York Times*, was as often my expert of choice as was Julia Child. His *The New York Times Cookbook* and *The New York Times Menu Cookbook* joined my collection early.

"Did you know Craig Claiborne is from Mississippi?" someone asked me about fifteen years after I had been using his cookbooks.

Speechless, I shook my head No.

Only in 1987 did Craig Claiborne publish a southern cookbook, *Craig Claiborne's Southern Cooking*. By that time I had come back full circle in my food tastes, ordering a southern country ham from a farm in Virginia for my Christmas preparations. His late-life nostalgia matches mine at this stage of life. He writes in his preface:

> Nothing rekindles my spirits, gives comfort to my heart and mind, more than a visit to Mississippi and environs, to sit down to a dinner (the meal, as any Southerner knows, taken at midday) and be regaled, as I often have been, with a platter of fried chicken, field peas, collard greens, fresh corn on the cob, sliced tomatoes with French dressing (that's what we call a vinaigrette sauce), and to top it all off with a wedge of freshly baked pecan pie. With vanilla ice cream or without. The beverage for that meal being, more likely than not, sweetened iced tea.[26]

Like foodways, which I knew in childhood as a nourishing provision of everyday life and only as an adult came to understand as an intriguing form of art, needlework was a part of my daily environment growing up, something I rejected as a pursuit for myself and in later life came to see as an art form. Quilting is the best example of this. Quilting, like cornbread dressing and orange-section-and-fresh-coconut ambrosia at Christmas, was so much a given of my childhood that I paid scant attention to it until picturebooks and scholarly articles about it began to cross my professorial desk in the books and announcements about women's art, in my new specialty of women's studies. But by fall 1987, I was making my first priority on a trip to New York a visit to the quilting exhibit at the Museum of American Folk Art in midtown Manhattan. Contemporary fabric artists, most of whom are women, have rediscovered quilting and have made a bridge between the fine art of museums and displays in homes and public buildings and the folk art of the practical everyday objects our female forebears made to keep their families warm.

My aunts quilted long hours of every winter. Our beds were covered with the everyday quilts of their making and ones that their mother had made before them, as well as quilts from my mother's family. My aunts gave me a quilt as a wedding present. It was a beautiful patchwork pattern known as Dresden plate, which was made up of connected circles of colorful cotton print scraps, connecting at a point and edged in half-circles. They were imposed upon large squares placed in a symmetrical design upon the top. The borders and lining of the quilt were a bright solid yellow. Another quilt was given to me when Aunt Bessie died, one that her mother and three sisters had made for my grandmother's trousseau. It is an appliqued quilt with a repeated yellow tulip design.

There are essentially two types of quilts, patchwork quilts and appliqued quilts. Patchwork quilt tops are made with small pieces of cloth cut into geometrical designs and sewed together to make an overall design to the top of the quilt. The cloth is almost always scrap cloth left over from other sewing or from good pieces of worn-out clothes. Basic blocks of squares or rectangles provide the essential outline of the design, and pieced combinations of small pieces of cloth are put together on each block to form the details of the pattern. There are a number of common patterns, and many variations on these patterns with colorful names like Log Cabin, Star, Wedding Ring, Pot of Flowers, Rose of Sharon, Pineapple, Dresden Plate. A Crazy Quilt still has a regularity to its pattern in the form of its blocks or squares, but it is pieced together with no deliberate attempt to make a repeating design out of the relationship of the pieces to each other.

Appliqued quilts have tops made with cut-out pieces sewed onto the top of single cloth covering according to a single design. Sometimes a single design is repeated in several squares across the entire quilt. The pattern might be a pot of flowers or a wreath or a vine. Sometimes each square is different. The applique stitch is close and precise so that no frayed ends of the small pieces of cloth in the design will ravel out in washing. Some quilts employ embroidery as well. Embroidered patterns might tell a story or picture activities or commemorate an event. For some patterns, embroidery is central to the design, as pictures are made on squares or rectangles of cloth and sewed together to make the quilt.

The pattern of many pieces of cloth is the quilt top. A plain piece of cloth is put on the bottom, and a middle layer of cotton batting or some other warmth-providing material is put between. Quilting itself is the stitching of the three layers together in still another pattern of fine handwork across the entire surface of the material. The stitches must be fine and regular to hold all the materials together in an even fashion. The most usual pattern is to follow the outlines of the patchwork pieces on top. Some quilters would follow the outline around only one edge, but more fastidious quilters like my aunts would follow the outline on both sides of the edge of each small square or diamond or half circle. Other designs for the quilting itself are imprinted on the entire face of the quilt and then the quilt is quilted with scrolls or circles or lines that add an additional pattern to the one the quiltmaker designed with the scraps of cloth.

Both black women and white women of earlier generations made quilts in Mississippi and still do today. The quilt form is of European origin, but black women adapted it with some of the design motifs of their African heritage. For example, scholars of this form of artistic work have noticed that black women do not make a Crazy Quilt like whites, rather, they make what they call a "string quilt" with rectangular pieces repeating a kind of non-pictorial color scheme and design movement that is strikingly similar to West African Islamic textile art. Maude Southwell Wahlman writes:

> In Africa, piecing is used to sew strips of woven cloth together and to make complicated designs on ceremonial costumes and funerary banners. Applique techniques are used in sewing large symbolic cut-out shapes onto costumes or large wall hangings. . . . Black women remembered African textile techniques and traditions when they came to the New World. They combined their own traditions with the Euro-American traditions of piecing, appliqueing, and quilting fabrics for bedcovers, to create a unique, creolized art— the Afro-American quilt. . . .
>
> In Africa, when woven strips with many patterns are sewn together to make a larger fabric, the resulting cloth has asymmetrical and unpredictable designs. These characteristics are also retained in Afro-American quilts. Lines, designs, and colors do not match

up, but vary with a persistence that goes beyond a possible lack of cloth in one color or pattern.

Afro-American quilters have taken this African tradition one step further by introducing improvisation. Black quilters often adopt traditional Euro-American quilt block patterns and "Afro-Americanize" them by establishing a pattern in one square and varying it in successive squares. Typical Afro-American quilt blocks do not repeat but change in size, arrangement, and color. While ostensibly reproducing Euro-American patterns, Afro-American quilters maintain African principles of multiple patterning, asymmetry, and unpredictability; through improvisation in this sense, the Afro-American quilt can be considered the visual equivalent of jazz music.[27]

A gallery exhibition of black women's quilts in Mississippi was held in 1983, sponsored by the Center for the Study of Southern Culture. Appreciation of quilting also has been demonstrated by scholars and journalists conducting fine interviews with some Mississippi quilters, getting them to tell about their art. In the Mississippi folklife journal, *I Ain't Lying*, interviewer Darryl Warner asks questions of Mrs. Artemeasie Brandon in the excerpt below:

Q: How did you start quilting?
A. My mother started me off at quilting. My mama, she would cut the blocks. The first quilt we worked on was something we call a plate. We pieced those little squares up and you put it on a solid piece of material. Then when we would get through with it, we would take embroidery thread and embroidery it around. I was about fourteen or maybe fifteen when I started doing that one. . . .

Sometimes I just get a gang of little pieces and sit down here and work 'em together. And when I get through with 'em I joins 'em all together and I just got a little top for my quilts. Some of my patterns are string, nine-patch, stars, and cow-catch. . . .
Q. Do you quilt in any pattern?
A. Just start in little rows just like that. When I get it far enough, I can reach out of this corner. Then after I reach out of the corner, I'll catch up here and run me off a row. See? Then I run that off . . . See how that is there. You call it a shell. . . .
Q. How do you finish the ends?

A. When you get through with it, you may have to trim the lining. You trim it down as small as you want it. Then you just
take it and turn it just like you hemming a dress.

A star is my favorite pattern. It's much easier to piece. . . . I
take an old sheet and then I cuts my legs—the star legs. Then I
take my material and sew it on the sheet. . . . You have to piece
the eight legs up first. . . . After you get these legs all pieced,
then you have to take some square pieces and put a square here
and a point here. . . . Then I take just straight strips and go
around it. Then I measures it on the bed. If it's large enough
I'm through with it. But if it's not, then I put some more strips
around it. Call it stripping your quilt.[28]

My interviewee Mrs. Jeannie Griffith also told me about quilting:

JG: Then my mamma like to piece quilts. You know, she wasn't
able to work in the fields like the other ladies. And so she,
she would do most anything like that. She would piece
quilts. She'd have little string, and she would take a piece of
paper and she'd piece the big one. And then she'd take the
string and put in on, sew it on a paper and make quilts. And
she had some of the prettiest quilts. And then she'd take
those sacks and make the lining and get some clay dirt and
dye the lining, so it'd be a color.

GGY: Did she make lots of quilts? Did you use them for your—

JG: Yes, she made a lot of quilts. For ourselves, and different
people.

GGY: Did she give them to you?

JG: Yeah.

GGY: Were there lots of different designs?

JG: Yes, all—whatever color of material she could get. I mean,
she wouldn't just have a certain design, and she made some
of the prettiest blocks. But she would get two or three
pieces, you know, to one block. You know, she'd have it
right, but she'd have it all over that quilt. You know, different colors.

GGY: Made up her own designs?
JG: Sure did. Maybe she'd have a solid piece and then a print together, you know, and make that block.
GGY: Yes, that would be pretty. Did you or your sisters quilt?
JG: We would quilt when we were home. You know, she taught us how, but that's as far as it went.[29]

Quilting bedclothes from the scraps of fabrics on hand was a part of the subsistence living that raised necessity and practical accomplishment to an art. At other times quilting rose from impoverishment and coping with it. Women made both useful and beautiful quilts from what they had available to them. What resulted was a transformation of their poverty into plenty and a transformation of their creative response to their daily needs into artistry that provided visual grace and satisfaction along with physical warmth.

Education in Mississippi too frequently also has been impoverished. Before the 1970s, the dual public school systems of white schools and black schools in each district and of separate state colleges and universities was very expensive. Maintenance of the separate systems meant lack of facilities and funds for other areas. In a location already lacking in economic resources, this was a very serious problem. There were no public kindergartens in many places until the 1980s, no uniform certification standards for teachers or centrally approved statewide curriculum supervision for the public schools. In a very real sense, educational reform in Mississippi can be seen as a consequence of the civil rights movement. After the establishment of desegregation and with it abandonment of the expensive need for two sets of schools in each school district, it became possible to move forward to new foci for education statewide in Mississippi. The Education Reform Act of 1982, under the leadership of Gov. William Winter with the legal counsel of Ray Mabus, provided that needed benchmark for improving education across the state. The new law made kindergartens mandatory in all school

districts for the first time, provided for the consolidation of
school districts, and set up new provisions for the certification
of teachers and new restrictions limiting teachers from teaching
subjects in which they are not trained. The act provided a permanent state commission to oversee state teacher education and
a School Executive Management Institute for advanced education of school administrators. Organizational mechanisms were
created for program and curriculum development and staff
training in local school districts. This comprehensive, forward-
looking legislation put Mississippi on a track of improvement of
its entire system of education that would have been inconceiva-
ble even fifteen years before.[30]

Even so, though the resources have been scarce and the opportunities sorely limited, in Mississippi there have long been
educators who care and institutions that have tried to provide
good education for their students. In the Jim Crow years of the
twentieth century, one such unique place was the Piney Woods
Country Life School, and one such person its founder and director, Dr. Laurence C. Jones. For many years it, along with Prentiss Institute and the Utica Institute, provided one of only three
settings for private industrial and agricultural secondary education available to Mississippi blacks. My informant Mrs. Jeannie Griffith told me of her schooldays at the Piney Woods School,
a church-related boarding school, which was founded in 1907.

JG: And then when we finished eighth grade, we went to Pi-
    ney Woods Country Life School at Piney Woods, Mississippi,
    for four years, and that is where I finished in 1942.
GGY: Yes. Now what was Piney Woods School like? I read
    Professor Harrison's book about Piney Woods School, and I
    know that all the students had work opportunities, and
    school subjects, and religious education. What kind of job
    was yours?
JG: I didn't stay in the dormitories; I stayed in the community.
    The boys that lived in the dormitory, they were the workin'
    students. And we lived in the community, and we paid a dol-

lar. That's what we had to pay (laughs). A dollar a month to go to school. Sure did. And, ah, well—they had different chores to do. The girls would cook and sew and whatever. Some played in the band, and some learned to dance. They had a group that sang—went from the school to sing, the Cotton Blossom Singers and the International Sweethearts of Rhythm, that was the orchestra. The Cotton Blossom Singers—they would go all over the United States and sing, and people would send money to the school, and some would send clothes. Some people would come from different places—retired teachers would come and give their services to the school. We had good teachers, and, I mean, we had all kinds, uh huh.

GGY: What was your favorite subject at school?

JG: (Laughs) Arithmetic.

GGY: Arithmetic!

JG: Uh-huh, sure was. That was my *best* subject. I liked that.[31]

Piney Woods School graduate Alferdteen Harrison earned a Ph.D. in history at the University of Kansas. As a graduate student, she was the first director of black studies at her graduate university. She did her dissertation in European history on the French slave trade in the French West Indies. She came back to Mississippi and became a professor at Jackson State University, because, she said, "I always wanted to teach at a black school. All my later education was at white schools."[32] At Jackson State, she directs the Institute for the Study of the History, Life, and Culture of Black People. She did a major research project on the Piney Woods School, *Piney Woods School; An Oral History.*[33]

I asked her why she did the book on Piney Woods School. "I was born and raised in Rankin County," she said. "I had gone away to Kansas and been away for fourteen years. When I came back, I was struck by the way the school looked. All of my high-school professors were still there. It was the same as it was when I had been there. When I returned in 1972, I was sur-

Alferdteen Harrison.
Photo by Gayle Graham Yates.

prised to find them the same people. Dr. Jones was still in control of the school. He was ninety-two years old. I thought,
'Gosh, this is like walking through history!'" Harrison noted
that she "had been out of the state of Mississippi for fourteen
years. I had experienced the 1960s and those changes. Piney
Woods didn't change a lot. I didn't see how Piney Woods had
changed a lot. I could look at it in a different light. I could look
at it almost for the first time. I had never had time to talk to the
high-school professors before. How can this school still be here
when everything else around it has changed? I asked myself. I
thought I had a good subject for oral history. Others before
writing about the Piney Woods School had not put it in the black
context."[34]

Harrison's book immediately sets the educational context of
the school in the tradition of vocational training for blacks, as it
was espoused by Booker T. Washington:

This is the story of an extraordinary school in the piney woods of Mississippi and of the enduring people of Piney Woods Community who forged on against incredible odds to make a better world for themselves and their children. To these poor, backwoods, turn-of-the-century blacks of Rankin County, Mississippi, Laurence C. Jones (1882–1975) brought the Booker T. Washington model of training blacks to be good workers.

. . . Because the school followed Jim Crow social codes and mirrored what were then expedient race relations in the South, Piney Woods School thrived without controversy and with encouragement from Mississippi whites. It served a noble purpose by opening its doors for the educational training of underprivileged rural black students, as well as for the colored blind and cripples of the state at a time when there was no other institution for them.[35]

Harrison writes of the opening of the school and its founder's philosophy:

Piney Woods School was founded in 1909 with the aim of giving impoverished rural blacks an industrial education. Laurence C. Jones (1882–1975), its founder, recommended that all graduates of his school acquire no fewer than three skills for earning a living. . . . Although Jones was himself a product of the liberal arts tradition, he believed that manual labor education could help people on society's bottom rung, or as he put it, the "bottom rail." He said, an "old-time rail fence . . . would fall down, no matter how many good rails were inserted, unless the bottom rail was strong, substantial, and properly placed." . . .

At the time when Jones was emerging as an advocate of industrial education, the philosophies of W. E. B. DuBois and Booker T. Washington were being widely discussed. Whereas Washington advocated an education for blacks that combined manual labor with academic training, proponents of DuBois's views argued that a "talented tenth" should be educated specifically for leadership of the black race and that improved conditions for blacks generally would result from political agitation. Although the two approaches were not necessarily incompatible, disputes often made them seem so.[36]

On its location, Harrison writes:

The Rankin County Piney Woods region, in which the Piney Woods Country Life School was located, was considered to have the poorest land, cattle, and people. As a result, in 1909 the name "Piney Woods" was often used derisively. For Jones, however, the words beautifully described the area. Later, however, reflecting on his choice of name, he wrote, "It was as though we had chosen to christen a baby 'useless' or to name a stately mansion 'shanty.'"

The school was located in the sparsely populated northwest edge of the region, forty-two miles southeast of Jackson, Mississippi, where tall pine trees with long needles rise from sandy soil. This land [is] . . . a place of great poverty, in stark contrast to the rich, fertile soil of northwestern Mississippi's Delta.[37]

Recognizing that the personality of Jones had dominated the school throughout its history, Harrison first set out to write a biography of Jones, from whom she had authorization. However, she came to believe that she needed to write of both the whole school and the community. She said she believes that Jones's direction of the school was strict and regimented, but she appreciated the way he worked with people and raised money. The support of the school was a community effort, she learned, even though it was important for Dr. Jones to raise money in the North.[38] On support for the school, Harrison writes, "Although Laurence Jones founded the school at Piney Woods, its actual construction and growth, as I have shown, resulted from community effort more than from the labors of any one individual. Lumber, geese, and a piano were some of the largest gifts that the school received in its early days."[39]

Concluding her book, Harrison suggests that the school faces very different challenges in the new era after the civil rights movement. Yet, remembering its origins is important: "As the twentieth century gives way to the twenty-first, so do the challenges facing Piney Woods change, particularly those that relate to the survival of ethnic and racial groups in America. During his administration Laurence C. Jones led blacks through an era of racial segregation, a time during which adequate state or federal support for black education was lacking. In the last year Jones was still building relationships for Piney Woods."[40]

Another post–civil-rights Mississippi book of great signifi-

Charles Sallis.
Photo published by courtesy of
Charles Sallis.

cance is *Mississippi: Conflict and Change* by James W. Loewen and Charles Sallis. It is a ninth-grade history book that arose out of desire to teach and to write history in a more inclusive and nonracist way.

Mississippi history is a subject required in the ninth grade in Mississippi public schools. Up until the 1970s, all of the available textbooks were written from the point of view of the white male leadership of Mississippi—a viewpoint not unlike that of most textbooks and scholarly works in history throughout the United States. What had been studied and taught was the experience of the dominant culture, with emphasis on political and military facets of history. By 1970, discontent with this situation had risen both within and without the profession of history and the settings of schools and colleges. This was the case in Mississippi, especially.

In Mississippi a new textbook was conceived and written to take into account the experience of people of all classes, of all races, of all national origins, and in all settings in the state of

Mississippi. Still, a federal court case was required to get the book adopted as one of the texts available for Mississippi ninth graders to use in their schools. Professor Charles Sallis (CS), one of the senior editors of the project, told me about the book and its creation in an interview.

CS: One of the courses I had to teach when I came to Millsaps was Mississippi history, so I had to, in a sense, begin doing research and drawing up a course. I'd been looking around for texts that I might use, and I could find no textbooks. And in my classes I remember talking about the necessity of good textbooks, and I found by quizzing the students in the class about what they knew about Mississippi history—I was appalled at their lack of understanding—really at the misinformation that they had. Well, in 1970, one of the students in my class [Bruce Adams] who was graduating, who was a senior in history, was planning to go to law school a year hence. He wanted to take time off, he said, Millsaps had kind of burned him out, he was not wanting to get back into an academic situation. But he wondered what to do in that year. And he asked me if I thought he might try to get a grant from some fund or some agency to write a history of Mississippi. I guess I had talked about it enough that he wanted to do that. And I told Bruce Adams that I didn't think anybody could write a history of Mississippi in one year, but that you could get started, that the research would be certainly interesting, that I felt he could get a grant to do that. And that I would be happy to help him out. He was taking a sociology course at Tougaloo, and Jim Loewen was teaching this, and I think Jim had recognized the fact that Mississippi needed this, too. And Jim had been in the state for a number of years—he's a native of Illinois—had written a very fine dissertation at Harvard on the Mississippi Chinese. So he had looked a lot at Mississippi history. Bruce then, being in both classes, heard the same thing and said, "I want you two to get together." I didn't know Jim. Jim was in a field other than mine, and he was at Tougaloo, and I didn't know him.

So we got together. I think Jim came to my office one afternoon, and he said, "Look, we both know that this needs to be done. Why don't we form a project, a group of professors and students and hammer this thing out in a year or two, and come up with a good, objective history of the state." I was very much eager to do that. So Jim and I formed the Mississippi History Project, insisting on Millsaps students and Tougaloo students, black and white, male and female, northerners and southerners. . . . So we started right in. We started in the spring of 1970. We finished it in 1974. It took us four years to do it. We did all kinds of things . . . [and] we went to schools to test what we were doing, to see how a ninth-grade class [would use it] because it had been quite a while since we'd been in that [level] class. And we had to also write on a ninth-grade level.

GGY: That's the year it's required in the public schools?

CS: Right. We had gotten affirmation from the pilot schools, [from our] history class. . . . And we looked at state histories from all over, and by and large they are just like Mississippi's was, Chamber of Commerce. Things that present the best foot forward. And we wanted to show the good and the bad—namely, what had happened in Mississippi.

GGY: You have a lot of kinds of information. It's social and political history, it's military history, it's literary and artistic history and cultural history in the widest sense of that. How did you go about doing the research in that midperiod while the project was going on?

CS: We looked at the history of the state, and I was very familiar with this—

GGY: By this time you'd taught it several times?

CS: I'd taught it, and I had kept up with Mississippi historians. So we just sort of put a timeline and divided up areas of research and had different students and professors responsible for certain areas to do research in. We met together in

group sessions . . . [T]hat was before the days of Xerox, so
we had to use the old mimeograph or ditto machines, so that
gave us trouble. We just hammered it out. We criticized each
other. We said at the beginning before we all met, we're all
equals. We have students and we have professors, and we
wanted the students to meet each other. [Most Millsaps students were white, and most Tougaloo students were black.]
We wanted black and white to treat each other as equals, as
we were. Looking back, these were very good sessions. You
know, some of my ideas were refined, because I had been
made to really think through a lot of things. So at these
give-and-take sessions—I can remember some sessions becoming somewhat angry and frustrated!

GGY: Can you remember some examples of content that got
changed?

CS: Yeah. For example, Jim, from Illinois, in terms of slavery,
tended to be somewhat soft on the southern planters, in
terms of their treatment of slaves. This was something I
could say to Jim: look, let's be honest about this, don't soft-
pedal things. One thing [about] the group process is [that] a
lot of people [participate]. We had to choose pictures to go in
the book, and one of the pictures that we debated about long
and hard was a picture of a lynching. And Jim did not want
to put that picture in. He was somewhat against it. And I
said, no, I think it belongs in there because we need to
dramatize the fact that we had lynchings in the South. As it
turned out, that got us into a lot of trouble because some of
the people who rejected it felt that students [would find it
too sensational]. But if you look at it in our book, it's not
gross. It shows a black man burned, but the features are not
distinguishable, it's not a repulsive picture. But that's just
an instance of one of the things we did, what pictures we
would put in there. [We asked] How do we deal with this
material? And we just sort of kept it up until we had it hammered out. Jim and I pretty much had the final word. Because I was the historian and he was the sociologist, he de-

ferred to [my views] some of the things that he had
questions on, so I was pretty much the historian in charge of
the project.

So we finished it in 1974, then we submitted our book to
the Mississippi Textbook Purchasing Board, which has to ap-
prove all texts that are used in the public schools. The State
of Mississippi could adopt as many as five. Only two were
submitted—our book and the John Bettersworth book. The
Textbook Purchasing Board rejected our book. They approved Bettersworth's book. We wondered why, because we
thought we had done a good job. They wouldn't tell us why
we'd been rejected. They would not tell us the vote. We
were not allowed to appeal the decision. We were told, in effect, "Come back in six years when we adopt history books
again." And we just decided that we would sue. We filed suit
in federal district court. We filed suit in 1975 against the
State of Mississippi, on the grounds that our due process
rights [were violated]. It was the first time that the federal
courts had become involved in a textbook suit. [Judge Orma
Smith of the U.S. Northern District found in their favor.]
The ruling just simply says "State of Mississippi is charged
with rejecting history books on any visible grounds, namely,
race."
GGY: The grounds were clearly—?
CS: Clearly . . . inadmissible. They [the State of Mississippi]
    rejected our book because it [included material about race].
GGY: About race?
CS: About race. And yet we had gotten good reviews from all
    over.[41]

In 1984, in a retrospective issue of the Jackson, Mississippi,
Sunday newspaper twenty years after the Mississippi Freedom
Summer of 1964, a reporter used Sallis's book as an illustration
of progress made toward a more equal treatment of blacks and
whites in education, as well as in other aspects of Mississippi
society in the twenty-year interval:

In contrast to earlier texts that seldom mentioned blacks, *Mississippi, Conflict & Change* writes about Mississippi blues artists B. B. King and Bo Diddley, saying they helped make the state the "birthplace of the blues." . . . The book attacks numerous "myths" such as "slave loyalty" and "white supremacy." Slaves lived in "crude huts with dirt floors and no windows." Masters often whipped them and rubbed salt and pepper in the wounds, it says.

Mississippi, Conflict & Change says white Mississippians usually viewed slavery as a "positive good" and white churchgoers thought it brought the benefits of Christianity "to savage, heathen blacks."

Black accomplishments are also noted, including the election of Revels as the state's first U.S. senator during Reconstruction and his appointment as president of Alcorn State. The book says the Ku Klux Klan burned black schools and committed other terrorist acts and that many whites were afraid to speak out against the Klan and Citizens Council.

The Sallis book indicated problems in the recording of Mississippi history itself in years past. The writers were "usually members of the upper and middle classes of society" and "to some extent" their history books "may not tell what actually happened." But rather it is "what they think happened."[42]

Charles Sallis and his project associates prepared a book that is an excellent educational contribution to a new understanding of Mississippi society. It, like so much else emerging from Mississippi in the years since the civil rights movement, has given insight and understanding about a Mississippi that has, instead of just one, many ways of life, many features of its past as well as its present.

5

Gender and Sexuality

When I was a girl, my mother used to say, "The most important thing a woman ever does is get married." We would be riding along in our Willys car, Merrell in the front seat with Mother and Daddy, me in the back seat with Aunt Bessie and Aunt 'Cile, and something would trigger Mother's need to declaim about our future. Since we did not ride in our car for pleasure, we were most likely going to or coming from church, for that is where the six of us usually went together at least half of the times we were out.

To my brother, I am sure she said many times, "There is nothing that would please a mother more than to have a son who is a preacher." I remember this most vividly because I myself harbored in my fervent and devout young heart ambitions to be clergy, ambitions I could confide to no-one because never in my life had I seen or even heard of a woman preacher, but the preachers were the most publicly prominent, best educated, and most powerful people I observed in my Deep South rural fundamentalist child's environment, and to be like them was what I most wanted for myself. Not so, according to my mother. After my brother was told his destiny in my mother's view, she would turn to me, sitting squished against the car door in what was left of the carseat after my two ample-bottomed maiden aunts had claimed their share, and she would say, pointedly I always thought although I did not ever gather the nerve to discuss it with her, "Gayle, the most important thing a woman ever does is get married."

Besides my discomfort on account of my beloved aunts' single status and my own rather different hopes and dreams, even as a child I found this viewpoint conflictful on my mother's part, for it appeared to me that our family income and our social opportunities in the community were both much enhanced by Mother's position as a schoolteacher, given that very little cash came into our home from Daddy's farming. But I didn't argue with her. Her absolutism was complete. Forged by her own teenage choice to be Baptist, joined in marriage to a country Methodist tradition, tended by the rural public political piety of 1940s Mississippi, her viewpoint was unbending. Then as now, the destiny of a woman was her man, she thought. It was the creed she believed in most deeply, the public policy to which she subscribed most willingly, the education she inculcated most freely: "The most important thing a woman ever does is get married."

Sometimes I imagined Aunt 'Cile rising forward from her place opposite me by the other car door, grabbing up the wooden crutch beside her that she had always walked with since she suffered from polio in infancy, and hitting her over the head with it. But Aunt 'Cile, often sharp-tongued and usually ready with Bible quotations and religious injunctions for any wrongdoers in her vicinity, was silent when Mother made that statement.

Aunt Bessie, too, said nothing. I did not expect her to. Her bosom ample like her bottom, she had already nurtured two generations in her arms and with her handiwork—her six younger siblings, including my father, and her many nieces and nephews, including my brother and me. In the trinity of mothers my brother and I in our childhood simplicity saw that we had, we named Aunt Bessie our "first mother," Aunt 'Cile our "second mother," and Mother our "real mother." Perhaps Aunt Bessie was too shy, perhaps she saw no relation to herself in what Mother was saying. It was in character for her not to speak, for she did not call attention to herself. But perhaps the tyranny of the truism Mother spoke was so deep in Aunt Bessie as in us all that it overwhelmed our lives without our knowing

it, Daddy's and Merrell's as well as the women's. Mother did not
mean to be cruel. She only meant to instruct me on the right
thing to do. Then and now, she would find much agreement.
Many other people in Mississippi, women and men, would have
agreed with her. Many other people in the U.S.A. Many other
people all over the world.

Mother would sometimes add, "Some kind of marriage is better than none at all." And we would all fall silent. Mother's assumption embodied the uncritical expectation of many cultures
of the world for women. Marriage and motherhood are definitive
of who we women are. For men, public performances give them
meaning and identity. No-one would disagree with her as we
rode in our Willys car, but we were all uncomfortable in our
silence.

It is most curious what passes for knowledge among human
beings. And some of the most potent and controversial knowledge among humans of all classes, all races, all manner of folks
is knowledge about sexuality and gender. The two kinds of
knowledge, often even convoluted, are intertwined and inter-
acting, but they are the two kinds that forge the most heat,
right up there next to war. How to behave in your sex life? What
to do as men? And what to do as women?

I learned a lot about sex and gender from Libby Leard the
year I was six years old and started to school in the second
grade. Second grader Libby Leard was a learned child, a wise
child, well schooled in the ways of the world, the best informed
in our class. I was the smartest, hands down, could read and
recite, write in print and longhand, add and subtract better than
all the other children. But Libby Leard *knew the most*, no question about it.

My mother said to me, "You let Libby Leard lead you around
by the nose, and she's not half what you are." That's not the way
I saw it. She may have lived in a shack, and her father may have
been a tenant farmer, but she had knowledge, and knowledge is
power. "Do you know about F-ing?" Libby Leard asked me one
day at recess when we two were playing alone together out

around the girls' outdoor toilet. That's what she said, "F-ing." I soberly shook my head, no.

"It's when a man gets on top of a woman and pees in her," she told me, "and then they get a baby." The condition that created, she told me, was "pergency," making the woman "pergent," and for some years, even after I saw the correct spelling of that condition in print, I talked knowingly among my peers about "pergent women," a vocabulary item I had no need for with any form of pronunciation, either hearing or speaking, in conversations with my adults.

Libby Leard also told me about Santa Claus. My disbelief ran to tears. That one I could take to Mother, if "F-ing" I could not. As soon as Mother, Merrell, and I got off the schoolbus that afternoon and had the privacy of our walk up the road to our house, I blurted out, "Libby Leard says there is no Santa Claus." Nine-year-old Merrell looked as shocked as I felt.

"Oh, my dear child," Mother replied, "I wish that li'l ole girl hadn't told you that. Santa Claus is the spirit of love, and for as long as you have someone to love you, you will always have a Santa Claus." Which is approximately the same thing she told Merrell and me when, some years later, we together got around to asking her about "F-ing," though she had a rather harder time getting her words out on that subject than she had had on Santa Claus. And eventually I had to read a book about sex to get the pertinent fluids sorted out.

By the 1980s, there had been change in the sex and gender expectations that our mothers taught us. The sexual revolution of the 1960s had as its province sex, and the women's movement of the 1960s and 1970s had as its province gender roles, including the politics and cultures of being women and men. The sexual revolution and the women's revolution have questioned, changed, and reorganized much that we thought and did sexually and as women and men. Yet, much still lingers in our consciousness of the attitudes that we learned in the 1940s and 1950s.

The place where sex and gender collide is in marriage. There are other arenas, but this is a big one in symbolism and in practice. Marriage has long been both wonderful and awful for women, and, as sociologist Jessie Bernard showed early on in the women's movement, "his" and "hers" marriages were different. Women often gave more and gained less, while men gained more and gave up less for effective marriages.

For marriage, the ritual, symbolic, and pivotal moment is the wedding. And when marriage is the achievement-goal for women, the greatest day of one's life is the wedding day, the greatest role of achieving womanhood that of The Bride.

In recent years feminists have sought and sometimes earned for women both a public and a private equality with men. They have also gained a societal affirmation and public validation of the experience and achievements of women that have been connected historically to the gender-specific, woman-specific role of women. However, feminists at times have also been ambivalent about affirming women's childcare and cooking and housecaring work, while at the same time advocating for women a public prominence, opportunity, and decision-making power in public workplaces. Calls for equal time, responsibility, and sacrifice from men in both home and public work have been forthcoming, even sometimes heeded, but domesticity has remained a testy arena for new gender formations.

It has been the same with personal style and ceremony. The wedding is a prime example. Women of my daughter's generation have a genuine choice about weddings. They first have a greater choice about whether to be married and a choice about the realms of their focus. If they choose marriage, they have a choice about doing it in a traditional style or a style all their own, though a traditional style is returning for many. For our mothers, there was an ideal which my own mother yearned for and did not have: the formal wedding with all its trappings and all that it stood for. It was the ideal she instilled in me, and she probably was proudest of me on the day I stood at the altar in my white satin gown.

My mother and father were married in the Depression era in

Ruth Winfield Love.
Photo by Gayle Graham Yates.

a very private ceremony presided over by a relative who was a minister on the campus of Mississippi Southern College. Being a college graduate and having lived in the small cities of Columbus and Hattiesburg as a student, my mother had had exposure to more elaborate wedding ceremonies, but they could not afford one. She wanted for me the "church wedding" that we did in fact have at my beloved Shubuta Methodist Church, with five bridesmaids, fresh flower bouquets, candlelight, organ music, and song.

Ironically, however, the model story of The Bride of my mother's generation I heard in my Mississippi interviews, from an esteemed woman professor whom I knew in Boston. Ruth Winfield Love grew up a southerner, a Texan, and spent the first few years of her teaching career at a small college in Mississippi, during which time she was married. Her father was president of the college, and she was married in the president's home in Brookhaven, Mississippi. Her story of her courtship by Joe Brown Love, the wedding preparations, and their marriage ceremony is one full of a whole range of feelings, beginning with the death of one fiance, moving through tender and loving preparations with three of the parents, and reaching its finale with her being the bride before the glowing, watching eyes of the assembled women college students. Yet, hers is also a 1920s story of a working woman as well as a bride, the story of a woman with a career as a theater artist. Hers is the story of a woman satisfied, satisfied on her own terms, which included being the bride. She was my professor for a period I spent as a student at Boston University in the early 1960s.

Miss Ruth's Wedding

RWL: At Brookhaven, I lived at home [in the President's Home of Whitworth College]. Joe and I were married in Brookhaven. . . . I had gone to graduate school at SMU [Southern Methodist University]. So, that put me at SMU at 26 or 27.

GGY: And enter Joe Brown Love.

RWL: Yes, and he was a seminarian. I thought that my life had been so marvelously understood and affirmed by a boy who had been down in my father's college a number of years before. [Her father had then been president of a two-year college in Texas.] He was a graduate student in landscape architecture at Texas A & M. His name was Frank Moon, and I got a message that he had died. I really had not confronted death this close before, and it had never occurred to me that there was anything except that Frank and I, who had done so many projects together, were just going to keep

on doing those things. Suddenly to have it cut off was an
acute experience.

GGY: How did you receive the news?

RWL: By telephone. His sister, with whom I had gone to college, called. Those were days when you didn't travel easily,
and besides, nobody had a great deal of money. Besides,
what would have been the use of going to mourn with his
family? . . . [T]he frontier world that we lived in didn't demand that your physical presence need be there. . . . [But] I
needed to experience this thing for myself. First I climbed
the steps of the main building at SMU and sat up there for a
long time trying to understand . . . and I'm sure I cried a
great deal. It was then twilight when I came down so I
thought I couldn't go back to the dorm. I didn't know really
whether I was going to call Mother or what I was going to
do. . . . I went to walk across [the campus] and on the other
side of Arden Forest just off the campus was the big High-
land Park Church. Suddenly I realized that I was seeing in
the playground the fellowship ring of that church. It was
Saturday night, and I had planned to go to a party that
night. There were the young people gathered. I had to decide without deciding, to allow myself either to go in and
test it or not. I did go in, and I don't altogether know why.
As I came in the door it seemed unbearable to see people
alive, just as it was unbearable to think of Frank dead. As I
turned away, across the room several steps away came this
smile. I only saw the smile with a bunch of hair around it.
And then an extended hand, and that was Joe, and in the
time that it took him to get his hand to mine with his smile, I
knew that this was something as real as Frank was real. I
had to test that because I wasn't sure that I was reading my
grief or my sense of loss into a situation that wasn't really
there. So it was four years. Besides, I wanted a career. You
remember that women in the early twenties were now the
inheritors of all the hard labor that had been done by the
early feminists. Even southern women whose agrarian cul-

ture didn't require the same kind of declarations of their independence, were acutely aware of their independence. . . .

GGY: So it was clear to you that you needed to establish your career before you could develop your relationship with Joe Brown?

RWL: Yes, but if you'd have asked me then, I wouldn't so much have said I wanted a career. I think I would have said I want to do something in the arts. . . .

The spring [of the wedding] the seniors [I was teaching] at the college were going to perform scenes from Shakespeare, and that was to be four days before our wedding! But that didn't bother me. I loved that! I didn't see any distinction between completing what I wanted to do in the arts and joining with Joe in what *we* wanted to do on campuses. It didn't seem incongruous to me. It was also logistically workable. He was through at Yale and it was time to come down, and it all worked real well. His family could get there. And Jerry and Louise [her brother and sister-in-law] were going to China that fall, but they were still there. The sooner we got all of us together [the better] . . . Joe and I had an assignment to go up to North Carolina for the summer for the General Board [of the Methodist Church].

Four days before the wedding I did the show. Joe wasn't there yet.

But in the days before, we had—Mother and I had had—a wonderful time planning the wedding. And I had made lingerie. Hand made. And as I cut the scraps—you might like to see this, too. Scraps were left over of the pink crepe de chines or whatever—I cut them into relatively organized shapes and embroidered in with silk threads little designs of flowers and jar vases on them because I was going to make a baby carriage robe. And I did. And my children used it. And my nieces and nephews have used it. And my grandchildren have used it.

GGY: Oh, lovely!

RWL: So you see how sentimental I am! But I think this has

to do with the texture of southern living. It's not an isolated thing. These are feelings that belong to the warmth of the ecology, to the kinds of people who came south—I don't know where all it comes from, but it's a part of the texture.

Among the things that Mother and I wanted—we hoped we could have a garden wedding, but it began to be clear that the weather wasn't going to cooperate. So, how were we going to get inside the two hundred guests plus the two hundred college girls, though the house was a big one? How were we going to manage it? So, what we planned was to take all the furniture out of the huge drawing room, as we called it, with the huge dining room back of it and a large entrance hall. And then the windows from the drawing room out onto the veranda at the front were ceiling to floor, so when they were not draped, and we didn't keep them draped—we liked the light—there were trees outside—the girls could come upon that veranda, see? And they could see me coming down the stairs and hear the ceremony with the windows open. So we thought it would work pretty well for them to be on the veranda and out on the front lawn. And that's where they were. And then, by taking everything out, two hundred people could get in there without killing each other. The only thing to decorate—because I didn't want to do any elaborate stuff—but Mother did put smilax ropes down the staircase with a clutch of blooms at the newelpost and one lovely arrangement on the mantle. And that was it.

We were going to have the breakfast for Joe's family from Texas, who had come, several of his sisters—his father couldn't come because he was busy at his professional job and couldn't get off. And so a family breakfast was in order. I had painted little miniatures of flowers. One of them is over here. For the sisters, for my attendants. One of my attendants was Margaret Dunkle, who was the Latin teacher, and she was my age, and I loved her very much. She was very beautiful as well as gifted. And it pleased me very much for her to be in the wedding. And then I had one student, a student who came from two or three towns down, who had been doing that for several years. Frances Friedler. She came from Crystal Springs. And she was a petite, charming little person. And so I made her a little hat. It just sat over one eye, and it had to have a rubber around it to hold it on. And everybody just wore the formal that she wanted to. We didn't have to be lockstep about it.

And Mother had made my wedding gown. She, of course, wanted me to help plan it. It was flesh satin crepe, satin-backed crepe, the crepe side out. And it was made princess [style]. The bodice sewn onto the flared skirt with train. And then it had a puff sleeve with a flowing cuff on that. And I wore a Brussels lace bertha. It could be worn either as a collar or a bertha. One of the art teachers had bought [the Brussels lace bertha] in Paris, and it was museum quality. I paid thirty-five dollars. She also had a short veil to match. But I thought it was extravagant to buy the veil too, so, regretfully, I didn't do that. My sister-in-law, Joe's brother's wife, had a Brussels net veil with a little bit of lace in it, so I wore it. And the making of that gown was to Mother and to me a very beautiful thing. She wrote a poem about it. And— I love the gown to this day. And, of course, I wore pale pink pumps—white ones tinted pink. And Joe gave me a pearl lavalier. He had already given me the pearl ring with the little diamonds around it. . . .

GGY: Have other people worn your gown? Has either of your daughters-in-law worn it?

RWL: (Laughs.) It's too small! I only weighed about ninety pounds. And I couldn't even get into it a little while after. But it's lovely. And I doubt if it will ever be worn as a wedding gown again. Especially around. And, by the way, we didn't have any zippers, and it had to be snapped to get into the silly little thing. It is a great chore to know how many snaps to put in so you don't get gaps in between. And then it is a great chore to snap and unsnap (laughs).

GGY: Yes!

RWL: But the wedding gown mattered to me a lot, and so did
the scraps. Because again, I took the scraps and made little
slippers about an inch-and-a-half or two inches long of the
satin, and bound it around the edge with the satin face and
then made a little heel carved out of paraffin and attached it
to the slipper and then put a few little forget-me-nots in the
toe of the slipper. And those slippers were at the ladies'
places.

GGY: At the breakfast? At the family wedding breakfast?

RWL: Ah-hah. And then the miniature paintings of the flowers, the campus flowers, were at the attendants' places.

GGY: Yes.

RWL: It was at that breakfast, then. And maybe this is
[where I can] get into—my experience with Mama Love.
Mama Love—this was one of the first times I really had
some conversations with her.

GGY: Oh, I would love to hear it.

RWL: Well, it was about a very important [event] in Joe's life.
It explains more about Joe to me than any other one event.
And I think Mama Love so thought. Because after breakfast
she found a way to interrupt me. Without seeming to do.
And then she told me that when he was three he had pneu-
monia. He stopped breathing and was blue and cold. She
wrapped a blanket tightly around him, kicked the burning
logs on the fireplace aside, and put him on the warm ashes.
And, as the warmth hit him, he gasped for breath and began
to turn pink. But as she put him down, even before she saw
that he was reviving, she said, "Take him if you must, Lord,
but if you leave him here, I promise he will be a good man." I
appreciated it then, but I had a lot of other things on my
mind!

GGY: Yes!

RWL: And now I know that the man I have lived with for
fifty-three years was made in that second birth. And his—it
was a faith commitment—well, you've got it! (Laughs.)

GGY: Yes!

RWL: At the time of the wedding—before the breakfast.
There was something terrific before the breakfast. Joe, of
course, was in one of the guest rooms in the house. And so,
first thing we heard that [wedding day] morning before
really time to wake up was the Girls' College Glee Club.
They were singing, "This Is Thy Wedding Morning." They
had found the music somewhere. I have to admit that the
Glee Club and my Drama Club were a little bit in competition, so I understood it to be very gracious of the director of
the Glee Club to go to the effort of finding the proper music
and getting those girls down there that morning.

When it was time for the wedding itself, Jay McGrath [the
violinist, who owned the clothing store and lived across the
street] came from across the street, and for thirty minutes
he, on his violin, and Miss Mutton on the piano—and she
was a superb pianist—she had played in Berlin when that
was the mecca of music in the Western world. So, the concert was a real concert. It was not just music that you had to
have before the wedding started.

And with the windows open, people were stopping out in
the street even to hear it. Now the Brookhaven [people]
were invited inside, our friends and the people in the community to whom the college had some sort of responsibility.
[And the college students stood on the porch and on the lawn
in front of the house.] . . .

[The music was quite important.] I left the choice of the
music for the concert up to the two musicians, but somewhere I had heard Miss Mutton play in one of her concerts,
and I knew that one of the things that she did very well was
Schumann's "Bird as Prophet," which is a programmatic
piece, and she very seldom played programmatic music. But
in this piece the writer takes you, the listener, through the
woods to hear the birds and then come upon a chapel, and
you hear the hymn being sung in the chapel, and then you
walk away from it all. And I wanted that during the ceremony. Piano music—we went on and on about this—piano

music doesn't stay in the background very easily. My dad has a big voice, and he was going to do the ceremony [officiate as clergy], so, okay, there is that on him. He can just get over the music. So, the bird arrived, and I heard it, but, of course, mostly I heard my father's voice. However, before I even heard that, as I came down the steps and looked at those upturned faces of those lovely Mississippi girls who knew me as "Miss Ruth," I knew that they were seeing "Miss Ruth"—and I believe that there was love in their look—but I also knew that they were seeing "The Bride." They were seeing themselves. This is a major role that may be played, that is assigned to play, there is no question that it may be played by *me*. And so, there it is. And I think that that was perhaps as precious a "view" as I have ever seen.

Then, when I turned, there is my brother who has been more than a brother always. [When Joe Brown Love phoned to tell me about Jerry Winfield's death, he said, "You know to Ruth he's like a piece of her."—GGY] And there was my dad. And my mother right close. And then Joe's family. And then, of course, Joe came. Who was black-haired. Now he is white-haired. When the ceremony was finished—and it *was* the ceremony. Nobody dickered with the rituals in those days [wrote their own services]—didn't feel the need to— the language is elegant, magnificent in fact. It has been used for centuries. It never occurred to me that you would want to do anything else. I don't think "obey" was in there, because my father didn't—he, for a long time, he hadn't done that.

And, so, when it was over, the moment the ceremony was finished, he held my eyes, caught them again, and he didn't move, until they said, "Okay, Dad," and he put his arms around me and [her voice catches] said, "You see, Ruth, I didn't shed a tear" [laughs]. Because he loved to cry. And he taught me to cry. And I had said, "Dad, I don't know whether I can handle your crying or not. Will you please not cry?" [Laugh.]

So, then, of course, my wedding bouquet, which was sweetheart roses and a shower of lillies-of-the-valley, I handed to my matron. The ring ceremony had taken that already. But we didn't have a photographer. That wasn't one of the things you did. But my brother Jerry made some pictures, but he thought of Louise, his wife, so he gave her the bouquet and she stepped out on the front porch. So the picture of my bouquet is in my sister-in-law's arms! But that was all right.

Then we got in. I went up and changed to my McGrath's dress outfit. [She had bought her trousseau clothes at McGrath's store.] And Joe's brother had bought for him a Chevrolet—a used Chevrolet—Joe's brother was a mechanic, and he knew if one was a good car. He had driven it over. He paid $225 for it. It was out front. I guess Jerry got it out front, and then all the kids were tying tin cans on and so on. People were throwing rice, and we did the traditional thing of going through the rice and getting in the car and driving away. We went to Jackson and spent our first night at Jackson. In the room Joe had a bouquet—a clutch—of red roses.

So Mississippi has all of those deeply significant moments [in our lives]. My parents are buried in Mississippi, and I guess there is a way in which I am really a Mississippian.[1]

So it was that another of my beloved mother-women told me how she was The Bride in Brookhaven, Mississippi. We sat at her dining-room table in Newburyport, Massachusetts, fifty-three years later, while a late March snow fell gently on Lake Artichoke in the distance. This woman had taught me much. The same many-faceted mother-woman had come to me when I was twenty-three and, rocking my fretful baby, said, "Now, Hon, it is time for you to think of something else besides the baby." And she, the theater director, cast me as the Virgin Mary in the Medieval Mystery Plays at Christmastime. And she had me dance. I—who could never dance before or since—danced the Virgin Mary to Benjamin Britten's "Festival of Carols" that

Christmastime in Marsh Chapel, and it all came together, in this splendid woman's classroom, what meaning and love and work and joy were all about. As my teacher in Massachusetts, she it was who taught me to reconcile the apparent contradictions of womanhood and work given to me by my Mississippi heritage: loving them both is her answer. The one need not be forsaken for the other. Yet her own life had not been easy. For many years she was the unsalaried second worker in a "two-person career." She and her husband left several settings because the radicalism of their work made their employers too uncomfortable. When she was employed "in her own right" on a contract in the university, she was not rehired by her all-male faculty group, even though we students attested that we learned more from her than from most of her colleagues. She confided in me, without bitterness, I thought, but with a sad wisdom, "They didn't know what to do with a woman."

It was, however, about privilege we spoke when we talked about a lavish wedding, and both Ruth Winfield Love and I knew it. To be this bride, as both she and I were allowed, was not possible for many Americans.

The story of another Mississippi woman's marriage is more sparse of gowns and song if similarly filled with work and joy. Mrs. Jeannie Griffith, who is black and was poor at the time of her marriage just as World War II began, has a very different story of courtship and marriage. She too was a working woman. She told it to me in this way.

GGY: Tell me about your getting married. How did you meet your husband? And what did you do for fun with him when you were courting?

JG: The only thing we had to do—I met him at Sanitorium, Mississippi, the [tuberculosis] hospital down at Magee. He was working at a hospital there and I went. A lot of the students would go out in the summer, when school was out, to work. And I went to work that summer. The only thing we had to do was to go to a movie. That's about all we had to do other than work. We didn't have too much time. That was in the evening. We'd go to work in the morning, and we served breakfasts and snacks. I worked in the preventorium with the children whose parents had tuberculosis. We were trying to prevent them from getting it. And I'd work with them and serve them a little snack. I worked with them, and then you'd go home and then come back. There were two different shifts, then you'd come back and serve supper, and then I was off for the evening. Maybe go to the show or play cards. We did a lot of card playing. That was about all we had to do. The fellas had a ball team, and we would watch them play ball. That was about it.

GGY: Now how did you get married. Did you decide and go get married, or did you do some planning?

JG: No, I'm not going to tell you.

GGY: OK, we'll go on. I won't ask you those private things! That was during the war?

JG: That was in 1942. I'll tell you this. We married at two o'clock on the seventh of December, and he went to Camp Shelby at seven on the seventh.

GGY: Oh, yes.

JG: Yes, that was a hard time. And he was away then. He was in boot camp. The next time was the next March. Then he went overseas, and I didn't see him any more until December of 1945. When the war was over. He came back from overseas.

GGY: Where was he overseas?

JG: In Germany.

GGY: And you worked during that time?

JG: No, I didn't. I had a little one, and I didn't get a chance to work. So now you know![2]

These are some stories of marriages from Mississippi, and then there are those for whom marriage is not the object. Julian Rush's story is one of those.

Julian Rush

When we were students at Millsaps and conference officers—serving the judicatory covering half of the state—in the Methodist Youth Fellowship (MYF) together, Julian Rush was my "big brother." Julian was enormously popular with those of us we then called "the college girls" and "the college boys." He was president of his fraternity. Socially, he was a good dancer, a creative and fascinating conversationalist, and a wonderfully kind and attentive companion; he had lovely manners and a most winning charm and sense of humor. He was a Big Man on Campus, as both a leader and a dramatic artist, holding many student offices and annually writing and producing his fraternity's skit for Stunt Night, a dramatization that every year was considered to be the best on campus, whether or not it took prizes. (One year, one of my sorority sisters and I wrote and produced a musical for Stunt Night parodying Religious Emphasis Week under the title "Sexual Emphasis Week," shocking and outraging some of our faculty who had theretofore thought very highly of us. "The Chi Omegas?" they exclaimed. "Gayle Graham and Patti Patrick? But they have always been such nice girls!" That, however, is another story. A good one, but another story.)

Julian was from the Meridian family associated with the Rush Memorial Hospital; the family name Rush I had long realized belonged to one of Meridian's most prominent families. I counted myself very fortunate to have access to this marvelous man and gladly traded the amatory relationship I would have preferred for a fraternal one, rather than have no relationship at all.

In my wedding scrapbook, I have a letter from Julian, then a seminarian in Dallas. The newspaper clippings from the *Wayne County News* there say that he was a guest at my wedding and at a "dinner for couples" that my college roommate, Martha Ray, had in her Meridian home for my bridegroom-to-be and me two nights before the wedding. In fact, he did not come from Dallas, cancelling at the last minute, after the wedding copy had gone to the weekly newspaper. Thus, any archivist, any roots-searching descendant of Julian's or mine, searching the files of the *Wayne County News* or perusing my wedding scrapbook, unless rigorously trained to be a skeptical historian, would believe that Julian Rush was at my wedding on 21 July 1961 and at the prenuptial dinner party given by Miss Ray in the Ray home in Meridian in honor of Miss Graham and Mr. Yates. This impression would be bolstered by the fact that the scrapbook contains a letter of congratulations on my engagement to me from Julian Rush. "Dear Hon," he wrote,

> I haven't forgotten you. I merely made the mistake of taking an *over* full load this semester along with working, so I'm going quietly but surely out of my mind. The news you wrote me is *wonderful* and actually, I was surprised. You talked as if this was one of those idle dreams that could never happen, but darn if it didn't. I'm still shopping, but I've had enough of this window shopping nonsense. *I am ready!* I'm glad you've already purchased and I'm so happy for you. Tell all my friends hello and write when you can.
> Love,
> Julian

Oh, I so loved Julian Rush, and I am sure he loved me. Ours was the communal love of "our group," the Methodist Youth Fellowship and its liberal leaders, and then the Methodist Student Movement in our later years together. We earnestly canvassed Mississippi together on various campaigns on behalf of good behavior, the Methodist Church, and not a little unstated late adolescent sexual attraction. Up and down Mississippi, we and our cohorts went. Such wonderful young people as Warren Day, Jim Waits, Kay Ayers, Margaret Sylvester, Rufus Peebles, John Sharp Gatewood, Kent Prince, Mary Elizabeth Waits, up and down Mississippi, our hormones jiggling and our piety firm, we preached and campaigned, persuaded and taught. "Leadership Workshop," "Recreation Laboratory"; conferences on "Drinking and Christian Living," "The Church and Race Relations,"

"Christian Social Relations," and "Dating and Christian Living"—these were some of the arenas in which we led the youth of Mississippi Methodism and even occasionally its adults.

Late one night some twenty-five years later, sitting up reading the *New Yorker* on my side of the bed, I started an article by Calvin Trillin datelined Denver, Colorado. Suddenly, a startled recognition came, and I cried out to my bedmate, who until then had been sitting up silently and peacefully with his sleepy-time reading. "Listen!" I cried out, "This is about *my* Julian!"

The last time I had seen Julian was about four years before, when I had been invited to give some lectures at the University of Denver and our mutual friend from our national Methodist Student Movement days, who was then president of Iliff Seminary on that campus, had invited Julian and his wife Margaret to lunch with me after one of my lectures. He had on a bushy toupee that day, but, other than his hair loss, little about this handsome and gracious man differed from the one I had known as a "college boy."

"Listen!" I, now wide awake over the *New Yorker*, exclaimed to my unwillingly awake spouse, "Julian has come out as a gay man! And there is a great hullabaloo in the church about it!"

The hullabaloo turned out to be not only in the local church which Julian served as a minister to youth. Julian's coming out had forced the issue of clergy homosexuality into the fully public context of the national Methodist Church. It not only did that; it made the church of our childhood and youth examine its conscience nationwide regarding its treatment of gay men and lesbians, and made it examine the attitudes toward these people it fostered among its members. Our church's struggle over Julian's decisions paralleled to what state and local governments and courts were doing about homosexuality in political institutions all over the United States. The situation was the same in Mississippi as in Denver or New York or San Francisco.

In Julian's local church, First Methodist of Boulder, Colorado, the issue of the conflict between service to the church and his homosexuality was addressed by the congregation in an explosive meeting on 12 October 1981. The focus of the church meeting was on whether Julian's public declaration of his gayness made him ineffective as a minister to youth. The head pastor, Ben Gilbert, had set this debate in motion. He said, "Julian Rush and I are friends. Julian Rush and I disagree very strongly on whether or not a youth minister in the church can be a declared gay." Bishop Melvin Wheatley and his cabinet of district superintendents were in attendance at the meeting. The bishop has a final say in the appointment of ministers in the Methodist structure, though the recommendation of the congregation weighs heavily in the decision a bishop makes.[3]

The night of the meeting, the congregation was deeply divided in their statements. Young people from Julian's youth group spoke for him. One teenager said, "The only bad effect [of the case] will be if you take Julian away from us."

Another said, "By getting rid of Julian, we are not getting rid of the problem. Julian fits no stereotype and never had. What kind of Christian attitude is it to get rid of Julian? One argument is that the Bible teaches that homosexuality is wrong. Does not the Bible also teach that women should obey their husbands?"

One of the adults commented, "[People are saying] 'I love Julian, but . . .' I wonder if I might be the next to have certain conditions tied to your Christian love."

The other side was equally vocal. One older man said, "I am not a Biblical student, but I think I understand what I read. And I read into the Bible that homosexuality is wrong. And you people who are arguing here tonight for us to accept it are asking me to compromise my moral issues . . . my religious issues! And I don't believe I can. Julian, the solution is with you. If you want to save this church with the polarization that is here tonight, you must resign!"

Though that meeting ended in indecision, Julian was shortly terminated in that position.

But that was not the last word. Methodist clergy "in good standing" are required to be given church assignments by the bishops of their regional jurisdictions. Bishop Melvin Wheatley continued to make a clergy appointment for Julian Rush in the jurisdiction which he served. This was challenged in the national Council of Bishops of the United Methodist Church, but the bishop's authority was upheld.[4]

In summer 1987, a national news service report discussed the recent adoption of a modest inclusive language policy of the United Methodist Church in the Colorado judicatory. A closing addendum to the story said, "The clergy body also voted to verify the moral character of each minister in the regional conference.

"This vote cleared the way for announcement of clergy assignments for next year, including the reappointment of the Rev. Julian Rush, who is gay, to St. Paul's United Methodist Church in Denver."[5]

A woman friend of ours at Millsaps has not been so fortunate. If it is fortunate to be able to make a public declaration of one's fundamental sexual orientation, have a very public battle fought over the issue, and, out of one's commitment, end up making a modest change in the institutional order of one's church.

The woman who was my best friend our freshman year in college left college mysteriously before our senior year. She was creative and bright, eager and disciplined, the "model pledge" in our sorority in which we knelt at initiation on the white satin pillow and vowed that we were "white Christian virgins." Not a word about heterosexual. She, like Julian, was very popular, but unlike Julian, she was socially awkward, loud, and earthy. She had a wonderful sense of humor, which was expressed in quick-witted one-liners and clever, sometimes raunchy repartee. All through college she had intense, short-lived one-to-one friendships with other women students. Though I had my turn as her closest friend and then she moved on to others, I remained a loyal friend all through college, even going to visit her in her town some distance from mine in the summer after our sophomore year, when she had serious illness and surgery. When she left college, I was never quite sure what happened—and I might not have understood if someone had told me, for I don't think I understood what "lesbian" or "homosexual" meant until well into my twenties, white Christian virgin that I was in mind, spirit, and body, in those pure days of innocent youth at Millsaps College.

Years later, a graduate student in our university who is from my college friend's Mississippi town and I were visiting. "Do you know [my friend]?" I asked him. "She's from [your home town]."

"No, but I've heard about her," he said. "She got into some kind of trouble, having an affair with a doctor's wife, I think it was, and had to leave town."

She is in New Orleans now, I have been told, but I have not been able to reach her. The troubles she has gotten into, beginning in our college days, I have been told, are because of her lesbian relationships. She has found it necessary to remain private about her choices for partnership for sexuality and love.

My friend could have been the model for a wonderful novel by Mississippi writer Ellen Douglas, *A Lifetime Burning*.[6] Douglas's reputation for insight extends far beyond Mississippi to a nationwide audience. Reviewers say of her work: "There can be no question about it, Miss Douglas is . . . one of the best of our contemporary American novelists . . . an artist who sees, who understands and who grieves over the sorrows of life,"[7] and "Miss Douglas's exploration of hearts and lives is at once passionate . . . powerful and disturbing."[8]

A Lifetime Burning is a compassionate, tender, and yet forthright treatment of bisexuality and the lives of two married people for whom gay and lesbian love becomes a reality. I have told the ending and thus spoiled the reading for readers who have not yet read the novel, for the novel is about the deceit and ambiguity, the agony, jealousy, fear, and shame that sixty-two-year-old Corinne and her sixty-year-old husband George experience in relation to their sexual preferences and desires. Douglas uses a technique of gradual and layered; tentative, tenuous, and retractive revelations of the truth. Using the device of two journals, Douglas presents the entire text as a journal written by Corinne in episodes of disclosure meant for the couple's three

children to read after her death. Within Corinne's journal is
given an account of another journal that Corinne found in the
attic, this second journal written by their much-admired great-
grandmother.

Corinne had discovered that the great-grandmother had committed suicide, and one of the mysteries she seeks to resolve is
why. Simultaneously, she tells the children in episodes she
writes in her journal of the sexual and emotional coldness that
has come between her and George. Gradually she reveals that
George is having an affair with a woman she calls the Toad. Then
she retracts that revelation, saying that it is not true. She reveals, though by this time the reader is on guard about what to
believe, that she herself had a long affair with a married man
before she and George were married and that, while her marriage to George at first had been a marriage of convenience, she
soon came passionately to adore George. George, a surgeon, has
never been demonstrative of feeling, but he, two years younger
than Corinne and a distant cousin, loved her deeply as an adolescent, and she interprets their marriage as, for him, a marriage of friendship. Sex for him is a component, but one not so
important as companionship, she thinks.

Soon, however, in another episode in Corinne's journal, Corinne reveals that, rather than the Toad, it was a man George
loved, a young man her children's age who is a technician at
George's hospital, a man she dubs the Musk-Rat. George has
carried on his love affair with the Musk-Rat while remaining
married to Corinne, and while the relationship has caused Corinne great pain, it has paradoxically kindled in her a new passion
for George. She falls in love with him again.

Then she finds the diary of the great-grandmother and in it
the explanation of the suicide. The great-grandmother hated
her husband, and some years after his death, she invited a beloved woman to come and live with her. Shamed by both their
families because of the two women's relationship, she felt she
had no way out.

And then Corinne tells that she too had an affair with a

woman many years before. Both she and her woman lover were beautiful and energetic mothers of young children, indistinguishable from other well-heeled wives and mothers in their southern river town. The affair broke off when the woman's husband became violent.

Throughout the journal entries, Corinne imagines the children's responses as they read what she says. She imagines judgment, feels guilt over being so revelatory, wishes for their understanding. She writes to each one individually, warmly, out of her particular relationship with each one. In the end, she addresses her adult children as a group:

> Now it's as if all of you are here with me again in this room, around the dying fire of a late winter evening.
> You look at one another and at me. You reach out to me . . .
> "Never mind your motives, Mama," one of you says. It doesn't matter which one speaks, for it seems to me that you are acting as one. "Never mind your character or, for that matter, ours, or Daddy's. What can we do, any of us, except reach out to one another, stay within reach?"
> Ah, children, ah, George, here I am, then, and here is this. Waking and dreaming, I reach out to you all.[9]

During my stint as a graduate student of religious drama with Ruth Winfield Love, I also studied with Harold Ehrensperger. Love was known to her students as "Lady Love" or "Lady," and Ehrensperger invited us to call him by his first name. Harold was a warm and dear, cosmopolitan and courtly gentleman who was gay but private about it. One of the plays we studied in their team-taught class was Christopher Fry's *A Boy with a Cart*. I learned the play well, for I also had acted in this play in a summer I spent in summer stock with a company called the Bishop's Company. One of the precepts of my later life has come from that play. The boy-with-a-cart says of the strangers he has met on his way, "They are not bad fellows, once you get to know them."

They are not bad fellows, once you get to know them. That is the truth of it for many people, gay men and lesbians among them. The hard part is getting to know them. Or even knowing that you know them, when they are the people you love.

Beth Henley, Mississippi Playwright

Beth Henley is a playwright who grew up in Jackson, Mississippi. Her grandparents were from Brookhaven, Mississippi, and Hazlehurst, Mississippi, and she set her first two plays in those towns that she knew from her grandparental visits. *Crimes of the Heart* is set in Hazlehurst, and *The Miss Firecracker Contest* is set in Brookhaven.

Born in 1952 and a mere twenty-five-years old when she wrote *Crimes of the Heart*, Beth Henley is a postfeminist female writer. It was her mother's generation who did the slugging through women's liberationist battles in the 1960s and early 1970s. What their work yielded for women of Henley's generation was the comfortable assumption that women writing about women is fully appropriate. That assumption need not necessarily be either self-conscious or articulated, as it appears not to be in Henley's case. Both *Crimes of the Heart* and *The Miss Firecracker Contest* are wonderfully implicitly woman-centered, and, while the two plays, like all good literature and art, do many things, both plays instruct us in gender dynamics, between and among women and between women and men. And they do so while at the same time being a great deal of fun.

I noticed in the movie of her *Crimes of the Heart*, for which Henley wrote the screenplay adaptation of her play script, that the town sign locating the setting said "Hazlehurst"—as a child, I had playmates from Hazlehurst who would come and visit their grandmother in my town—and I paid attention to the credits at the end long enough to learn that it was filmed in North Carolina, not Mississippi. But *Crimes of the Heart* is a Mississippi play, and it is a woman's play.

There is a 1981 interview with Henley by a gifted young man from the Mississippi Department of Archives and History named John Griffin Jones. That was the year that *Crimes of the Heart* was opening on Broadway after its Off-Broadway stint and just before she was to win the Pulitzer Prize. Beth Henley told Jones about herself in a refreshingly open and unselfconscious way. The interview took place in her mother's home in Jackson, where Henley and her rock-music-performing boyfriend were paying a short visit from their home in Los Angeles. Expressing delight that the play had been successful in Louisville and Off-Broadway, Henley said she had enjoyed the Jackson performance of *The Miss Firecracker Contest* more than the New York one. She had spent three years in Los Angeles trying to find work as an actress and working as a temporary office worker after her graduation from SMU, where she majored in acting. She called those years "that many years of destitution," and she admitted to writing *Crimes of the Heart* as a workshop piece for her unemployed fellow actors in Los Angeles—a piece in which she expected to play the part of Babe.[10]

Jones told her that reviewers had likened her work to the works of Flannery O'Connor, Tennessee Williams, Chekhov. Had she read those writers? Did she deliberately try to write like them?

No, Henley said,

> I hadn't read Flannery O'Connor. Like, in my first review in Louisville they compared me to her. I hadn't read her. Now I love her. I think she is great. I had read Tennessee Williams and Chekhov, and I think they're great. Now what did you ask me?
>
> JONES: If you drew that parallel consciously, or if that tradition meant anything to you when you sat down to write?
>
> HENLEY: Chekhov and Shakespeare, of course, are my favorite playwrights. Chekhov, I feel he influenced me more than anyone else, just with getting lots of people on stage. I don't do anything close to what he does with orchestration. That fascinates me. I also like how he doesn't judge people as much as just shows them in the comic and tragic parts of people. Every-

thing's done with such ease, but it hits so deep. So I guess I've got to say he influenced me more than I guess anybody.[11]

Peppering her sentences with extra instances of "I guess" and "like" and "like how," as many young people her age do, Henley gamely took any question Jones gave her, saying at one point, when asked if she would like to write fiction or poems or other forms of literature, "I still don't have good grammar for putting like a whole novel or whole story together. I can just write dialogue."[12]

"What about the literary tradition of Mississippi?" Jones asked her. "A lot of the humor you use in the two plays I've read is taking that Gothic Southern heritage and turning it upside down—you know, with the mother who hangs her cat and then herself. Do you take that old Southern eccentricity as something you are trying to satirize? Are you really conscious of that?"

Henley replied, "Well, I didn't consciously like say that I was going to be like Southern Gothic or grotesque. I just write things that are interesting to me. I guess maybe that's just inbred in the South. You hear people tell stories, and somehow they are always more vivid and violent than the stories people tell out in Los Angeles. It's always so mellow. . . . The South just suits me better. . . . I like to write about the South because you can get away with making things more poetic. The style can just be stronger. If I could figure it out I'm sure I could do it with any place, but I haven't."[13]

Throughout the interview, Jones asked her questions leading to how much of her work was autobiographical. She said the idea for *Crimes of the Heart* came from an incident in which her Hazlehurst grandfather got lost in the woods and there was a three-day search for him. There was much publicity, and family members came home from distant places, but eventually he just walked out of the woods. She thought that would make a great play. Eventually, though, she couldn't write a play about her grandfather being lost in the woods, but the part about the family gathering back at home around a crisis was put into the play.

She said, "I don't think *Crimes of the Heart* was as autobiographical as [a critic] was implying. It's true I'm from Mississippi, and I have two sisters, but my mother isn't dead with
suicide, my sister hasn't shot her husband, you know, my sister
doesn't have a missing ovary. All the characters were imaginary.
I guess it is biographical in the sense that they were sisters and
they are from Mississippi."[14]

When asked how much of the stories in her plays was from
her memory and how much from imagination, Henley said:

> Some of the things I might not have heard from my family but have
> heard from other people in Texas or even in New York that I trans-
> posed down to the South, to Mississippi; or even to Los Angeles
> because that's where I live now. But a lot of them are from stories
> I've really heard, more in *Miss Firecracker* than *Crimes of the Heart*.
> I totally made that up about being hung with the cat. I never knew
> anyone who would shoot their husband because they didn't like
> their looks, and then go fix lemonade. I made all that up.[15]

Crimes of the Heart is about three sisters and their relationships. Lenny, the oldest, whose thirtieth birthday is a framing
event of the play, has stayed home, remained single and in service to the family needs, and has taken care of Old Granddaddy,
who took them and their mother into his home when they were
children. Meg, the second sister, has gone out to Hollywood to
seek the singing and acting career that Old Granddaddy wanted
for her. Babe, the youngest, married Zachery Botrell, "the richest and most powerful man in all of Hazlehurst," a lawyer and
state senator from Copiah County. Lenny remembers, "She was
the prettiest and most perfect of the three of us. Old Granddaddy used to call her his Dancing Suger Plum. Why, remember
how proud and happy he was the day she married Zachery."[16]

As the play opens, Babe has shot Zachery. She wounds him
in the stomach and then goes and makes lemonade and offers
him some before she gets medical help for him. She is arrested,
admits she did it, "'Cause I didn't like his looks. I just didn't like
his looks."[17] She is brought home from jail on bail by their
society-matron cousin from next door, Chick, for whom the

McGrath sisters are a great embarrassment and toward whom she behaves with condescension and disdain, using them for her needs and abusing them with her words.

The Babe-shoots-Zachery crisis draws all the sisters home together. All the action of the play takes place in the kitchen, that center of so much of women's lives; and this kitchen has a cot in it, which Lenny has put there for herself to sleep on, to be available for sick Old Granddaddy's calls in the night. In this play, an action counterpoint to the legal and matrimonial woes experienced around Babe's attempted murder is the offstage hospitalization and decline of Old Granddaddy.

The three sisters re-remember their mother's sensational suicide, at which time she hung the cat along with herself in the cellar. They return to their pattern of quarreling with one another over who was the family favorite: Babe the beauty, Meg the talented, or Lenny the reliable. Meg goes to the hospital and lies to Old Granddaddy about successes she has had as an entertainer in Hollywood, when really, she admits to Lenny, "What I do is I pay cold-storage bills for a dog-food company. That's what I do." [18] In the midst of everything else, Lenny unthinkingly submits to a demand from Chick to drive Chick's children to the hospital for a minor emergency. Babe submits to her young male lawyer's efforts to use her case to carry out his own personal vendetta against Zachery.

It is revealed that Babe has had a loving sexual relationship with fifteen-year-old black Willie Jay and that Zachery has found out about it. Zachery, for his part, has physically and verbally abused Babe, and the lawyer has medical records to prove this, though Zachery has damaging photographs.

It is also revealed that Meg went crazy at Christmastime and was in a psychiatric hospital, lying to the family about glamorous work obligations keeping her in California when Old Granddaddy sent her money to come home. It is remembered that Meg's actions have permanently damaged family friend and her former boyfriend, Doc Porter. She had loved him but would not commit herself to a relationship with him. Seeking excitement, she exposed them to danger during Hurricane Camille in Biloxi, a building collapsed on them, and Doc's resulting injury crippled him for life as well as caused him to give up his aspirations for a medical career, but Meg left him that night after having made him risk the danger of the hurricane by staying there with her.

The two days of crisis that comprise the play's action also bring resolution. Resolution comes for each sister. It also comes for them together. Babe's lawyer, though exacting the price of sending Willie Jay away, gives up his own vendetta and moves to defend Babe in earnest, on the basis of what Zachery did to her. Babe, attempting suicide in two raucous episodes, one with a rope and one with a gas oven, is physically saved by Meg and emotionally saved by learning about love: "Mama. I know why she hung that cat with her. . . . It's 'cause she was afraid of dying all alone. . . . So it wasn't like what people were saying about her hating that cat. Fact is, she loved that cat. She needed him with her 'cause she felt so all alone." [19]

Meg goes out with Doc. There is a spark between them as before, though Doc now has a wife and two children. They spend the night driving in the moonlight together, and Meg too learns about love. In a newfound ecstasy in the new morning, she tells her sisters, "Everything's all right with Doc. I mean, nothing happened. Well, actually a lot did happen, but it didn't come to anything. . . . But for now it was . . . just such fun. I'm happy. I realized I could care about someone. I could want someone. And I sang! I sang all night long! I sang right up into the trees! But not for Old Granddaddy. None of it was to please Old Grand-daddy!" [20]

Old Granddaddy has died in the night. Meg will not have a chance to tell him she lied to him. Inappropriately, irreverently, even rudely, the sisters get the giggles. All of them no longer lie to themselves. Chick comes over with her usual orders concerning what they should do, criticizing Meg for staying out all night with Doc and calling her a slut. Lenny assails her and drives her out of the house, beating at her with a broom. "I said for you to get out!" she says, "Do you hear me, Chick the Stick! This is my home! This is my house! Get out! Out!" [21]

The three sisters together celebrate Lenny's birthday with a huge decorated cake, ordered by Meg and Babe, saying "Happy Birthday, Lenny—A Day Late!" In the opening of the play, Lenny had surreptitiously crept into her own house with birthday candles and slipped cookies out of the cooky jar on which to place her candles and make a wish all alone. Only Chick had brought her a present, and it was a cheap box of chocolates with Christmas cellophane on it. On this new day, her sisters give her a cake with thirty candles and "one to grow on," and her sisters empower her to make a wish. "The more candles you have on your cake, the stronger your wish is," Babe improvises to fit the situation—Babe, "the regular expert on birthday wishes."

Meg and Babe insist that she tell them her wish. Lenny says, "Well, I guess it wasn't really a specific wish. This—this vision just sort of came into my mind. . . . It was something about the three of us smiling and laughing together. . . . it wasn't forever; it wasn't for every minute. Just this one moment and we were all laughing."[22]

And so it was. They were together. It was temporary. But it was real.

Mississippi white middle-class women have, for the most part, been trained, as I was, to see marriage to a suitable man as their foremost goal for a successful life. Beth Henley's artistic and unselfconscious breakthrough beyond this idea is an important yardstick for the gains that have been made by feminism for interpreting and understanding women's lives as multidimensional, as based on choices made by the women themselves, as sometimes connected to men and sometimes not, as sometimes bonded to other women and sometimes not, as sometimes confident and sometimes not, and as capable of setting their own directions for career, love, hate, or crime.

Another of the goals of young Mississippi women of my day, one that was tacitly subsumed under the preparation-for-marriage goal, was to be beautiful. And the beautiful Mississippi woman had in the beauty queen a model for appearance, talent, hip-waist-and-bust measurements, skin care, hair style. And the greatest of all the beauty queens was Miss America. It

went unstated that she was white. Teenaged girls of my acquaintance trained to participate in the local Miss Hospitality
contest or the local pageant for the Miss Mississippi contest, and
Miss Mississippi, of course, was our representative in the Miss
America contest. An evening gown competition, a swimsuit
competition, a talent presentation, and a brief interview on
stage were standard.

Though I was the state president of the Future Homemakers
of America (FHA—a high-school home economics club with a
national structure) and valedictorian of my high school class,
those accomplishments paled before the fame and glory that
came to Mary Ann Mobley, my fellow state president of the
FHA who went on to be Miss Mississippi and then Miss America. My predecessor by two years in the state FHA, Mobley and
I attended state conventions together and in 1955 were members of the seven-girl delegation to the national convention of
the FHA in Ames, Iowa. Mobley has gone on to have an outstanding career as an actress in New York and Los Angeles,
and, like many Mississippians, I thrill with special local pride in
this celebrity whom we once knew. I have probably said three
thousand times, "Mary Ann Mobley and I went together to
Ames, Iowa, to the national convention of the Future Homemakers of America." For those of us who have yearned for public
rather than domestic success as adult women, it helps that *she
too* was one of us in the Future Homemakers of America. *She too*
went to those all-girl meetings in those Mississippi towns. *She
too* went on a speaking tour of the district conventions with Miss
Funk as her chaperone. *She too* said those same words of those
same club pledges in honor of domesticity. And when I see her
on my TV screen, in a movie or as broadcast commentator from
the Los Angeles Olympics or in a magazine modeling clothing in
Thailand with her entertainer husband, I can think smugly, "*She
too* did not stay home and become a housewife!"

The beauty contest has changed in the years since Mary Ann
Mobley and I were teenagers, she a success and I a flop by the
beauty-queen standard. The standardized white middle-class

version of beauty that we all longed to embody has changed. Though a black Miss America preceded her, it was history-making in Mississippi when black Toni Seawright won the Miss Mississippi pageant in 1987 and represented Mississippi in the Miss America pageant.[23] The racial barrier to opportunity had been breached in one more place. Even so, the standard of female beauty has remained constant. The beauty contest still goes on as the place where the-most-beautiful-of-us-all is named as the representative of young womanhood.

As the playwright created it, Beth Henley's *Miss Firecracker Contest*, much like her *Crimes of the Heart*, was theatrical and fun. But as a reflection on the culture out of which it came—American or Mississippian—it provides a useful index to the current challenge to the ideal of standardized virginal female beauty as the model for contemporary young womanhood. A story of the annual beauty pageant at a small-town Mississippi fair, the play satirizes the sexual purity, moral uprightness, social grace, aesthetic physical appearance, and trained talent that are norms for contestants in the beauty pageant. In the character of Carnelle Scott, with her red-dyed hair and her very name suggestive of carnality, Henley creates an anti–beauty queen, and with her a deteriorated situation of callow rudeness and ineptitude that ridicules the entire process of judging the-young-woman-most-beautiful-of-all.[24]

Boys and Men

Best-selling Mississippi author Willie Morris called his 1980 memoir of his Mississippi Delta youth *Good Old Boy*. His title is a term that grown men call one another in affection and trust, a term of bonding and cooperation. There is jesting to the term, too, a half-serious suggestion that the men so called never quite have to grow up, that they can be perpetual boys. Men do not call each other "old boy" with somber faces; rather, they smile, speak with animation and even glee as they refer to some good old boy or other whom they know or love, hunt with, or, at the very least, conspire with to play pranks. Women and northerners use the term only as a descriptive label for a classification of southern men, revealing that the category marks out the boundaries of a class of men from which not only women but other men are excluded. The grouping has to do with being buddies and hunting, drinking, taking risks, and playing sports together. Its members must be white and male, privileged and prosperous. Such men are members of an implicit club with an invisible charter and unwritten rules. Extremists at one edge of the club's membership use their accumulated power to hate, murder, and destroy. At the other extreme within their group, societal good will; family, religious, and civic duty; and moral responsibility are the male norms shared in the exercise of their collective power. Good old boys are the southern version of the white male elite around the world. For those females of us also privileged by birth group or education or money, they are our fathers, husbands, and brothers, their heirs our sons and nephews. *Human beings all. Beloved human beings.*

In 1945, thirty-five years before Willie Morris published *Good Old Boy*, another Mississippian published another best-selling autobiography with another male-specific title. Richard Wright called his book *Black Boy*. "Black boy" is a term of contempt for an adult male black person. If perpetual boyhood of the good old boy is chosen, the eternal state of black-boy is dictated *to* the black man. He is not allowed to grow up, not allowed to be adult, not allowed by the system, not allowed by the Man. "Boy" as a means of address to the black person is a term of condescension, a command, a relegation to servitude, or a sign of disrespect. When the good old boy said, "I take care of my boys," he was being patronizing. For a black man to call himself "boy" or to say that to one of his fellows, while sometimes clever insider-humor, often reflects self-hatred, often self-abnegating and defeatist obedience to outside rule. The black boy is the counterbalance to the good old boy. If one must be down for the other to be up, then neither will be free to be full human beings facing one another on a level. What is true for the group is true for the individual.

Richard Wright was a black Mississippian bitterly angry about the hunger, poverty, misery, ignorance, and abuse of his people wrought by segregation and white supremacy. Richard Wright was a very gifted writer. He chose the title *Black Boy* for the autobiography of his youthful years, published in 1945, when he was already an acclaimed writer.

Wright was born in Natchez, Mississippi, and lived with his mother and brother in dire Mississippi black poverty, often without enough to eat, without adequate clothing or housing, and with very limited education until he was nineteen. At nineteen he moved to Memphis, and subsequently he settled in Chicago. Publishing first in the late 1920s, he attracted wide attention with a volume of stories called *Uncle Tom's Children*, published in 1938. These stories dealt with the black man's quest to find meaningful identity in American society, but most of the heroes in the stories met death instead.

Wright was involved with other talented writers with national reputations and received his first opportunity to write full-time in Chicago in the Federal Writers' Project in the early 1930s. In Chicago during that time, he also joined the Communist Party and in 1937 went to New York to become, for a time, an editor for Harlem of that party's newspaper, the *Daily Worker*. Wright's fame and greatest stature came from his 1940 novel, *Native Son*. The novel's hero, Bigger Thomas, learns of the antagonism of the white world after accidentally killing a white girl. In his decision to defend himself, to fight, Bigger comes to maturity and the realization of his humanity, of his manhood. This theme of maturity gained through fighting reiterates an account from early in Wright's autobiography. Wright describes there how his mother sent him out into the street to buy groceries and he was beaten and robbed by bullies on the street. His mother sent him back, and back again, and finally locked him out of the house until he was able to fight the neighborhood boys with a cane, until they were all beaten and their parents threatened, until he became the ruler of the street, able to walk to the grocery store and back without fear of having his money stolen and being beaten.[25]

The autobiography *Black Boy* is at times lyrical in its expression of Wright's love for, as well as his outrage over, his homeplace South. He writes:

> There was the yearning for identification loosed in me by the sight of a solitary ant carrying a burden upon a mysterious journey. . . .
> There was the thirst I had when I watched clear, sweet juice trickle from sugar cane being crushed . . .
> There was the speechless astonishment of seeing a hog stabbed through the heart, dipped into boiling water, scraped, split open, gutted, and strung up gaping and bloody.
> There was the love I had for the mute regality of tall, moss-clad oaks.
> There was the hint of cosmic cruelty that I felt when I saw the curved timbers of a wooden shack that had been warped in the summer sun.
> There was the saliva that formed in my mouth whenever I smelt clay dust potted with fresh rain.
> There was the cloudy notion of hunger when I breathed the odor of new-cut, bleeding grass.
> And there was the quiet terror that suffused my senses when vast hazes of gold washed earthward from star-heavy skies on silent nights.[26]

Near the end of the book, Wright describes his departure for Chicago and, with it, his realization of what his "place" meant, what location in the South, his Mississippi, signified for the young black man:

> The white South said that it knew "niggers," and I was what the white South called a "nigger." Well, the white South had never known me—never known what I thought, what I felt. The white South said that I had a "place" in life. Well, I had never felt my "place": or, rather, my deepest instincts had always made me reject the "place" to which the white South had assigned me. It had never occurred to me that I was in any way an inferior being. But in what other way had the South allowed me to be natural, to be real, to be myself, except in rejection, rebellion, and aggression?

Not only had the southern whites not known me, but, more important still, as I had lived in the South I had not had the chance to learn who I was. The pressure of southern living kept me from being the kind of person that I might have been. I had been what my surroundings demanded, what my family—conforming to the dictates of the whites above them—had exacted from me, and what the whites had said that I must be. . . .

I was leaving the South to fling myself into the unknown, to meet other situations that would perhaps elicit from me other responses. And if I could meet enough of a different life, then, perhaps, gradually and slowly I might learn who I was, what I might be. I was not leaving the South to forget the South, but so that some day I might understand it, might come to know what its rigors had done to me, to its children. . . .

Yet, deep down, I knew that I could never really leave the South, for my feelings had already been formed by the South, for there had been slowly instilled into my personality and consciousness, Black though I was, the culture of the South. So, in leaving, I was taking a part of the South to transplant in alien soil, to see if it could grow differently, if it could drink of new and cool rains, bend in strange winds, respond to the warmth of other suns, and perhaps, to bloom.[27]

Richard Wright went to Paris, France, in his later years made his home there, and grew to believe that integration would never work in Mississippi. Even when he died in 1960, he was not accorded honor in the South. His membership in the Communist Party was one of the factors in the suspicion held toward his reputation. Yet a number of major American writers had been communists or favorable toward communism in the 1930s, and Wright, like many of the others, had rejected it early in the next decade. However, for many Americans, especially southerners, this "red flag" was reason enough to obliterate his memory. The fact that he was black and wrote about black experience kept him from honor in his native Mississippi.

Richard Wright was born in 1908, died in 1960. He was William Faulkner's (Faulkner: 1897–1962) age-peer, his junior by eleven years, but until recently, little has been made of their common origin. There was local suspicion of Faulkner, too, in his lifetime, but by now many Mississippians have come to honor

Faulkner with great patriotic pride. Faulkner's home in Oxford, Mississippi, is now owned by the University of Mississippi, and it is now a shrine to which travelers come from all over the world, as well as from all over Mississippi.

At long last, in the 1980s, Richard Wright, too, came to be honored by Mississippi, at the University of Mississippi. Twenty-five years after his death, his memory was honored with a conference on his work, a conference sponsored by the Afro-American Studies Program and the Center for the Study of Southern Culture, under the leadership of black Professor Maryemma Graham. Scholars came from around the world to read papers on his work and to discuss his literary legacy. A dramatization was even written for the occasion, *A Tribute to Richard Wright*. The keynote speaker was Wright's friend from his Federal Writers' Project days and his most recent biographer, Dr. Margaret Walker Alexander.

Richard Wright's daughter, Julia, was invited to Mississippi as well, and she presented the university library with a letter written by her father on receiving the Springarn Medal in 1941 for writing *Black Boy*. The letter, now in the archives of the formerly all-white University of Mississippi, says that Wright accepts the award on behalf of the countless Negroes whose lives and whose brave efforts for freedom he has tried to represent faithfully in his fiction. He accepts the medal for his father who was a Mississippi plantation sharecropper and his mother who lost her health at work at hard jobs that did not pay her decently. He hopes to do honor to all the nameless black people like his parents who have suffered much and been little rewarded. On behalf of all of them he accepts the medal.[28]

Julia Wright, to whom, along with her mother, *Black Boy* is dedicated, came from her home in Paris to donate the letter, to visit the family graveyards in Mississippi, and to seek her paternal home. She received a warm reception and was generously hosted in an official public ceremony by both blacks and whites. In memory, the black boy rightfully had come home to Mississippi as an internationally honored man of letters, an author in company with the best of peers.

Man-of-letters Willie Morris is a fine writer. His *North Toward Home* is a contemporary classic. Greatly influenced by William Faulkner, Morris claims that Faulkner was prescient in foreseeing racial reconciliation in Mississippi. *Prescience* is one of Morris's favorite words. He states in an interview:

> There's a long way to go, though. Of course, the person who really understood [that Mississippi would be the land where racial reconciliation, in whatever form it was going to take, could occur] so well in his generation was Faulkner. There's no more revealing a story—it's one of my favorite short stories—"Delta Autumn." You know, the story about Uncle Ike McCaslin's last hunt, and the mulatto woman who comes with the baby to the hunting camp. There's a resonance in that story. Mr. Bill knew what he was talking about. And of course the Northern liberals gave him hell. There's a word called *prescience*.[29]

Richard Wright, a man of Faulkner's generation, might well have been prescient, too. His stories, too, alongside Faulkner's, have their particular truth. But Wright had reason to be far more pessimistic than Faulkner.

Morris himself is prescient about men and race. He sees very clearly the breaking of the past power-grip of white male ascendancy based on race. As weddings, beauty pageants, foods, and domesticity have been the gender-charge of women, so hunting, drinking, government, commerce, and sports have been the fields of men. Perhaps the greatest of these is sports. Nothing is more male in American culture than football, and in the heyday of the good old boy's unrivaled rule in the South, even if blacks could play well and did, white males were in charge of football. That has changed. When he first heard about Marcus Dupree, Willie Morris knew that he had the symbol and the story of how that dominion has changed after the civil rights movement and after what was perhaps its most important accomplishment in Mississippi, the desegregation of the public schools. His book is a fascinating, detailed account of the redemption of a chastened and shamed Mississippi town, after the civil rights movement and federally-mandated public racial integration, by its having the best high-school football player in the United States, the one most sought by colleges nationwide, a black student in the first high-school graduating class that had been triracial—blacks, whites, and Indians—from kindergarten through twelfth grade. The town is Philadelphia, Mississippi; the football player, Marcus Dupree. Willie Morris, former good old boy, called his magnum opus about the social deconstruction of racial malice *The Courting of Marcus Dupree*.

Marcus Dupree was a senior and a running back for the Philadelphia, Mississippi, High School football team in fall 1981. He broke famed Georgian Herschel Walker's high-school record for running and touchdowns. Dupree was an intelligent, serious boy, almost shy, who made Bs and As in school. He was devoted to his single-parent mother and to his younger brother, Reggie, who was crippled and about whom Marcus said, "I run for both of us." Marcus started kindergarten with the first class of totally desegregated Mississippi schools. His was the first class of students who knew nothing but integration from start to finish in their schooling.

Mississippian Willie Morris begins his chronicle of Mississippian Marcus Dupree in this way:

> I had heard about him for many months, ever since I came back from the North to live in Mississippi. Going into his senior year, he was the most sought-after and acclaimed high school football player in America, a swift and powerful running back whom many were already comparing with the legendary Herschel Walker of Georgia. The town of his past and his people—Philadelphia, Mississippi, in Neshoba County—as in the Biblical sense certain places sometimes are, was suffused with its remembrance of self-destruction . . .
> . . . On this hot September night, Number 22 [Dupree] walked through the door of the gymnasium with his fifty or so teammates. He stood there beyond the end zone and waited with them to run onto the field. They were a small-town Mississippi football team. . . .
> He was big. He was carrying his helmet, which he put on now over a copious Afro haircut kept in place by a red hairnet. He was seventeen years old and he was wearing glasses.[30]

Lacing his book with his own observations and memories and his own comprehension of the historical significance of the excitement surrounding Dupree, Morris skillfully interweaves these with the story of Dupree's senior year in high school and the national attention given him by recruiters and coaches from college football teams. Morris makes much of the location in Philadelphia, where three civil rights workers had been killed less than twenty years before. Ever the skillful reporter, Morris blends the stories of townspeople with that of the football player. He interviews and describes the Choctaws from the Neshoba County Indian reservation. He appreciates the irony in the fact that law officers who killed Schwerner, Chaney, and Goodman are now freed from prison and participating in an integrated society. For example, at the decisive game in the Choctaw Bowl, when Dupree breaks Herschel Walker's record, the son of the sheriff who participated in the killings, Cecil Price, Jr., is the team's water boy who brings Dupree his drinks of water during the game, and Cecil Price, Sr., is seen in attendance at the event, cheering.

Morris also pays tribute to Florence Mars, a woman who was one of the few white voices of reason in Philadelphia during the civil rights era and who wrote her account of it in *Witness from Philadelphia*.[31] Willie Morris is the self-appointed chronicler of that year in the life of Marcus Dupree, that year in the life of Mississippi, that year in the saga of men and football, that year of symbolic demonstration that the walls of racial segregation and white supremacy had indeed come tumbling down.

The recruiters and coaches came from all over the country to watch Dupree play. While they could not officially recruit him until after the end of the football season, the media and the coaches were there to see him. Willie Morris came, too, with his dog Pete, and became well acquainted with Dupree's home in the Independence Quarters section of town, and with the seventeen-year-old manchild, Marcus Dupree himself.

Dupree let it be known that he was interested in the three major predominantly white Mississippi universities, Ole Miss, Mississippi State, and the University of Southern Mississippi. Among the alumni of these universities, alumni groups encompassing the vast majority of the most prominent citizens of Mis-

sissippi, as well as among their coaching staffs, there was much
hot discussion and fierce competition for Marcus to choose their
university. Dupree was also interested in the largest predomi-
nantly-black Mississippi university, Jackson State. He fluc-
tuated widely in his out-of-state interests: University of Southern California, Texas, Alabama, Oklahoma, UCLA.

The climax came the night of the Choctaw Bowl, the last
game for the Philadelphia High School team and the last game
for Dupree. That day he had announced that he had narrowed
his list to twelve. The surprise was that Ole Miss was left off.
The coach from Ole Miss came to the Choctaw Bowl game anyway, looking haggard and tired. "I just wanted him to know I
was here," he said.

With eight minutes and fifty-three seconds left to play in the
game, Dupree tied Herschel Walker's record. Morris writes:

> A silence fell on the crowd as Marcus took a pitchout to the right,
> slowed for the briefest instant, swerved toward the sidelines, de-
> ceived a linebacker with a motion of his head, reversed his field,
> and sped unmolested into the end zone.
>
> The entire stadium was joyous. I believed I heard war whoops.
> Even the Union people across the way stood and cheered. Over the
> pandemonium, the loudspeaker announced that this touchdown,
> number eighty-six, had tied Herschel's figure. The referee gave the
> football to Marcus. He ran off the field with it, holding it in one hand
> high in the air. The band played the fight song, and his coaches and
> teammates embraced him at the bench. Two white and two black
> cheerleaders embraced and kissed him. Another white cheerleader
> sat on his lap and hugged him. Cameras recorded these scenes. The
> crowd continued to stand, and little white, black, and Choctaw chil-
> dren ran down out of the stands and surrounded him for his auto-
> graph.[32]

And then the record-breaker:

> Four minutes, thirty-five seconds remained. Philly got an off-
> sides on the next play, moving the ball to the Union eighteen.
>
> The handoff went to Marcus. He crashed down the middle for
> sixteen to the Union two-yard line, 4:24.

A hush descended once more on the spectators, about a hundred of whom were at the goal line. Everyone was standing.

He carried up the middle to the six-inch line. There was 3:57 left when the Philly team came out of the huddle.

The silence was eerie now as Number 22 ran the ball for the last time in his high school career. There was nothing spectacular about this play. He merely bulled his way across the double-stripe for the touchdown.

There was a re-enactment of the impassioned scene of five minutes before. Once again he ran off the field and was engulfed in children, and the crowd applauded for long minutes.[33]

Dupree had broken Herschel Walker's record. The coach asked, "Do you want to go in for one last one?" "Naw, Coach," he replied.

The recruiting was fast and furious, and at last the day came that he would announce his choice. Strongest speculation was that he would go to Mississippi Southern. With media, coaches, and townspeople present, he came to a press conference in his high school gym:

At last Marcus, his mother, and Joe Wood were walking across the basketball court again. When they finally entered the hall and sat down at the table under the glaring lights there was loud clapping. The TV cameras were grinding away, and people stood on tiptoe to get a better look. A silence fell as Marcus leaned into a microphone.

There was a span of eternity to me from that midnight of seventeen years ago on Rock Cut Road to this hallway of Philly High on this day when he said: "Next year you'll see me at the University of Oklahoma."

The applause echoed down the corridor. Several people dashed out the door.

The reporters asked their questions. "Why did you choose Oklahoma?"

"They have a winnin' tradition. They'll be on TV a lot. They'll be a national contender. I can win the Heisman. I enjoyed the trip. I believe I can fit in there."

"When do you make up your mind?"

"Last night?" . . .

There were other questions. Then Marcus' mother, her eyeglasses reflecting the hard artificial light, her voice husky and emotional, said, "I'd just like to say to the people of Mississippi and especially to the people of Philadelphia that we appreciate very much the support they's shown. It was a difficult decision for Marcus. Very difficult."

"Let's make it official," Joe Wood said. Someone brought in the papers from Lucious Selmon outside, and Marcus and his mother began signing them one by one.[34]

Morris speculates with William Faulkner's sister-in-law about what Faulkner would have thought of the desegregation in his hometown Oxford:

> I would begin with his sixteen-year-old-great-nephew whom we know as "The Jaybird," grandson of his younger brother Dean. One night recently I was sitting at the old table in the house on South Lamar where Dean Faulkner Wells, The Jaybird's mother, and her husband, Larry Wells—publisher, editor, and janitor of the Yoknapatawpha Press, located over the Sneed Ace Hardware Store, now lived. Much of *Absalom, Absalom!* had been written on this table, during Faulkner's grief over his brother's death. The Jaybird had just departed to play in the high school basketball game. I was talking with Miss Louise—Faulkner's sister-in-law, Dean's widow. "Miss Louise," I asked, "if Mr. Bill were sitting here tonight and knew that The Jaybird was the only white boy on the starting five for Oxford High School, what would he think?" Miss Louise thought for a while. "I think," she finally replied, "he'd be honored that The Jaybird made the team."
>
> To me The Jaybird's warm comradeship and day-to-day proximity under the official auspices of the public schools of Mississippi with Topcat, The Hawk, Toad, Scott, Calvin, and the others went to the heart of a different South.[35]

Willie Morris provided a postscript on Marcus Dupree's life after his senior year in high school. He stayed until the middle of his second year at Oklahoma, then dropped out and returned briefly to Mississippi Southern. Shortly, at nineteen, he signed with the New Orleans Breakers in the United States Football League. In 1982, the only teenaged player in the history of American professional football, he averaged 4.7 yards per carry and became a New Orleans hero. He owned and drove a Mercedes.[36]

A post-postscript is not so happy. Although Dupree had signed his $6 million contract with the New Orleans Breakers to be near home in Mississippi, the team moved to Portland, becoming the Portland Breakers. In his opening game for Portland, Dupree severely injured his knee and did not play again. He watched the games from the sidelines in a hip-to-toe cast. He wound up with an insurance lawsuit to obtain the money that the Breakers had guaranteed him and insured him for.[37]

It was in this way, then, that Marcus Dupree broke the color barrier for himself and young Mississippians. The school, commercial, and athletic desegregation that came in his lifetime allowed him to do something that no black Mississippi youth had done before. The terms of his success, however, while entirely new for blacks, were thoroughly traditionally male. The game of football itself is a male-invented, male-performed, and male-dominated sport; and the professionalization of football, as well as its commercialization, has been a male achievement. In a very real sense, then, and in a gender-specific way, it was American manhood that Dupree achieved with both his running-back prowess and his multi-million dollar contract.

Peggy Prenshaw: A Woman's Way

In the jigsaw puzzle of gender, race, and class in the United States, it is nearly axiomatic that the man has been the key piece. Afro-American people's language abstracts and capitalizes "the Man" to signify the white male owner and landowner and boss who historically has held power over black people's livelihood, location, and movement and, with these, all too often their freedom, safety, rights, opportunities, and very lives. He is not the man of suffering and brotherhood. The Man is white and authoritative. He belongs to the collectivity of power and precedence. One by one, as human individuals, some white men have been compassionate and kind, have made just laws, have fought for the liberty of persons other than themselves, have exercised power judiciously. Some saintly ones of them have given up themselves and their own wills for the cause of improving the fortunes of other people, for one beloved person or one group, for dedication to abstract justice, for a vision of a greater good in the world beyond the limits of their own interests, or for an attitude of loving as the better way to live. Some other white men have been mean, cruel, personally violent. Some white men have been atrociously destructive. But whoever they are as individuals, white men as a group have had the topmost place of privilege and have been accorded the assumption of authority and power throughout all the spheres of modern civilized life. In the past twenty years, this hegemony of the Man has begun to crack. It has begun to crack over race, as Willie Morris shows so skillfully in his story of Marcus Dupree in the male domain of football. It has begun to crack, too, over gender.

My longtime friend, Alabamian Katie Thompson, for more than twenty years has repeatedly told a story from her wedding reception that is guaranteed to make me blush. Over the years, however, my blush has slowly matured from modesty to shame.

Katie and I were first friends when we lived in Cambridge, Massachusetts, as young adults. I, the younger of the two of us, had been married for several years when she was married, and I was a hostess for her wedding reception—and apparently the day's expert on etiquette. Katie and Thom were preparing to cut ceremonially the first slice of their wedding cake and were expressing confusion over whose hand should go where on the cakeknife, when I interjected conclusively, "Katie, you know the man is always on top!"

It brought the house down. And I have never lived it down. Both of us already had achievements of national student leadership, both of us were soon to read *The Feminine Mystique* and eagerly identify ourselves as feminists, but the truth about

Peggy Whitman Prenshaw.
Photo published by courtesy of
Peggy Whitman Prenshaw.

women and men has never been clearer for me than it was on that day.

I was only talking about cakeknife etiquette, of course. But I believe that etiquette, like everything else, is linked in our minds and habits, in our feelings, observances, and behaviors, to everything else that we do and think and believe and practice. Thus I named, unwittingly, the root cause of the gender justice battles that were to rage everywhere in the United States and around the world for the next two decades.

Katie's and my Mississippi counterpart on that wedding day in the 1960s was Peggy Whitman Prenshaw. Ours had been three parallel white women's lives. Thinking that, as mid-life colleagues in scholarly circles, we had come to know each other, I interviewed Dean Peggy Whitman Prenshaw in her office in the Graduate School at the University of Southern Mississippi on my Mississippi homecoming journey. It turned out that I had seen her on stage as a high-school girl when she presided over the first state convention of the Future Homemakers of America I attended. Mary Ann Mobley—the Miss America with whom I had gone to Ames, Iowa, for the national FHA convention when I was fifteen—had been elected state president of the FHA at the state convention Peggy Whitman served as president.

When I interviewed her in the 1980s, Peggy Whitman Prenshaw, like me, was a university professor. Like me, she had a husband and two children. Like me, she had been deeply affected by the civil rights movement and had become a feminist leader in her area. Like me, she was a scholar of American women's literature and culture. And, like me, she had left Mississippi to go to graduate school thinking she would never come back.

When I interviewed her, she spoke of the 1960s, of familiar family dissension in which every discussion centered on racial conflict and in which nearly every family in Mississippi was engaged. "They were hard, hard times. At one time my dad said all he could figure out was that I was a Communist."

Prenshaw recently had attended a conference at Jackson State University on the life and work of Fannie Lou Hamer, "With black colleagues, it was a time of public witnessing, of remembering those days. My role was utterly private. I had no public role to remember, as did those at Jackson State and at Tougaloo. Those were the years when I was a student. I was also married and had a child. The times finally got so painful. I felt that I had to leave Mississippi because there absolutely was no middle ground."

She told of choosing to be an English major in college. Wanting to study "everything," particularly physics as well as literature, she had postponed a decision about a major until the last possible time and was forced by a college official to declare a major. English it would be: "Why would you press yourself to a test tube or an inclined plane if you could sit around and read?" She had learned a lot in high school home economics and had won an FHA scholarship in home economics, so at first she had thought she might be a home economist: "I had seen home economists give speeches wearing nice suits." And when she discovered the student newspaper, "I decided to be a girl journalist." But in the end it had been English: "I think English and history are the two most comprehensive disciplines." She did a master's thesis at Mississippi College on Eudora Welty, one of the first, and then she did her Ph.D. dissertation at the University of Texas on Welty, too. She did a study of "place in [Welty's] own fiction, how she made those Mississippi environments carry so much weight in the story."

At Texas she found graduate school "relentlessly masculine." At her first literary seminar, on Melville, "My professor asked me—there was a sizeable number of women in graduate school, but no other woman in this class—he asked me what I was doing occupying a chair that some man could be sitting in.

"It was the first time I was *really* conscious of the masculine bias. . . . And then at the end, when we were graduating, when many professors were writing references for me, I remember one telling me how that year at Texas they had grouped all the job applications by male or female, one pile for male and one pile for female. And they did not read the female ones unless they decided that year they were going to hire a woman. Women were not professors, they were invisible. I just denied the discrimination was there, wouldn't believe it."

Faced with what it would mean if she and her husband could not get a job in the same place, "We had a spirited discussion, a horrible argument. He said, of course, we would go where he got an offer. It really came home to me. It was painful, really painful. But it was only theoretical. Dick was offered a position here. They offered one in the English Department to me as well. My parents were wonderfully happy! When we came back here. I wasn't a radical anymore, I guess. The ones who noticed were the children."

Back in Mississippi, Prenshaw found that "race relations didn't have the power to raise the deep divisions the subject had had before. In a few short years, attitudes had changed dramatically, and in 1969 there seemed a great many possibilities for building bridges. All these opportunities for really contributing to the state."

Peggy teaches southern literature: "From the very first year here, I taught an overflow course on southern literature, taught a Faulkner seminar. With my work on Welty, I had taught myself what I know about how to read modern literature. With women's studies, I have learned the role of women in southern fiction. I have published two collections of essays on Welty and recently edited a book of her interviews—also an essay on Welty, 'Woman's World, Man's Place.' Too, I have been interested in the portrayal of the family in modern literature. That has been a way to teach about women without the topic's seeming so threatening. Several years ago the MLA and FIPSI funded a project on 'Teaching Women's Literature from a Regional Perspective,' and that provided a way for me to get to know women in my region."

Prenshaw was, she said, "only briefly involved with politics in the state, a precinct delegate to the 1976 convention for the reorganization of the Mississippi Democratic Party. But what I did do was help organize the League of Women Voters in Hattiesburg. Also, working with the Mississippi Committee for the Humanities has been a little like Eudora Welty's WPA days, an opportunity to get out and see the people. I have done a great many programs for the committee—now the Mississippi Humanities Council—as one of the scholars in the field."

There is one story that is illustrative of what all of this means today, personally, socially, and professionally for Peggy. I heard it from at least two other Mississippi sources before she told it to me:

"Early in the days of the Humanities Committee [the early 1970s, when feelings of racial conflict were still high], I went to Lexington to talk about kindergartens. The question was, should Mississippi have public kindergartens? My opinion was yes, but I tried to approach the subject with as much objectivity as possible. I worked a month to prepare and became a minor expert on public kindergartens."

When the day arrived, "We were to go to the Lexington Attendance Center [the public school]. I asked my mother and father to drive up there with me. It was a long way, and I didn't want to drive back late at night alone. Part of the reason my father went was to go to a large family burial plot in the area. So we did that. Took photographs. Did all this Confederate stuff. I went to the radio station. Then I headed to the Lexington Attendance Center.

We stopped at a service station, and my dad asked, 'Where is the Lexington Attendance Center?'" Astonished, "the service station operator said he thought we must be mistaken. We must want the Lexington Academy. Because the Lexington Attendance Center was 'all niggers.' I said I was sure I was going to the Lexington Attendance Center. And we went."

When the three arrived, "sure enough, the audience was 100 percent or 99.8 percent black. My mother and father and I went in. And, bless them, both parents and audience were genuinely interested. We had a good evening's discussion at the Lexington Attendance Center about kindergartens. And this was one of many such programs."[38]

An eloquent speaker, Professor Prenshaw was the spokesperson for the national Federation of State Humanities Programs before the House Appropriations Committee of the U.S. Congress in 1987. She echoed some of the speech she had given at the tenth anniversary celebration of the Mississippi Humanities Committee, when she said, "My topic this morning is: why the humanities in Mississippi? If I were a foolish wag, I might suggest that the humanities and Mississippi are natural companions, both in low cotton in the eyes of their competitors among disciplines and states. But I am not a foolish wag, I hope, and to my eyes the association of the humanities in Mississippi is entirely a worthy one."

Reading. Learning to read. Learning that there are books. Learn-

ing to know, to know books. Learning what the books have to say.
Learning. Knowledge. Books. People. Richard Wright. The kinder-
garten children. Peggy Prenshaw. Marcus Dupree. Willie Morris.
And me. Our fathers and mothers, sons and daughters, husbands and
brothers, sisters and enemies, lovers and friends. Human beings all.

The original speech ends: "Why the humanities in Mississippi? In 'Little Gidding' in the *Four Quartets*, T. S. Eliot wrote,
'We shall not cease from exploration,/ and the end of all our ex-
ploring/ will be to arrive where we started/ and know the place
for the first time.'"[39]

> *the end of all our exploring*
> *will be to arrive where we started*
> *and know the place for the first time.*

6

Spirituality, Religion, and Belonging

To be rooted is perhaps the most important and least recognized need of the human soul.[1]

Simone Weil, *The Need for Roots*

A football cheerleader at the University of Mississippi in 1982, a black man named John Hawkins, the first black male to be elected a cheerleader there, refused to wave the Confederate flag as part of the university's football-game school-spirit crowd-rousing that was its tradition. His action triggered significant protest by the Black Student Union, defense by many whites, heated discussions repeated over and over again about current use of Confederate symbols in schools, colleges, and communities throughout the South—my godson at the University of Florida, a transplanted New Yorker, told me about the controversy—and eventual removal of the Confederate flag as a school symbol for the University of Mississippi.[2]

Several such vestiges of white Civil War memory had attached themselves to the University of Mississippi and become representative of it. Largely in an unconscious way, persons privileged by society are upheld in privilege by routinized actions and also by familiar and established things and language, used and repeated over time to hold a cluster of meaning, historical, social, personal, imagistic, spiritual, and aesthetic. In short, an object, a word, or an action potentially bespeaks deep layers of values. Often it takes protests by excluded persons even to call attention to the import of many objects, words, and actions to those who are left out.

One such Confederate era symbol for the University of Mississippi is the nickname, "Ole Miss." As nicknames are, it is an affectionate name for the school. Also as nicknames are, it is a diminutive name. Shorter, easier to say, less formal, it also potentially lessens the dignity of what it stands for. (Think of the women who as adults insist on being called Beatrice instead of Buffie, Julia instead of Julie—but, it's okay, they qualify, for intimates to continue the diminutive. Think of the men who want to cease being Georgie or Johnny or Billy as grownups—or the precocious ones who as small boys would fight if a brave schoolyard fellow said Willie for Wilson or Jimmy for James.) As a symbol, the name "Ole Miss" comes from the title given to the plantation mistress. In the nineteenth-century vocabulary of the Deep South, white women were entitled to the titles "Mrs." and "Miss" but an oddity, by twentieth-century urban standards, was that respect was conveyed not only by reference to marital status, but also by first names. The plantation mistress might be "Mrs. Phelps," but she would be "Miss Sarah," sometimes even to her husband (who might be "Mr. Phelps" to her, even intimately and certainly publicly) and always to persons of lower social status, including children and slaves. Thus, the plantation mistress would be "Miss Sarah," and when she would have a daughter, perhaps also named Sarah, the daughter would become the "Little Missy," and the mother would be "Old Missy" or "Ole Miss." Thus, the affectionate title bestowed upon the University of Mississippi carries with it the authority—and femininity (*alma mater*)—of the white plantation aristocracy of the South.

Ole Miss's husband, as it were, at the University of Mississippi is Colonel Rebel. Colonel Rebel, a figure dressed in a Confederate military uniform, was for many years the mascot of the football team, called the Ole Miss Rebels, and a symbol for the university in print, in the form of its logo on signs, banners, posters, books, and stationery. Colonel Rebel's descent from the

Confederate States Army is less difficult by far to trace than that of his "wife." As, in the Civil War, the Army of the United States was called "the Yankees," the Confederate Army men were the Rebels. There was a battle-cry to go with the name, the Rebel yell, also approximated as a sound accompaniment for football games at the University of Mississippi. And the university mascot is an officer, not a footsoldier, no buck private. All this begins to sound very elite and exclusive.

Another football game tradition that took on mythic proportions was the singing of "Dixie." Written on the eve of the Civil War, 1859, the song was a war song of the Confederate soldiers. At Ole Miss (as well as at countless other schools and colleges for white students across the South) it became an anthem of regional white patriotism, sung ceremonially on a regular basis at the football games after the national anthem, "The Star Spangled Banner," and sung with the same ritual posture of respect and standing—indeed, sometimes sung with more vigor and enthusiasm than the national song. Traditionally the song ended with the Rebel yell before the football players, that squadron of young male warriors in sport, ran out onto the stadium's field to face their opponents.

All these very symbolically living words, material objects, and familiar ritualized actions formed part of the preserved Civil War legacy of Mississippi culture when John Hawkins took a cloth piece of that material culture, the Confederate flag, and refused to wave it in ostensibly playful ritual as a part of the cheerleading ceremony for the Ole Miss football fans. Thereby, he illuminated the two sides of a fact: ritual and patriotic honor are as full of meaning as argument; fun-seeming lively athletic play is as surely significant in implication as prayer or law. A human-made object, custom, or manner of speaking can select and dignify, or exclude and repel, as deeply as a statute or a governor.

The name Ole Miss, the drawings or costumed figures of Colonel Rebel, the song "Dixie," the Rebel yell, and the Confederate flag, all symbols drawn from the Confederate past, signify a pride in that past. On first blush, they might seem harmless reminiscences of a dead past. Yet in their original forms, that pride only could be white, for it was whites who rebelled on behalf of slavery. That bondage of slavery was the collective past of the Mississippi blacks; and when blacks joined whites in such Mississippi institutions as the university, it became essential for the university to recognize their past as black people, understood from within their own experience and cultural memory. There might be several choices, since the university will still need logos, mascots, affectionate names, and banners for its community-building efforts. There could be black ones alongside white ones, or black ones replacing white ones, or new ones that "integrate" Mississippi experience. For the time being, the University of Mississippi has removed the Confederate flag as its school symbol and with it made the acknowledgment that that flag has been a symbol of white power. Also, many faculty members of my acquaintance at that university very carefully refer to their school as the University of Mississippi, without a diminutive substitute.

This flag-waving (or flag-not-waving) incident is an illustration of what scholars of American society call "civil religion." It is a Mississippi version of the idea of civil religion at work. Civil religion is not the same as Protestant Christianity or Judaism or Catholicism, nor is it the same as government or civil law. It is "religion," in that it is a set of beliefs, practices, affirmations, images, symbols, rituals, and revered writings and people, as all religions are. It is "civil" in that its reference point, its transcendent reality, is a unity of state or nation, the peoplehood of members of a particular political society. It is closer to patriotism than to church, yet it has a "God," a calendar of commemorative days of celebration, past leaders held in special reverence, and commonly held images drawing forth powerful meaning for the people as a collectivity.

The civil religion thesis was proposed by sociologist Robert Bellah in an influential article published in *Daedalus* in 1967.[3] In the article, Bellah analyzes the inaugural addresses of the

American presidents and concludes that Americans have a public "God" who is not the God of Christianity, though the God of
the civil religion is derived from the concept of the deity of Protestantism that the leaders of the early American nation brought
with them from Europe. This civil religion also has prayers, said
to the civic deity at public events, and U.S. presidents or other
public or community leaders call upon "Him" at national ceremonial events such as inaugurations, dedications of public buildings, or war memorial events. The time of origin, the point at
which the people of the American nation began to "belong" to
this civil religion is the time of the American Revolution. This
time when the civil religion established the national uniqueness
or community separateness is the symbolic time that members
can look back to, cherish, and worshipfully remember as their
time of coming together, their holy time of beginning. Like an
institutional religion, the American civil religion has a time of
trial, the Civil War, from which it emerged "saved," revived as
a nation, "revitalized."[4] These wartimes—the holy time of beginning, the Revolutionary War; and the holy time of trial, the
Civil War—have their heroes, who have become holy people,
the Fathers of the Nation, the "saints"—in particular, George
Washington in the first case, Abraham Lincoln in the second.
The nation and its civil religion also have their holy days, their
holidays, particularly the Fourth of July or Independence Day,
Thanksgiving, and Memorial Day, on which days there are ritual
celebrations commemorating the achievements of past victories
and the peoplehood of the Americans. At these ritual celebrations, prayer and thanksgiving are offered to the God of the
Americans, but an explicit attempt is made to avoid any partic-
ularity of reference to Jesus Christ or Jehovah, such as would
make that reference Protestant, Jewish, or Catholic, and thus
less than comprehensive of all of the Americans. Near the end
of his article, Bellah says, "the American civil religion is not the
worship of the American nation but an understanding of the
American experience in the light of ultimate and universal reality."[5]

Language, Images, and the Civil Religion in Mississippi

As the civil religion idea shows us, three of the ways we can get to know a people, ways into the cultural meaning and symbol systems of a society, are: learning their language, identifying their images, and becoming acquainted with their religion and spirituality. We must acquaint ourselves with them as these three factors appear to members from within the culture and society, to those people who *belong*. All cultural systems are equivalent, both in their being manifest by the group and by the individual member of the group, and in their being partly unselfconscious and partly obvious to their practitioners, the people who belong.

Language, images, and spirituality all have affinity with one another and all are parts of the same cultural whole that includes politics, economics, family structures, and community life. But these three dimensions of culture—language, images, and spirituality—are more private in their interpretations and accessibility, while the practices such as politics, that necessarily originate socially, more often automatically are understood by insiders and more difficult for outsiders to comprehend. If a foreign language is hard to learn, so is a foreign imagery and spirituality. Foreign imagery is more subtle and more difficult to grasp than foreign politics or economics. And, like language, the images, spirituality, politics, and other features of culture, too, have regional variations, "dialects" that locals know and use innocently, knowing no other. Cosmopolitan members of the region know and use these dialects of cultural systems also, but, in addition, cosmopolitan members are fluent both in their own "dialects" of image, spirituality, and politics and in those of other regions or people, and they know the differences among them.

Local or innocent outsiders often ridicule the "dialect"— whether it be language, image, religion, politics, or other cultural practice—of a given locale other than their own. Outsiders who are cosmopolitan travelers, educated participant-observers, or sensitive people try to learn the dialect of religion or language or politics or imagery or whatever cultural system of the people other than their own whom they are visiting or studying, working with or living beside. There are both tomes of social science methodology and lots of folk wisdom to support this position. Growing up, I often heard an American Indian saying that one should "walk a mile in another man's moccasins before deciding what he thinks." At the time I did not know enough to ask: Choctaw or Lumbee, Apache, Navajo, Cherokee, Sioux, or Winnebago? Or, what about the women? But I got the point. It was the same as the Jesus-lesson: "Do unto others as you would have others do unto you." Or the lesson some therapists teach their troubled patients: "Empathize. Try to imagine and act on the other person's feelings." To know Mississippi language, imagery, and spirituality, one must know them as Mississippians know them, both Mississippians who are local and innocent and Mississippians who are cosmopolitan and acquainted both with their own Mississippi and with the outside world. Like Miss Marple in St. Mary Mead, who, to know human motivation, thinks of what her fellow villagers would do, to learn what Mississippians know, we have to go to Mississippi to listen to Mississippians, or at least read what Mississippians say.

Mississippi professor of history Charles Reagan Wilson has analyzed southern history, society, and culture with the aid of the civil religion thesis. Wilson is a University of Texas Ph.D., a staff member at the Center for the Study of Southern Culture at the University of Mississippi, and the coeditor of a new *Encyclopedia of Southern Culture*. His book is *Baptized in Blood: The Religion of the Lost Cause, 1865–1920*, and he followed it with a series of lectures and articles demonstrating the usefulness of the civil religion idea in interpreting "the southern way of life," with its reverence, affinities, loyalties, motivations, and memories.[6]

Wilson proposes that in the post–Civil War South, the majority people, the dominant culture, created for itself an "afterlife of a Redeemer Nation that died." He sees the development of an ideology of the Lost Cause, the moral justification of the inherent holiness of the Confederate character and the separateness of the righteous southern people, as the basis for a regional piety that was not denominational but cultural, not of the church religion but of the civil religion:

> But the dream of a separate Southern identity did not die in 1865. A Southern political nation was not to be, and the people of Dixie came to accept that; but the dream of a cohesive Southern people with a separate cultural identity replaced the original longing. The cultural dream replaced the political dream: the South's kingdom was to be of culture, not of politics. Religion was at the heart of this dream, and the history of the attitude known as the Lost Cause was the story of the use of the past as the basis for a Southern religious-moral identity, an identity as a chosen people. The Lost Cause was therefore the story of the linking of two profound human forces, religion and history.[7]

Wilson goes on to show how, in the period from the end of the Civil War to the end of World War I, a combination of old Confederate soldiers and Protestant clergy led the South into a reverence and honor for the spirituality of the Lost Cause commitment. They participated, he says, in a "war of ideas" to retain southern identity: "The South's religious leaders and laymen defined this identity in terms of morality and religion: in short, Southerners were a virtuous people." He quotes Samuel S. Hill, a leading sociologist and historian of southern religion, as saying, "In a word, many southern whites have regarded their society as God's most favored. To a greater degree than any other, theirs approximates the ideals the Almighty has in mind for [hu]mankind everywhere. . . . For the south to stand, its people had to be religious and its churches the purest anywhere." Wilson goes on to comment, "Unfortunately, the self-image of a chosen people leaves little room for self-criticism. This deficiency has led to the greatest evils of the religion-cultural link in the South."[8]

Wilson then shows that the Lost Cause religion has all the features of the American civil religion, all the features that Bellah pointed out earlier as features of "an experience of . . . an ultimate and universal reality." These include the saintly heroes: Robert E. Lee, Stonewall Jackson, Jefferson Davis. Sacred monuments are built to these men throughout the South, and then monuments are built in many a southern courthouse square to "the Confederate dead," the unnamed ones or, more usually, the ones listed by name as from that county and fallen in battle. Ceremonies are held, sacred days are set aside. At first these ceremonies were reunions of the Confederate soldiers, held in Richmond or Charleston. Then Confederate veterans groups were organized. Later groups were established, made up of their daughters or sons. A day was set aside and made a state holiday throughout the South, Confederate Memorial Day, on which the Confederate memory was honored. Songs and poems were written, preachers pounded the points home from their pulpits. The most eloquent preachers of the Lost Cause were leading Protestant clergy. Mississippi's Methodist Bishop Charles B. Galloway, Charles Wilson tells us, "was perhaps the best-known Lost Cause paternalist in the post-1900 period." He describes Galloway:

> Born to pious Mississippi parents, he reached adolescence during the Civil War and he always remembered that the Southern preachers he had heard when young had "expounded the old prophecies and proved to my perfect satisfaction that the South was bound to win." He later became one of the most prominent second-generation ministers of the Lost Cause. . . . Galloway was a segregationist. In "The Negro and the South," an address delivered at the Seventh Annual Conference for Education in the South, he outlined his white supremacist views, advancing four principles for race relations: no social mixing, separate schools and churches, white control of politics, and opposition to the colonization of Blacks. Galloway claimed that whites still had a paternalistic responsibility to halt Black decline, although he had retreated on the issue of segregated churches. Galloway absolutely refused, though, to justify or to con-

done the lynchings that plagued racial relations after 1900. He blamed the resort to lynch law on political demagoguery and the sensation-seeking press. While these institutions had failed the South, he noted approvingly in 1904 that a Confederate veterans' camp in Mississippi had again provided the moral leadership for the South. These "heroic men, who feared not the wild shock of battle in contending for what they believed to be right, recently passed some vigorous resolutions against this spirit of lawlessness." He insisted after 1900 that Blacks were impotent and "the old cry that 'white supremacy' may be imperiled is a travesty on Anglo-Saxon chivalry."[9]

Wilson concludes his book with the 1917 Confederate Veterans' Reunion day in Washington, D.C., at which President Woodrow Wilson spoke to the veterans:

The place [Arcade Auditorium] was packed, the rebel yell greeted him [President Wilson] as he came to the platform, and his speech was interrupted by repeated cheers and applause. Wilson drew on the ideas of reconciliation that ministers and others had been developing for several decades. He first paid poignant tribute to the gathering and its "days of memory," but added that "the world does not live on memories." Noting that, in the days of the Civil War, there was one common passion among us, and that was the passion for human freedom, Wilson the Presbyterian then explained that God's mysterious ways with the South were becoming clearer. The South was to be part of "the great world purpose," which the United States was meant to fulfill. Southerners were now "part of a nation united, powerful, great in spirit and in purpose," and "we are to be an instrument in the hands of God to see that liberty is made secure for mankind."[10]

The reunion closed with the traditional parade, and the 1917 march was perhaps the grandest veterans' parade ever. It came down Pennsylvania Avenue, where, more than fifty years before, Lincoln had reviewed the victorious army shortly before his assassination. At the front of the marchers waved the Confederate Stars and Bars, alongside the Stars and Stripes. To the tune of "Dixie" the old veterans marched, or rode on horseback, or rode in that token of time's changes, the automobile. Seated on a float, the Confederate Choir sang patriotic songs and tunes of the Southland. The Children's Choir occupied another float, with the smiling little girls in red, white, and blue dresses. On the reviewing stand above the parade stood Woodrow Wilson, reviewing the troops. He smiled as some of the Confederate veterans yelled out their offers to go to France and whip the Germans. At one point Supreme Court Chief Justice Edward White, a Louisiana Confederate veteran and Ku Klux Klan member in his youth, left the reviewing stand to march in the parade. It rained during the march, a downpour. But the parade continued to its conclusion, and President Wilson remained until the last veteran had passed by.[11]

In this manner Charles Wilson ends the lively story of how the Lost Cause of the Confederate States of America became the central cultural and moral symbol of a way of life to be honored, revered, and perpetuated as a unique form of community identity for a people, as a way of belonging. He analyzes it as a civil religion.

A Gender Journey to Vicksburg

Newly acquainted with and admiring of Charles Wilson's work, I began to think about how little I know about the Civil War and its memorials. Taking a clue from the acknowledgments page of Charles Wilson's book, on which all the names of scholars and experts recognized are male ones, it occurred to me that that the lack of knowledge probably was because I am a woman. Little girls usually are not taught about war and battles and military heroes, while little boys are. I remember that my husband tells me that one of his favorite books as a boy was *A Boy's Life of Robert E. Lee*. Like other knowledge and education, as well as exertion of power, in situations and institutions that have been created by men, Civil War knowledge is gender-specific. Thinking of that, I set out on a gender journey for what was almost my first encounter with such knowledge—information and comprehension and authority for interpretation—about the Civil War. My journey took me to Vicksburg.

Vicksburg, as most southern white males and all Civil War

buffs can tell you, was the setting for a decisive battle of the Civil War in 1863. I doubt that most southern white females know or care about that fact or think about it very much. At least I had not before. By coincidence, however, I had found a female source for my information. The Mississippi Department of Archives and History holds a diary, which has been privately printed, describing the Vicksburg phase of the War. This Civil War diary is by Emma Balfour, a Vicksburg doctor's wife and hence mistress of one of the great houses in town. Fascinated, I read the short journal, covering the dates 16 May 1863, through 2 June 1863, for several hours in the library the week before I went to Vicksburg. Balfour describes the shelling of the city, the anxiety about the army, the noise, the roads filled with routed troops, the retreat to caves, the reports from the battle front, the feeling of the officers and their conversation. While this account is written by a woman, it predominantly reports the actions of men.

After reading Emma Balfour's diary, for more compensatory education I went to Vicksburg in my car one Saturday afternoon. My destination was the Vicksburg National Military Park. I drove out of Jackson the fifty miles to Vicksburg in a holiday mood. Besides being my first serious inquiry into the Civil War, this was my first visit to that old river town where that strategic maneuver of the Civil War was won and lost. My eagerness for knowledge at this stage of my life has a unity with my rejoicing in the natural beauty of the world, and I looked forward to seeing the river as much as the military park. At Vicksburg I stopped first at the handsome Georgian-style tourism center by the river near the bridge that crosses over to Louisiana.

First I acquired a guidebook to the park. Then I sat in a rocking chair on the center's porch for a long time, just looking at the river, loving it, feasting my eyes and soul upon it, belonging to it. I have known this river in many places, even though I had never seen it at Vicksburg before. I feel especially connected to this most American of rivers, which begins up in Minnesota where I now live, the northernmost central state of the United

States, and flows to the sea in Mississippi, a southernmost state where I was born. I think of the song about this river, "Ol' Man River," who "mus' know sumpin'" yet "don' say nuthin'" while he "keep on rollin' along." Connected to us, flowing through our lives every day of our lifetimes, this river is both oblivious to us and sustaining of us, present to us and removed. It is the source of commerce and property disputes and the agent of flooding and death, as well as the source of food and recreation, life and renewal.

"Ol' Man River" was a favorite bass solo, sung in my school when I was in the ninth grade by a most wonderful, talented, and handsome high school senior whose name was Donald Cassell. Donald Cassell and I played the romantic leads in a school play called *The Little Clodhopper* the year we were in school together. We had a "Hit Parade" production at school that year, too, patterned after the television program of the same name; and in one episode of our hit parade, Donald Cassell sang "Rags to Riches" to me, as I stood all dressed up in my iridescent taffeta party dress. He was our student body president. But, most of all, as I remember it, he sang, over and over again, in concerts and talent contests, "Ol' Man River," with its commands to black people to "tote dat barge!" and to "lif' dat bale" and with its lament at being "sick of tryin'," "tired of livin'," and "skeered of dyin'." Yet the "Ol' Man River," by contrast, "jes' keeps rollin' along."

I adored Donald Cassell and loved to hear him sing, as did most of the rest of the students in our school. Donald Cassell died of cancer when he was twenty-four-years-old. I read an account of his death in a book only this year. It said that, on learning of his impending death, Donald Cassell said, "I am not afraid to die, but I am so very disappointed." And he acknowledged life and the autumn sunshine on the day of his death, saying to his wife, "Oh, what a beautiful day!" [12]

Life and the river, "Ol' Man River" and Donald Cassell, the beautiful day, death and the Civil War—that's what I thought about, sitting by the Mississippi River at Vicksburg for my first

time that Saturday afternoon. That kind of thinking, such reverie as that, is all I know of meditation, all I know of mysticism.
Contemplating life and death, human happiness, destruction,
restoration, and the river is sufficient satisfaction, sufficient
healing in the face of devastation. Like Ol' Man River, and like
my friend Donald Cassell in his affirmation on the day of his
death, "one jes' keeps rollin'," one "keeps on rollin' along."[13]

In that frame of mind, I went to the Civil War battlefield. It
was along the river, of course, that the Confederates were entrenched at Vicksburg, and the Union forces under Gen. Ulysses S. Grant were determined to wrench control from them in
what many southerners still call the War Between the States.
And young men like Donald Cassell, alive in 1863, died there
before General Grant and General Pemberton could agree to end
the fighting on 4 July 1863.

This series of battles for control of Vicksburg took place
nearly two years into the Civil War, when, by holding Vicksburg, the Confederates still controlled transportation down the
Mississippi River. The Union army hoped both to gain control of
the river and to divide the Confederacy by gaining Vicksburg.
Vicksburg was an effective location for maintaining a hold over
the river because it had unusually high river bluffs and a bend
in the river was located there.

The Siege of Vicksburg took place 18 May–4 July 1863. In
October 1862, General Grant was given the assignment of gaining the Mississippi River for the Union. The commander of the
Confederate Army along the Mississippi River was Lt. Gen.
John D. Pemberton. Grant made five unsuccessful attempts to
gain the city and the river before the summer campaign that
won it for his army. The Confederate Army built strong fortifications along the river. The military park brochure describes the
campaign this way:

> Believing that the battles of Champion Hill and Big Black River
> Bridge had broken Confederate morale, Grant immediately sched-
> uled an assault on the Vicksburg lines. The first attack took place
> against the Stockade Redan on May 19. It failed. A second attack,
> launched on the morning of May 22, was also repulsed.

Realizing that it was useless to expend further lives in attempts to take the city by storm, Grant reluctantly began formal siege operations. Batteries of artillery were established to hammer the Confederate fortifications from the land side, while Admiral Porter's gunboats cut off communications and blasted the city from the river. By the end of June, with little hope of relief and no chance to break out of the Federal cordon, Pemberton knew that it was only a matter of time before he must "capitulate upon the best attainable terms." On the afternoon of July 3 he met with Grant to discuss the terms for the surrender of Vicksburg.

Grant demanded unconditional surrender. Pemberton refused. The meeting broke up. During the afternoon, the Federal commander modified his demands and agreed to let the Confederates sign paroles not to fight again until exchanged. In addition, officers could retain sidearms and a mount. Pemberton accepted these terms, and at 10 a.m. on July 4, 1863, Vicksburg was officially surrendered.

When Port Hudson surrendered 5 days later, the great Northern objective of the war in the West—the opening of the Mississippi River and the severing of the Confederacy—was at last realized. For the first time since the war began, the Mississippi was free of Confederate troops and fortifications. As President Lincoln put it, "The Father of Waters again goes unvexed to the sea."[14]

When I visited the Vicksburg National Military Park, I first drove my car through the long, woodsy road of the military park. Red markers showed the placement of the Confederate soldiers, blue markers showed the placement of the Union troops. Gropingly, I learned the vocabulary of the fortifications: redans, and redoubts, and lunettes. I wondered if, had I been to military college, these would be ready words in my vocabulary and I would know the subtle differences and how to visualize them on a live battlefield. This battlefield was strewn with peaceful grassy mounds and many monuments. At various locations there were names of men and names of armaments identified by states. The first tour stop was at Battery DeGolyer, where the guns had been commanded by Capt. Samuel DeGolyer, of the eighth Michigan Artillery, who lost his life there. I stopped and saw the grassy site and its monuments under the lush green trees, and then drove on. The Third Louisiana Redan came next. I saw Ransom's Gun Path. I saw the site of Stockade Redan Attack. Farther along, I stopped and got out of my car and walked down the path to the National Cemetery. The rows and rows of cold marble headstones there have a spectacular view of the river. Farther on still, I saw Grant's Headquarters. I read in my guidebook that it was a little-known fact that Grant's son was with him at Vicksburg, a twelve-year-old who later became a military officer.

There were not many other travelers on the park roads, and long before I reached the end, I began to feel very lonely, agitated, and confined. I became almost claustrophobic. Monument after monument with a state's name upon it seemed to try to outdo the last in cold monumental grandeur. Name after name after name on the marble slabs and statues were the names of men.

A picture in my guidebook leaped out at me and captured my imagination in morbid fascination. It showed dead soldiers, lined up with arms akimbo, put aside to be buried. They had on ordinary clothes, were ordinary men, almost boys really. I tried to think of my two great-grandfathers who fought in the War, but involuntarily pictured my own son instead—the male person whose hair grows like mine and whose face and spirit reflect mine back to me. My son in his blue uniform? My beautiful, winsome boy, blood of my blood? With his Mississippi cousins in gray? Lying dead together? No doubt some beloved son of some Jones ancestor of ours, with hair grown similar to ours, had died in that war. I shivered, cold at the maternal thought.

Emma Balfour says in the 30 May entry of her diary, "Conversations occur nightly between friends on the opposite sides. Two Missourian brothers held a conversation very friendly— one sent the other coffee and whiskey. Then they parted with an oath and an exclamation from one that he would 'blow the other's head off tomorrow.' The commanders object to this intercourse, but it is impossible they say in two armies so near to prevent it altogether."[15]

I had had enough. I did not go to see the battleship *Cairo* or other sights in the park. I drove out of the park as quickly as

I could. As I turned my car back to Jackson, I realized how very male was all that I had seen. And how female was my response.

And how white they both were.

Especially about the institution of slavery, the Civil War is still too little commemorated with monuments to black people who were subjugated by slavery. There is a Mississippi literary monument, however, that represents the Civil War from the perspective of blacks and especially of black women. Margaret Walker's masterpiece, a historical novel, is called *Jubilee*. The novel is set before, during, and after the Civil War in a plantation location in Georgia, and the central character, Vyry, a young slave woman, is based on Walker's own great-grandmother. It is a brilliant and moving account, courageous and life-affirming.

As I drove back to Jackson, I was consoled by remembrance of Margaret Walker's book. As with the river, I have a spiritual affinity with such a book by such a woman. Though white, I am more connected with such literary knowledge conveyed by a woman who is black than with the male-centered cemetery. Walker's title came from a song—this one, however, not by a lyricist attributing a sentiment to black people but by black people themselves, in a traditional spiritual call "Jubilee":

> We are climbing Jacob's ladder . . .
> Every round goes higher, higher . . .
> Do you think I'll make a soldier?
> Do you think I'll make a soldier?
> Do you think I'll make a soldier?
> In the year of Jubilee?[16]

The Civil Religion and Founded Religion

The civil religion that Robert Bellah identified and Charles Wilson describes in its southern manifestation contrasts with more familiarly known organized religion of the church or synagogue, what scholars call "founded religion" or a religion that has a time of origin with a specific founder—Moses in the case of Judaism, Jesus in the case of Christianity. In addition, founded religion has writings such as the Torah or the Bible; a fully articulated set of doctrines, practices, and interpretations; an affiliated set of believers and participants; officers, holy designates, and teachers (priests, theologians, and officials); and a fully developed institutional framework—for Judaism, branches such as Conservative, Orthodox, Reconstructionist, and Reformed, and worship settings such as temples and synagogues; for Christianity, branches such as Protestantism and Catholicism, with their many denominations and orders, and worship settings such as churches and cathedrals. In Mississippi, founded religion is most prominent—particularly Protestant Christianity and, within that, particularly evangelical Protestantism. It is "church religion," founded religion, of which Mississippian Florence Mars is writing when she tells about the churches in Philadelphia, Mississippi:

> Evangelical groups came to the square to preach, either under the magnolia tree on the courthouse lawn or on the steps of the courthouse. Every week Miss Nannie Ogletree from the Linwood community preached on the east courthouse steps, across the street from Mars Brothers' Department Store. . . .
> Miss Nannie Ogletree was a Pentecostal. The most well-to-do families in the county tended to belong to the regular denominations—Baptist, Methodist, and Presbyterian; the tenants and some of the poorer farmers congregated in the Pentecostal and primitive sects, sometimes moving up to regular denominations as their circumstances improved. There was a tendency among the membership of the first churches of the regular denominations to look down socially on the noisier sects. In Philadelphia, we uptown Methodists even considered the uptown Baptists more backwoodsy and harder against the sins of the flesh like drinking, dancing, and card-playing. The Baptists did seem to be more successful in keeping their children from slipping around to participate in these activities, and the Baptist ladies not as likely to belong to one of the several afternoon bridge clubs. There was an oft-repeated saying that "a Methodist is a Baptist who has learned to read; a Presbyterian is a Methodist who has moved to town; and an Episcopalian is a Pres-

byterian who has gotten rich." There were no Episcopalians in Neshoba County, and, literate or not, there were far more Baptists than members of all other denominations combined.

The few Catholics in the county had very different attitudes toward drinking. Roman Catholic priests did not preach about the evils of alcohol and even drank a little whiskey themselves. If nothing else, this difference set the Catholics apart from the Protestants. There was often anguish when a Catholic married into a fine old Protestant family.

There was not much difference between the Protestant denominations in the county. Once saved through immersion, the Baptists were always saved; Methodists could fall from grace; and Presbyterians were born into salvation. But we all interpreted the Bible literally and subscribed to the hellfire-and-brimstone preaching of fundamentalism.[17]

Florence Mars writes of the religion, religious attitudes, and social structure of denominations in white Mississippi. Black church religion was similarly structured by class and education, town and country, fervor and decorum. Its denominations were derivative from the white ones, although black churches, like other institutions, had been strictly separate from white ones since instigation of the Jim Crow laws and customs. In fact, churches remained segregated long after school integration and commercial desegregation in the 1970s and 1980s, causing political and religious leader Aaron Henry to lament in 1984, "Eleven o'clock on Sunday morning is still the most segregated hour in Mississippi."[18]

Religious leadership was extremely powerful on all sides of the race conflicts and the civil rights movement of the 1960s. As in many wars and crusades, a mutual deity was attested to as the standard bearer of the cause by both sets of fighters. The Ku Klux Klan and the Citizens Councils called upon their God, who they believed was the Christian deity, and they claimed to be doing His work. People who were called "moderate" whites, or called "liberals" by themselves or "communists" by their antagonists, also based their convictions on Christian teachings— people like Florence Mars; or the twenty-eight young Mississippi-born Methodist ministers who published a statement called "Born of Conviction" on 3 January 1963, the result of which was that nineteen of them had to leave the state; or the minister of Jackson's large "cathedral of Methodism," Galloway Memorial Methodist Church (its name had been changed early in the twentieth century from First Methodist Church to honor the bishop), Dr. W. B. Selah, who resigned his church in 1963, after eighteen successful years as a beloved and inspiring pastor. Dr. Selah's resignation sermon in that historic old church ended with the admonition, "There can be no color bar before the cross of Christ!"[19]

Most of the black leaders of the civil rights movement, in Mississippi as across the South, were greatly influenced by Christianity, were clergy or clergy children. For example, Martin Luther King, Jr., was a Baptist with a theology Ph.D. from Methodist-affiliated Boston University; Andrew Young is a Congregationalist clergyman from Georgia; Mississippians Medgar Evers and Charles Evers were children of a Church of God and Christ minister; Robert Clark was an African Methodist Episcopal member. And virtually all of them were church workers. Among the most devout was Fannie Lou Hamer.

Fannie Lou Hamer's Mississippi Spirituality

Fannie Lou Hamer from Ruleville, Mississippi, was on the losing side of an argument with U.S. Sen. Hubert H. Humphrey in the Credentials Committee at the 1964 Democratic National Convention. Their conversation ended with an arrangement known as the "two-seat compromise," by which the chair and co-chair of Hamer's black-dominated delegation from the Mississippi Freedom Democratic Party (MFDP), Aaron Henry and Edwin King, would be seated as delegates-at-large, instead of allowing the entire MFDP delegation to replace the all-white regular delegation of Mississippi Democrats. When this decision later was announced from the podium by Walter Mondale, then Minnesota's attorney general, the white Mississippi regulars walked out anyway. Not one for compromise any more than her Mississippi segregationist opponents, Hamer ended her conversation with Humphrey by shaking her head in implied judgment and saying, "I'll pray to Jesus for you!"[20]

Hamer, like most Mississippians, was a devout Christian. There were no niceties about separation of religion and politics for her, not even any fine lines of theoretical distinction regarding separation of church and state. Doing what was right was doing what God wanted. Truth and God's will and the seating of the MFDP delegation were one and the same. Her fellow Sunflower Countian in the departing white delegation, Sen. James O. Eastland, no doubt had an equally fervent Mississippi religious conviction that truth and God's will and the maintenance of white supremacy were identical.

Outside the Democratic Convention headquarters in Atlantic City, New Jersey, after their rejection, Hamer led the MFDP delegation in singing gospel songs. The political delegation became an impromptu choir, their training in their home black churches in Mississippi having prepared them to sing for the nation from the streets of Atlantic City, songs about Jesus, freedom songs, southern black work songs, protest songs learned from southern black religion. Hamer became famous for "Ain't Gonna Turn Me Round" and "This Little Light of Mine." After her celebrity at the convention, when she was seen on nationwide television telling her story of political and police brutality toward her, attempting to be seated as a delegate, and singing on the streets, Hamer, sponsored by national civil rights organizations, individually and sometimes with a choir group toured the country inspiring courage in civil rights activism with speeches and gospel-cum-movement songs.

Repeatedly beaten and jailed and battered for her attempts to desegregate public facilities and assure black people's political participation in Mississippi, Hamer would scream and cry through her ordeals, but then, in the jails, she would sing and lead the religious songs, the same songs that, out of the collective identification by many civil rights leaders of the justice of their cause with the foundation principles of their Christian faith, had become the movement's own. For any for whom the civil rights cause and their religious faith were not one and the same, the music provided community-building, solidarity, and strength like those that Hamer and the other black southern Christians had known in their churches all their lives.

Fannie Lou Hamer's music was a part of her religiousness that permeated her whole life. One of the last people who visited her before her death, her friend June Johnson, said of her, "She felt that her house was in place, and that everything was in order with God, because she was a very religious person."[21] Writer Alice Walker understood also how central her religion was to Hamer in the way that she dealt with all issues and events. Walker reports of Hamer, "When asked why she doesn't hate, she says, 'Ain't no such a thing as I can hate anybody and hope to see God's face.'"[22]

This religion informed Hamer's everyday experience in very particular ways and was personally sustaining for her during her catastrophes. Her religion gave meaning to death and gave an ethical basis for facing death with courage, just as it had provided the ethics of courage for confronting county voter registration officers, hostile plantation bosses, harassing sheriffs, and compromising government officials. Her religion was also shared and was the very basis of community through its beliefs, its rituals, its events, and its songs. It had been the source of her community in her growing-up time and in many years of private adulthood, and for her the same community remained unbroken when she became a public figure, for her civil rights movement had risen directly out of black churches and black Christian consciousness.

When Fannie Lou Hamer died in 1977, thirteen years after the Atlantic City convention, the ambassador to the United Nations, Andrew Young, came to Ruleville, Mississippi, and preached the eulogy at her funeral. At her death, Hamer's community had become a national one, her funeral a national ritual. Young had been to Ruleville before, as one of the leaders of the Southern Christian Leadership Conference (SCLC). In those days, he was known as "one of Martin Luther King, Jr.'s lieutenants."

At the funeral, in the crowd of an estimated one thousand people were several other officials of the administration of President Jimmy Carter, including white Mississippian Hodding Carter III, an assistant secretary of state who, like Young, had been an ally of Hamer's in the Mississippi civil rights movement. Young, an ordained minister in the United Church of Christ, explained at Hamer's funeral what both black and white southerners already knew—that the blending of religious devotion and politics in the South had yielded the victories that had come.

With the audience at times shouting out familiarly, "Tell it, Andy!", Young called Fannie Lou Hamer one of "those chosen people who changed the lives of all of us" and recounted how the civil rights movement had been successful. He claimed that President Carter's election was traceable directly to the civil rights movement. "Ruleville, Mississippi, got known before Plains, Georgia," he said. "And if it hadn't been for Ruleville, we might never have heard of Plains."

He said that on election night, he had been with the Carter campaign organization in which he had worked, and the election returns were showing a close vote. He said, "I heard that [the election] may depend on how Mississippi went, and I thought, 'Lord, have mercy.' But then when I heard that Mississippi had gone our way, I knew that the hands that picked the cotton finally picked the president." And then at the end of his eulogy, the United States ambassador to the United Nations burst out singing "This Little Light of Mine," and a thousand voices inside and outside the white-frame chapel joined him and sang out. They raised their voices and sang her song, the song she had shared with the nation. They sang and clapped their hands for the cotton-picking sharecropper from Sunflower County who prayed to Jesus instead of compromise.[23]

Mississippi Christianity

Christianity matters in Mississippi—for good and for ill.

When I was a small child on the farm, I loved religion. Among my earliest memories of great comfort, warmth, and belonging is the recollection of sitting under the quilting frame for many hours many times through long winter days, as my Aunt Bessie and Aunt 'Cile quilted and taught me Bible verses. Their skillful fingers expertly moved the needles down and back through the fabric and cotton in tiny, even stitches so artful and precise that the underside from where I sat under the plain-cloth lining just as perfectly displayed the beautifully stitched design as the patchwork or applique on the top which they outlined as they worked. As they stitched, I would watch the needles come down through the cloth followed by the length of cotton thread, turn, and with a deft gesture of my aunt's hand, return as quickly as it came, a minuscule portion of an inch away, up through the lining, the cotton batting, through to the colorful cover on top. Down again came the needle point from my aunt's companion hand. Up it would quickly return from the other. And as they worked these quilts, they taught me to say the Twenty-Third Psalm, the Lord's Prayer, the Creation Story, and many verses from the Bible.

When I was growing up, my church and my religious faith were the most important dimensions of my life. But, as in politics, education, and economics in Mississippi, there was one dominant form to the Christianity we knew. Intellectually, most Mississippi Christianity was fundamentalist. The core beliefs were literal interpretation of the Bible, literal belief in a seven-day Creation, a designated period of human history that could be counted up from the start of the Old Testament in Genesis to the end of the New Testament in Revelation, a judging God who got personally involved in human wrongdoing, an immaculately conceived Christ, his birth to a virgin mother, his death as God-human sacrifice for human sin, the personal accessibility of God to people through prayer, and the expectation of personal immortality after death—for good people in Heaven with God, Jesus, Saint Peter, and all of one's dead relatives and friends; and for bad people, those who had not repented of their sins and seen their evil ways and come to Jesus before it was too late, in Hell with the Devil. We never talked of these tenets of faith in my family or my community. They were givens. They were just there, like stones and earth. Preachers talked about them for an hour on Sundays or at revival meetings, but these men were the experts, not to be questioned. The prevailing wisdom on the matter of religious thought was very similar, whether in my childhood Methodist country church where the music was an off-key piano, or in the town churches where the music was the educated playing of an accomplished organist. Theologically, it was very similar in the black churches, too, though their songs had an African beat and their stories of God and the Devil had a sense of humor missing in the prim Calvinist preaching or fire-and-brimstone threatening of those of us with Europeans for ancestors. The truth of Christianity as they taught it was fixed, set, and established, no buts, ands, or questions about it. It made good absolutists out of all of us, true believers, literalists, authoritarians, orthodox.

There was, on the other hand, a social side to my childhood religion that bore little resemblance to the rigidity of the teachings. The singing in church was great fun, as was the visiting before and after church. Only on Sunday, in our otherwise isolated rural environment, was it possible for me to go home with children my age in the neighborhood and play with them. Getting dressed up and seeing all the relatives and neighbors all dressed up, too, once a week on Sunday morning was quite wonderful. Hearing the stories the ministers told of distant times and places that they knew about from reading or even sometimes from having been there was thrilling. Having the preacher and his family home for Sunday dinner and having on the table our very best food and our very best dishes and tablecloth and using our very best manners was a joy. The special days! Easter Sunday, when we sang "Up from the Grave He Arose!" Christmas, when some years we would have a pageant and dramatize the Bible story of Jesus' birth in our bathrobes. Dinner-on-the-grounds, when we had what was called "quarterly meeting." Graveyard-working-day at the cemetery at Hebron Church. Belonging, belonging it was, belonging peacefully and happily as only a child can know it.

Later of my own choice, I graduated to an organ-playing town church with a seminary-educated minister; but when I was a young child, my family went to the country Methodist church in our community, and in the summers we went to camp meeting. Camp meeting was not to my mother's college-educated liking, but my father and his family, led by Great-Aunt Sally, had gone to camp meeting all their lives, and it was a special time for them. I loved it. The preachers shouted and waved their arms till the whole place vibrated. Everybody sang at the top of their lungs, "Bringing in the Sheaves," "There Were Ninety and Nine," and "Washed in the Blood of the Lamb," and it was a jubilant event.

Some people, including Aunt Sally, "tented" at camp meeting. Tents weren't canvas, however, they were small camp houses, complete with kitchens, in which people lived for the duration of the revival-like series of services in August. There was a "tabernacle" for the services and a dormitory for young people. There were services with preaching several times a day and a gospel sing for the young people in the late afternoon. The preachers were called "evangelists" and were usually itinerant preachers, or preachers from small evangelical splinter denominations referred to by names like "Hardshell Methodist" and "Methodist Protestant." At every service, there would be singing of gospel songs, testimonials to one's salvation or to "what the Lord has done for me this year," and more preaching. And altar calls. One year one preacher who was some form of rural Methodist introduced a new wrinkle to altar calls. He asked all the people who had not been "saved" to come to the altar. Since I had been a church member since I was six, that didn't apply to me, I thought. But then he had another word, which he claimed to have gotten from John Wesley: would everybody who had not been "sanctified" please come. Eager to participate, Merrell and I looked at each other. That was a new one for us. We answered the altar call. Jumping out of our seats and going down to the altar and onto our knees, we went down the sawdust trail to be "sanctified."

Riding home that night in our family car, the six of us were more silent than usual. Finally, Mother said to us very deliberately, choosing her words cautiously, "I'm glad you children made a response tonight," she said. "Humph," our father snorted, obviously quite displeased at having sanctified children.

When I was a teenager, I loved theology. I went to the Methodist Youth Fellowship in the town church, and the Methodist Youth Fellowship and its national connections gave me access to the wider world, to a more gracious style of church life, and to a more open theology than that to which I had been exposed as a young child. But I went about this new church life with the same earnestness I had devoted to the more evangelical variety that I had first been exposed to. Influenced by ministers who traced their theological consciousness to Boston University idealism, I learned about that basic debate, the one that at fourteen years of age I thought all human and divine meaning hinged upon: Is "man" basically good or basically evil? I remember the vigorous discussions among our conference-wide Methodist youth leaders, such people as Warren Day or Julian Rush or Jim Waits. I always took the side of goodness: "he," "man" had to be basically good, it seemed to me, for us to accomplish anything. Those older teenagers, already influenced by neo-orthodoxy, thought otherwise: "man" had to be basically evil because of the Fall, but in this version of theology, unlike our fundamentalism, we could take the Fall symbolically. The most persuasive debater in "our group" was Warren Day, two years my senior and already a student at Mississippi Southern when we were conference officers together. He had been exposed to neoorthodoxy, which I had not, and he was sure that evil was the way of "man's" ways.

The nearest thing to "conversion" that I actually experienced as a teenager was not to religious doctrine or to beliefs such as sanctification but to knowledge of the human import of race separation. My realization came under the auspices of the church. When I was fourteen or fifteen, I was invited to go to Meridian to a church meeting of black and white youths. Meridian was the city nearest to our home, the place where Mother, when she occasionally had enough money for store-bought clothes, would go shopping for clothes or shoes at the Marks Rothenberg store, one of the few Jewish-owned businesses in the area. We would go Christmas shopping to Meridian, and Daddy took his cattle to the stockyard there. The best peach orchards around were near Meridian, and the second largest church in our Methodist conference was there. Hills rose just before we reached Meridian on Highway 45, and, when we were little, Merrell and I would squeal when we rounded the curve of the hill and first saw the city, "I see 'ridian! I see 'ridian!" To go to Meridian to a church meeting with my county MYF advisor, Margaret Norsworthy, was enough to tell my parents when I was fourteen or fifteen to be allowed to go. The particulars of the meeting didn't have to be told to the parents.

The meeting was a joint meeting of a few students of the Central Jurisdiction MYF and the Southeastern Jurisdiction MYF in the area—black young people and white young people, members of the same national church but members of separated local judicatories. At the time, state law in Mississippi prohibited such meetings between blacks and whites. I went the fifty miles to Meridian with Margaret Norsworthy, and those in attendance included some of my friends, such as Julian Rush, Jim Waits, and others. One of the out-of-town staff persons was a black man from our national church Board of Education named James Thomas, the first black man I had ever heard speak educated English and seen dressed in a suit and tie. As the meeting progressed and he talked to us, I realized: Here is a man I want to *be like*, not *marry*, *be like*. Role model, we were later to call it.

Here was a man like the person I wanted to be: educated, erudite, generous-spirited, soft-spoken, well-dressed in Sunday clothes on a weekday.

One of the other students in the small group was a black student from Meridian, a young high school student like me. That season our friend Julian Rush had written and produced a play at the Meridian Junior College, which had been playing very recently. "Did you see Julian's play?" I asked her innocently. She looked embarrassed, and then she said haltingly, as if embarrassed for me, "No, well, you see, they wouldn't let us in."

And it was in that instant, at that precise moment, that I understood racism. If she could not see Julian's play, why should I? And it was at that moment that I was "converted" to change myself and others with whom I might have influence to overcome the conventional rigidity of my society as I had known it up to that time, a rigidity that included my religion as well as the politics and social order as I had understood them as a child.

Years later, as a traveler in Europe with my own family, having learned and loved the German language as a college student and also having learned my American and European history with its World War II history of the Nazi Holocaust against Jews in Hitler's Germany, I visited the town of Rothenberg simply as a tourist and lover of architecture eager to see beautiful ancient medieval buildings. Rothenberg is an ancient walled city, with many of its medieval buildings within the walls intact. Suddenly, half the world away from Meridian, Mississippi, and the Marks Rothenberg store and my first racially-integrated meeting, I stood on the corner of Judenstrasse—the street of the Jews—in Rothenberg and had another flash of insight like the one I had had that day many years before in Meridian: this was the Jews' ghetto as far back as the Middle Ages. This is the place to which that merchant family in Meridian can trace its very roots. This was home to them for many centuries, this very street in this magnificent walled town. They could come here and stand and know from whence they came, as I can only go back to Mississippi, having no such Irish place, no such place in Wales. Yet, paradoxically, the American Rothenbergs in Meridian are safe and alive today, having left this beautiful place in the distant past, this place of their confinement to this street, long ago, long before Hitler and his destruction of their people. Safe in Meridian, like me, they were white in 1964, when fellow Meridianite James Chaney was driven off the road from Meridian to Philadelphia and killed. On Judenstrasse in West Germany, I was reminded that we all of us must be vigilant always. Our truth is never absolute. Whether understanding racism or religion, sexism or society, beauty or hatred, politics or philosophy, the best we can know is tolerance, the most we can see is ambiguity, the greatest lesson we can learn is clearsighted recognition. Whether cruel, distorted, and pinched, or beatific, the face reflected back from any vision is our own.

Eventually I learned that the particulars of belief or practice or interpretation in Christianity or any belief system can be relative. A religious belief system, like a political loyalty and not unlike the feminism of a later period of my life or the theories of culture of a still later one, is a commitment or an ideology. The particulars of any such framework, be it religious, political, or intellectual, can create a useful guide, a useful tool, but in the hands of a rigid practitioner, these same particulars can be as doctrinaire, and thus destructive, as any other. Yet at its best, each one potentially gives us useful tools to live our lives, to do our work, even to discover how to love and to learn how to overcome hate. The great religions of the world have given humans our greatest resources for peace, harmony, and community. They also have been the most powerful forces in whose names countless wars have been waged, people killed, and lands ravaged. As with religions, so it is with governments. And as it is with institutions such as religion and government, so it is with ideologies and belief systems about gender or race or any other human formation. They are ways to help us know and understand and live our lives, not ways to separate sheep from goats, not to make one sharp divider separating left and right, right and wrong.

It is the same all over the world as it is in Mississippi. When we traveled in Botswana with our Peace-Corps-Volunteer daughter, Botswana reminded me of Mississippi. So did provincial Yorkshire in the north of England when we traveled there. I loved them both. Botswana's dusty sand-orange roads, head-ragged women, and bare village stores visually brought back to me 1940s Mississippi. The odor of luxuriant growth and the china cups from a tea garden in Yorkshire similarly reminded me of my childhood Mississippi. And the Motswana headmaster at the new secondary school in Letlhakeng, Botswana, scolded the server in his home when she brought out native food for his foreign guests and sent her back for his English tea set and tinned English biscuits, however much we the guests were longing for the taste of new experience. He behaved much as people today would behave in Minneapolis or in Mississippi.

When I went to Mississippi in the 1980s, it was most of all a spiritual journey, but my Mississippi had taught me well that the social and the spiritual journey are the same. Politics, economics, education, and moral actions, as well as contemplation and reflection, are parts of spirituality. All the parts of human life are one whole, and human life is a part of the whole of greater life. What I had learned from midlife suffering was that people and all their doings, mean and good, and nature, too, all of nature, are a part of that whole of life. I had learned to sit and watch the sunsets, to celebrate the tall pine trees, to glory in the forsythia blooming when it is not yet spring, to remember the sound of rushing water from the creekbanks of my childhood, and to seek out the waterfalls.

And from such contemplation of nature, from which I have learned to be at home in the world, I am able to return both to work and to love.

Epilogue

One late February day I drove out of Memphis on my way to what was to be my last visit with my parents in their home

"Welcome to Mississippi" Sign at the Tennessee Border near Hernando, Mississippi. Photo by Gayle Graham Yates.

on the farm in southern Mississippi where my brother and I grew up.

There were patches of snow in Memphis and northern Mississippi. The water was up—floodwater in rivers and streams and even in low places along the highway. All Saturday afternoon on the highway, all I could hear on the radio was country music and evangelical preachers. Once I got a good piece of jazz and the sounds of a black station, but I lost it. Two stations were carrying football for a while. I missed the news if there was any. It was colder than I had hoped for. Mother had said on the phone the night before that their pond was frozen over, a rare occurrence any year.

I got tourism literature, a free Coca-Cola, and some exercise at an elegant state highway rest-stop building, decorated living-room style, just beyond Hernando, Mississippi. Realizing I would be late, I phoned my mother from Meridian, and then I chose to drive down the two-lane Highway 45 because it was familiar, having been my "street" my whole life, while I–57, the interstate, the other road that went by our house from Meridian, had been finished after I left home. Once again I noticed with tangible pleasure, pleasure inhaled with my breath of sweet, clean air, the tall pine trees standing among bare branches soon to bud their baby green and orange, soon to disclose spring's dogwood blossoms and redbud.

These later winter pine trees and their beds of straw were wonderful signifiers of home, this home, this beloved setting of my ancestry, my place of origin, my homeplace, here and in the world, in Mississippi and everyplace.

As I approached Meridian, the blood-red sun shone in the blue haze obscuring the Meridian hills just before sunset. The eternal child in my soul cried out, "I see 'ridian! I see 'ridian! I'm home! I'm home!" These were my hills and my sunset, and I knew who I was. "I'm home! I'm home!" I whispered softly into the thick, rich solitude illuminated by the dazzling light of the setting sun over the Meridian hills. And the dropping sun shone back its clear red welcome as it fell from sight into the peaceful dusk.

Notes

Chapter 1

1. Mrs. Betty S. Chapman, "History of Hebron Church," n.p., n.d. Xeroxed newspaper clipping from the family archives of Erma Gay Mathers, copied on the same sheet as an obituary of Mrs. Bettie Stanford Chapman, datelined "Waynesboro, Miss.," and dated 7 June 1945. A likely source is the county weekly newspaper, the *Wayne County News*. Another possibility is the conference (judicatory for the southern half of Mississippi) Methodist Church newspaper, the *Mississippi Methodist Advocate*.
2. From my photographs of the gravestones.
3. Rosellen Brown, *Civil Wars* (New York: Knopf, 1984), 56.
4. Yi-Fu Tuan, "Concepts of Region: A Commentary," paper presented at the biennial meeting of the American Studies Association, Memphis, Tenn., 31 Oct. 1981.
5. Widely quoted. Displayed in large painted print in the twentieth-century permanent exhibit room, Old Capitol Museum, Mississippi Department of Archives and History, Jackson, Miss.
6. Margaret Walker, "My Mississippi Spring," *Southern Review* 23 (Summer 1985):827.
7. Also widely quoted. William Faulkner, "Interview with Jean Stein vanden Heuvel," *Lion in the Garden: Interviews with William Faulkner, 1926–1962*, ed. James B. Meriwether and Michael Millgate (New York: Random House, 1968; rpt. ed. Lincoln: Univ. of Nebraska Press, 1980), 255.
8. Eudora Welty, "Place in Fiction," *The Eye of the Story* (New York: Vintage, 1979), 118. First published, *South Atlantic Quarterly* 55 (1956):57–72. Originally a paper delivered at the Cambridge American Studies conference, Cambridge, England, 1954.
9. Interview with Mrs. Jeannie Griffith, in her home in Jackson, Miss., 23 Mar. 1985. Emphasis in her intonation in the tape recording.
10. Interview with Martha Bergmark, in her law office, Hattiesburg, Miss., 26 Mar. 1985.
11. William Faulkner, *Absalom, Absalom!* (New York: Modern Library, 1936), 346.

12. Ibid., 378. Punctuation and italics are Faulkner's.
13. Ralph D. Cross, editor; Robert W. Wales, co-editor; Charles T. Traylor, chief cartographer, *Atlas of Mississippi* (Jackson: Univ. Press of Mississippi, 1974), 133.
14. Dawson A. Phelps, "The Natchez Trace: Indian Trail to Parkway," pamphlet reproduced from *Tennessee Historical Quarterly* 21 (Sept. 1962):3–18. "Natchez Trace," brochure from National Park Service, U.S. Dept. of the Interior, n.d. David G. Sansing, *Mississippi: Its People and Culture* (Minneapolis, Minn.: T. S. Denison and Co., 1981), 85–86, 100–102. James W. Loewen and Charles Sallis, *Mississippi: Conflict and Change* (New York: Pantheon, 1974), 38, 76, 79, 83. Patti Carr Black, *The Natchez Trace* (Jackson: Univ. Press of Mississippi, 1985). Jonathan Daniels, *The Devil's Backbone* (New York: McGraw-Hill, 1962).
15. Loewen and Sallis, *Mississippi*, p. 60.
16. "Natchez Trace," Park Service brochure.
17. Cross, Wales, and Traylor, *Atlas of Mississippi*, 36–38.
18. Phelps, "Natchez Trace," 17–18.
19. Wiliam Least Heat Moon, *Blue Highways: A Journey into America* (New York: Fawcett Crest, 1982).
20. Copied from my photograph of the marker.
21. "Natchez Trace," Park Service brochure.
22. Copied from my photograph of the marker.
23. Loewen and Sallis, *Mississippi*, ch. 3, pp. 27–58; Cross, Wales, and Traylor, *Atlas of Mississippi*, 38; and Sansing, *Mississippi*, 41–45, 51–53.
24. See Patti Carr Black, *Mississippi Piney Woods: A Photographic Study of Folk Architecture* (Jackson: Mississippi Department of Archives and History). Henry Glassie's *Folk Housing in Middle Virginia* (Knoxville: Univ. of Tennessee Press, 1975) is the pioneering study of such housing in the South.
25. Eudora Welty, "Livvie," *The Collected Stories of Eudora Welty* (New York: Harcourt Brace Jovanovich, 1980), 228. First collected in *A Wide Net and Other Stories*. First published in the *Atlantic Monthly*, Nov. 1942.
26. Eudora Welty, *The Robber Bridegroom* (New York: Atheneum, 1963), 43–44. First published in 1942.
27. Interview with Erma Gay Mathers in her home, 23 Mar. 1985.
28. Interview with Jeannie Griffith.
29. Interview with Martha Bergmark.

Chapter 2

1. The thesis that the dominant item of regional identification of the South is attention to race and racism is a significant one among historians of the South. The leading proponent of such a view is C. Vann Woodward. See his *The Burden of Southern History* (Baton Rouge: Louisiana State Univ.

Press, 1968) and *The Strange Career of Jim Crow* (New York: Oxford Univ. Press, 1955). Historians' debate on what constitutes the South is summarized in the textbook by I. A. Newby, *The South: A History* (New York: Holt, Rinehart, and Winston, 1978), ch. 1, pp. 1–32.

2. Loewen and Sallis, *Mississippi*, 180.

3. Ibid., 178.

4. Tallulah Ragsdale, "The Lynched Man's Mother Prays," *If I See Green* (New York: Henry Harrison, 1929), 17–19.

5. James W. Loewen, *The Mississippi Chinese* (Cambridge, Mass.: Harvard Univ. Press, 1971). Also see Robert Seto Quan, *Lotus Among the Magnolias: The Mississippi Chinese* (Jackson: Univ. Press of Mississippi, 1982).

6. Loewen, *Chinese*, front matter opposite copyright page.

7. Quoted in Loewen and Sallis, *Mississippi*, 256.

8. Anne Moody, *Coming of Age in Mississippi* (New York: Dell, 1971), 123–26. First published in 1968.

9. Interview with William Bradford Huie, in Howell Raines, ed., *My Soul Is Rested: The Story of the Civil Rights Movement in the Deep South* (New York: Penguin, 1983), 392–93. First published in 1977.

10. Raines, *My Soul*, 13.

11. John Dollard, *Caste and Class in a Southern Town* (Garden City, N.J.: Doubleday, 1957); first published in 1937. Hortense Powdermaker, *After Freedom* (New York: Viking, 1939). George A. Sewell and Margaret L. Dwight, *Mississippi Black History Makers* (Jackson: Univ. Press of Mississippi, 1984).

12. Sansing, *Mississippi*, 317.

13. Vassor Joiner, in an audio cassette tape edited by Edwin Fox, "The Meredith Ordeal," 25 Feb. 1985. Archives of Sarah Isom Center for Women's Studies, Univ. of Mississippi.

14. Sansing, *Mississippi*, 317–18.

15. "Medgar Evers," in Sewell and Dwight, *Mississippi Black History Makers*, 117–22.

16. Eudora Welty, "Preface," *Collected Stories*, xi.

17. Interview with Dave Dennis, in Raines, *My Soul*, 276.

18. "Medgar Evers," in Sewell and Dwight, *Mississippi Black History Makers*, 122.

19. "Perspective: Freedom Summer, A Generation Later," a special report, *Clarion Ledger and Jackson Daily News*, 1 July 1984.

20. Anne Moody, lecture at Millsaps College, 26 Feb. 1985. Quotes from notes by Gayle Graham Yates.

21. R. Edwin King, Jr., "Foreword," in John R. Salter, Jr., *Jackson, Mississippi: An American Chronicle of Struggle and Schism* (Hicksville, N.Y.: Exposition Press, 1979), xiv.

22. Brown, *Civil Wars*, 23.

23. Ibid., 19.

24. Ibid., 418–19.

25. Ellen Douglas, *The Rock Cried Out* (New York: Harcourt Brace Jovanov-ich, 1979).
26. John Shelton Reed, *The Enduring South* (Lexington, Mass.: D.C. Heath, 1972).
27. Douglas, *The Rock*, 245.
28. Professor Vaughan Grisham, lecture, Southern Studies Program, Univ. of Mississippi, 19 Mar. 1985. Quotes from notes by Gayle Graham Yates.

Chapter 3

1. Steve Riley, "Heart Attack Claims Gov. Finch"; Dan Davis, "Ex-Governor Championed Underdog"; and "Cliff Finch Chronology," Jackson (Miss.) *Clarion-Ledger*, 23 Apr. 1986. James Young, "Populist Governor Is Recalled with Image of 'Working Man' Who Could Hear Black views," Memphis (Tenn.) *Commercial Appeal*, 24 Apr. 1986. Steve Riley, "'Work-ingman's Governor' Buried," *Clarion-Ledger*, 25 Apr. 1987.
2. Interview with Gov. William Winter, 23 Apr. 1986.
3. This biographical information comes in part from Dr. Gerald Lee, "Intro-duction of Governor William Winter," at Inaugural McLemore Lecture in American Studies, 10 June 1980, Mississippi College, Clinton, Missis-sippi, typescript in Mississippi Department of Archives and History. Also see *The Inaugural Papers of Governor William F. Winter*, ed. Charlotte Ca-pers (Jackson: Mississippi Department of Archives and History, 1980). Also, Erskine Alvis, "Winter's Young Men: The 'Boys of Spring' in Recent Mississippi Politics," typescript of paper, Center College, 12 Nov. 1984.
4. Lele Gillespie, "The Civil Rights Movement in Grenada, Mississippi, 1966," p. 4. Typescript paper in Mississippi Department of Archives and History.
5. Interview with Cora Norman, 28 Feb. 1985.
6. Thomas H. Brown, ed., *Ingredients for Survival: The Mississippi Commit-tee for the Humanities Tenth Anniversary Conference* (Jackson: Mississippi Committee for the Humanities), 24.
7. Dr. Sarah A. Rouse, speech quoted in Thoams H. Brown, *Ingredients for Survival*, 57–58.
8. Supplemental information for this interview comes from "Nine Women Who Excelled Are Honored by Radcliffe," *New York Times*, 31 Oct. 1985; the Mississippi Committee for Humanities, *Interlock: The Humanities and Mississippians, Report 1983–84;* and my interview with Peggy Whitman Prenshaw at Hattiesburg, Miss., 25 Mar. 1985.
9. This information is from "NAACP Plans State Meeting in Oxford," *Oxford Eagle*, 2 Nov. 1984. I also attended many sessions and was present at some of the sessions identified. See also, "NAACP Elects Henry," Mem-phis (Tenn.) *Commercial Appeal*, 11 Nov. 1984; Kevin Kittredge, "NAACP to Visit Oxford to Boost Northern Base," *Commercial Appeal*, 3

Nov. 1984. I have these articles in my clippings collection and personal archives, along with the programs from the convention's Freedom Fund Banquet, the Ministers' Luncheon, and the Summit on Black Education.

10. "Aaron Henry," in *Mississippi Black History Makers*, ed. Sewell and Dwight, rev. ed. (Jackson: Univ. Press of Mississippi), 86.

11. "Robert Clark," in Sewell and Dwight, *Mississippi Black History Makers*, 82.

12. Ibid., 83.

13. "NAACP Plans State Meeting in Oxford," *Oxford Eagle*, 2 Nov. 1984.

14. Raad Cawthon, "Black Rep.-Elect Mike Espy Basks in Mississippi Victory," *Atlanta Journal* and *Atlanta Constitution*, 23 Nov. 1986.

15. Notes taken by Gayle Graham Yates at the convention, 7 Nov. 1984.

16. Alexander P. Lamis, *The Two-Party South* (New York: Oxford Univ. Press, 1984), 44–45.

17. Ibid., quote on 44.

18. Ibid., 50.

19. Ibid., 52.

20. Ibid., 53.

21. Ibid., quote on 55.

22. Ibid., quote on 54.

23. Ronald Smothers, "Political Graft Charges Mounting in Mississippi," *New York Times*, 30 Oct. 1987.

24. E.J. Dionne, Jr., "Voting Produces Strong Evidence Of Importance of Racial Politics, Black Turnout Is Vital to Election of Governor in Mississippi and Philadelphia Mayor's Victory," *New York Times*, 5 Nov. 1987.

25. "Ross Barnett, Segregationist, Dies; Governor of Mississippi in 1960's," *New York Times*, 8 Nov. 1987.

Chapter 4

1. Paul Engle, "Miss Welty's Full Charm in First Novel," *Chicago Tribune*, 14 Apr. 1946. Clipping in the Eudora Alice Welty Memorabilia and Reference Collection, Mississippi State Department of Archives and History.

2. William Faulkner, *The Sound and the Fury* (New York: Random House, 1956), 7. First published in 1929.

3. Ibid., 246.

4. Ibid., 248–49.

5. Ibid., 249.

6. William Faulkner, "Nobel Prize Award Speech," in *The Literature of the South*, ed. Thomas Daniel Young et al., rev. ed. (Glenview, Ill.: Scott, Foresman, 1968), 1042. I have made an effort to add "inclusive language" to Faulkner's speech, replacing the generic "man" and the generic "he" in Faulkner's idiom and the English-language idiom of his time with the inclusive "human" or "he and she" and "humanity," in keeping with a

present-day rendering of language that feminists of the 1960s and the 1970s have brought into standard American English usage.

7. Interview with Eudora Welty in Jackson, Mississippi, 26 Feb. 1985.
8. James Curtis, *Culture as Polyphony* (Columbia, Mo.: Univ. of Missouri Press, 1978), v.
9. Ibid., 161.
10. Ibid., ix–x.
11. Ibid., x.
12. Ibid., 172–73.
13. "Farewell Role for Price: Verdi's 'Aïda' at the Met," *New York Times*, 31 Dec. 1984.
14. Loewen and Sallis, *Mississippi*, 219–35.
15. William Ferris and Mary L. Hart, eds., *Folk Music and Modern Sound* (Jackson: Univ. Press of Mississippi, 1982).
16. B. G. DeSylva and Lew Brown, lyrics, music by Ray Henderson, "The Birth of the Blues," *Reader's Digest Family Songbook* (Pleasantville, N.Y.: Reader's Digest, 1969, 110–11. Originally published in 1926 by Harms, Inc. Copyright renewed. Published by arrangement with Anne-Rachel Music Corps.
17. William Ferris, record jacket text for *Mississippi Folk Voices*, Southern Culture Records, SC 1700.
18. Ibid.
19. William Ferris, *Blues From the Delta* (Garden City, N.Y.: Anchor, 1979), xii.
20. Barbara A. Burch, "Ma Wailed the Blues for Beale," *Commercial Appeal*, 29 Mar. 1985.
21. Alice Walker, *The Color Purple* (New York: Washington Square Press, Pocket Books, 1983), 177–79.
22. James E. Akenson, "Jimmie Rodgers: An Educational Resource," *Jimmie Rodgers Memorial Association Newsletter* 2 (Winter 1984):1; Loewen and Sallis, *Mississippi*, 22, 228–29; Ferris, record jacket text.
23. Jimmie Rodgers, "Hobo's Meditation," lyrics on the record sleeve, *Mississippi Folk Voices*, Southern Culture Records, SC 1700.
24. Loewen and Sallis, *Mississippi*, 228.
25. Louis Dollarhide, "December 2, 1969 . . . Leontyne Price at Rust College," in Dollarhide, *Of Arts and Artists: Selected Reviews of Arts in Mississippi, 1955–1976* (Jackson: Univ. Press of Mississippi, 1981), 153.
26. Craig Claiborne, *Craig Claiborne's Southern Cooking* (New York: New York Times Books, 1987), xiii.
27. *The Afro-American Quilters Exhibition Catalogue* (Oxford, Miss.: Center for the Study of Southern Culture, Univ. of Mississippi, 2, 4.
28. Darryl Warner, "Interview with Mrs. Artemeasie Brandon," *I Ain't Lying* 1 (Winter 1982):35–37.
29. Jeannie Griffith interview.
30. Fred Anklam and Cliff Treyens, "Highlights of Education Reform Act,"

in *Miracle in Mississippi*, special supplement to the Jackson *Clarion-Ledger*, 7 May 1983.
31. Jeannie Griffith interview.
32. Interview with Alferdteen Harrison, 21 Mar. 1985.
33. Alferdteen Harrison, *Piney Woods School, An Oral History* (Jackson: Univ. Press of Mississippi, 1982).
34. Alferdteen Harrison interview.
35. Alferdteen Harrison, *Piney Woods School*, dust jacket.
36. Ibid., 3.
37. Ibid., 13.
38. Alferdteen Harrison interview.
39. Alferdteen Harrison, *Piney Woods School*, 91.
40. Ibid., 133.
41. Interview with Charles Sallis, Jackson, Mississippi, 2 Mar. 1985.
42. Andy Kanengiser, "Textbooks Now Giving Blacks Fairer Shake," in "Perspective: Freedom Summer, A Generation Later," a special report, *Clarion-Ledger and Jackson Daily News*, 1 July 1984.

Chapter 5

1. Interview with Ruth Winfield Love, Newburyport, Mass., 2 Mar. 1985.
2. Jeannie Griffith interview.
3. "Gifts, Graces, and Gayness," *Westword*, Denver, Colorado, 29 Oct. 1981.
4. Ibid.
5. "Methodist Clergy Suggest 'Inclusive' Ways to Refer to God," Minneapolis *Star and Tribune*, 20 June 1987.
6. Ellen Douglas, *A Lifetime Burning* (New York: Random House, 1982).
7. Orville Prescott, *New York Times*, quoted on dust jacket of Douglas, *A Lifetime Burning*.
8. Jonathan Yardley, *New York Times Book Review*, quoted on dust jacket of Douglas, *A Lifetime Burning*.
9. Douglas, *A Lifetime Burning*, 211–12.
10. John Griffin Jones, "Beth Henley," in John Griffin Jones, ed., *Mississippi Writers Talking*, vol. 1 (Jackson: Univ. Press of Mississippi 1982), 169–90.
11. Ibid., 181–82.
12. Ibid., 173.
13. Ibid., 182–83.
14. Ibid., 184.
15. Ibid., 177.
16. Beth Henley, *Crimes of the Heart* (New York: Viking and Penguin, 1982), 21.
17. Ibid., 17.
18. Ibid., 23.
19. Ibid., 119.

20. Ibid., 98–99.
21. Ibid., 113.
22. Ibid., 123–24.
23. "People," Minneapolis *Star and Tribune*, 20 July 1987.
24. Beth Henley, *Miss Firecracker Contest* (New York: Dramatists' Play Service, 1985).
25. Richard Wright, *Black Boy* (New York: Harper and Row, 1966), 24–26. First published in 1945.
26. Ibid.
27. Ibid., 14–15.
28. Ibid., 283–84.
29. "Wright Acceptance Letter Donated to Williams Library," *Southern Register* 5 (Spring 1987):8.
30. John Griffin Jones, "Willie Morris," in John Griffin Jones, ed., *Mississippi Writers Talking*, vol. 2 (Jackson: Univ. of Mississippi Press, 1983), 113.
31. Willie Morris, *The Courting of Marcus Dupree* (New York: Dell, 1985), 15.
32. Ibid., 13.
33. Ibid., 342–43.
34. Ibid., 456.
35. Ibid., 456.
36. Ibid., 284.
37. Ibid., 505–506.
38. "Take the Money and Run," *Sports Illustrated*, 12 Mar. 1984; "Dupree's Injury Makes Way for 'Bu-ing,'" *Sporting News*, 18 Mar. 1985; "USFL Losers: The Regretful Ones," *Sport*, May 1985; Norman O. Unger, "A Sporting Chance," *Jet*, Sept. 1986.
39. Peggy Whitman Prenshaw interview.
40. Peggy Prenshaw, quoted in Thomas H. Brown, *Ingredients for Survival*, 82.

Chapter 6

1. Simone Weil, *The Need for Roots* (London: Routledge and Kegan Paul, 1952), 4.
2. H. Bryant Ayers, "Flap Over Confederate Flag Ends in a Cultural Standoff," Minneapolis *Star and Tribune*, 2 June 1983.
3. Robert N. Bellah, "The Civil Religion in America," in Bellah, *Beyond Belief* (New York: Harper and Row, 1970), 168–189; originally published in *Daedalus* (Winter 1967):1–21.
4. Ibid.; Anthony F. C. Wallace, *Rockdale* (New York: Norton, 1978); Clifford Geertz, *The Interpretation of Cultures* (New York: Basic, 1973).
5. Bellah, "Civil Religion," 18.
6. Charles Reagan Wilson, *Baptized in Blood: The Religion of the Lost Cause, 1905–1920* (Athens, Ga.: Univ. of Georgia Press, 1980).

7. Ibid., 1.
8. Ibid., 7.
9. Ibid., 107.
10. Ibid., 179–80.
11. Ibid., 181–82.
12. Louis Dollarhide, "Don Cassell, 1936–1960," in Dollarhide, *Of Arts and Artists*, 78.
13. Oscar Hammerstein and Jerome Kern, "Ol' Man River," *Showboat* (New York: Welk Music Group, 1927), 161.
14. "Vicksburg," brochure, Vicksburg National Military Park, Vicksburg, Mississippi, National Park Service, U.S. Dept. of the Interior, n.d.
15. Emma Balfour, *Vicksburg, A City Under Seige: Diary of Emma Balfour, May 16, 1863–June 2, 1863*. Balfour Collection, Mississippi State Department of Archives and History.
16. Epigraph, in Margaret Walker, *Jubilee* (New York: Bantam, 1972). First published in 1966. The author is Dr. Margaret Walker Alexander, professor retired from Jackson State University.
17. Florence Mars, *Witness in Philadelphia* (Baton Rouge: Louisiana State Univ. Press, 1977), 3–4.
18. Aaron Henry, remarks at Minister's Luncheon, Mississippi NAACP Convention, Oxford, Miss., 7 Nov. 1984.
19. Often quoted. Appears in the thoughtful account of the racial crisis in that church by his successor: W. J. Cunningham, *Agony at Galloway, One Church's Struggle with Social Change* (Jackson: Univ. Press of Mississippi, 1980), 3.
20. Fannie Lou Hamer clippings file, Mississippi State Department of Archives and History.
21. Austin Scott, "Fannie Hamer, Civil Rights Leader, Dies," *Washington Post*, 17 Mar. 1977.
22. Alice Walker, review of June Jordan, *Fannie Lou Hamer*, in *New York Times Book Review*, 29 Apr. 1973; see also Walker's poem, "Revolutionary Petunias," in Walker, *Revolutionary Petunias and Other Poems* (New York: Harcourt Brace Jovanovich, 1973), 29.
23. Austin Scott, "A Tribute in a Delta Town: Early Civil Rights Worker Praised at Mississippi Funeral," *Washington Post*, 21 Mar. 1977; and Lonnie Wheeler, "They Gathered, Waited in Ruleville," Jackson *Clarion Ledger*, 21 Mar. 1977. Clippings in Fannie Lou Hamer file, Mississippi State Department of Archives and History.

Index

Aaron, Daniel, 149
Absalom, Absalom! (Faulkner), 15
Adams, Bruce, 189
After Freedom (Powdermaker), 69
Alexander, Margaret Walker. *See*
　Walker, Margaret
Allain, Bill, 117

Balfour, Emma, 258, 262
Baptized in Blood: The Religion of the
　Lost Cause, 1865–1920 (Wilson),
　253–57
Barnett, Ross, 117, 126, 128, 132
Basso, Hamilton, 154, 155
Beckwith, Byron de la, 76
Bellah, Robert, 250
Bergmark, Martha, 14–15, 45–46;
　interview with, 46–50
Bernard, Jessie, 198
Bettersworth, John, 192
Bilbo, Theodore G., 91–92, 95
Billingslea, Charles, 72
"The Birth of the Blues," 168–69
Black, Patti Carr, 61, 63
Black Boy (Wright), 228–29, 230–31,
　232
black people. *See* civil rights move-
　ment, race relations
Blue Highways (Least Heat Moon),
　22
Blues from the Delta (Ferris), 168,
　169–70
blues songs, 166–72

Borinski, Ernst, 68
A Boy with a Cart (Fry), 218
Brandon, Artemeasie, 180
Brewer, Billy, 117
Brown, Lew, 168
Brown, Rosellen, 12, 85–87
Bruce, Blanche K., 56
Busby, Jeff, 22
Bynum Mounds, 32

camp meeting, 272–73
cane, sugar, 27–30
Capers, Charlotte, 143
Carmichael, Gil, 127, 128
Carter, Hodding, 92, 269
Carter, Jimmy, 128, 129
Cassell, Donald, 259
Caste and Class in a Southern Town
　(Dollard), 69
Chaney, James, 51, 77
Childress, Alvin, 165
Chinese-Americans, 58–60
Chisholm, Elizabeth, 165
Chisholm, Peggy, 165
Choctaw Indians, 25–26, 51
Christianity. *See* religion
church. *See* religion
Citizens Councils, 66, 69
civil religion, 250–51, 252–57
civil rights movement: aftermath of,
　78–87; in Mississippi, 61–78
Civil War. *See* Confederacy; Vicks-
　burg, Miss.

Civil Wars (Brown), 12, 85–87
Claiborne, Craig, 176–77
Clark, Robert, 117, 119, 120, 130, 266
Clark, Sadie Schaeffer, 111
Cochran, Thad, 129, 130
COFO. *See* Congress of Federated Organizations
Cohen, Carla, 81
Cohen, David, 81
Cohen, Seena, 115
Coleman, J. P., 102
The Color Purple, 170–71
Coming of Age in Mississippi (Moody), 66–67, 80–81
Compson, Benjy, 137–40
Confederacy: as Lost Cause religion, 253–57
Confederate symbols, 247–51
Congress of Federated Organizations (COFO), 76–77
Congress of Racial Equality (CORE), 70
Conversations with Eudora Welty (Prenshaw), 144, 145
cooking, as art, 173–77
Cooley, Archie, 117
CORE. *See* Congress of Racial Equality
country music, 172–73
The Courting of Marcus Dupree (Morris), 234–39
Craig Claiborne's Southern Cooking, 176
Crimes of the Heart (Henley), 219–25
Culture as Polyphony (Curtis), 159–64
Curtis, James, 159–64

Dansby, David, 73
Dantin, Maurice, 129
Daughters of the American Revolution (DAR), 21–22
Day, Warren, 273
"Death of a Traveling Salesman" (Welty), 141

DeGolyer, Samuel, 261
de la Beckwith, Byron, 76
Delta Wedding (Welty), 145–46, 147
Democratic party, 125–32
Dennis, Dave, 76
De Soto, Hernando, 20
DeSylva, B. G., 168
"Dixie," 249
Dollard, John, 69
Donald, David, 148–49
Douglas, Ellen, 88–91, 216–18
Dowdy, Wayne, 117, 130
Duffy, Joe, 114
Dunkle, Margaret, 203
Dupree, Marcus, 51, 117, 233–39
Dupree, Reggie, 234
Dye, Brad, 117

Eastland, James O., 95, 128, 129, 267
Ehrensperger, Harold, 218
The Enduring South (Reed), 89
Engel, Lehman, 165
Espy, Michael, 120, 130
Evers, Charles, 74, 127, 129, 266
Evers, Medgar, 74–76, 266

Faulkner, William, 1, 2, 14, 15, 101, 134–41, 231–32, 238
Ferris, William, 168, 169
Finch, Cliff, 94, 99–100, 128
Ford, Gerald, 128
Fortune, Porter, 111, 117
Franklin, Webb, 130
Freedom Riders, 70
French Camp, Miss., 28
Fry, Christopher, 218

Galloway, Charles B., 255–56
Gandy, Evelyn, 95
Gilbert, Ben, 214
Gillespie, Lele, 100
The Golden Apples (Welty), 152–55
Good Old Boy (Morris), 227–28
Goodman, Andrew, 51, 77
Gorden, W. C., 117

Graham, Bessie, 7–8, 10, 174
Graham, 'Cile, 10, 174, 175
Graham, James, 8
Graham, Maryemma, 232
Graham, Merrell, 6, 7–8, 273, 274
Grant, Ulysses S., 260–61
graveyard-working-day, 4–7
Greensboro, N.C., 68
Griffith, Jeannie, 14; courtship and
    marriage of, 209–10; interview
    with, 41–45, 181–82, 183–84
Grisham, Vaughan, 87–93

Hamer, Fannie Lou, 70, 78, 266–69
Handy, W. C., 168, 169
Harrison, Alferdteen, 184–87
Hawkins, John, 247, 249
Haxton, Josephine. See Douglas,
    Ellen
Hearn, Betty, 113
Hebron Church, 4
Henley, Beth, 219–25
Henry, Aaron, 76, 94, 128, 129, 265,
    266; as president of Mississippi
    NAACP, 117, 118–19, 121
Hill, Samuel S., 91, 254
"Hobo's Meditation," 172
Holliday, Troy, 111
homosexuality, 213–19
Hope, Julius Caesar, 121–23
Howorth, Lucy, 112, 116
Hull, Marie, 165
Humphrey, Hubert, 266

Indianola, Miss., 69

Jackson, Jesse, 121
Jackson, Miss., 44, 53, 68, 69; as
    home of Eudora Welty, 141–42,
    158–59
Jackson, Mississippi: An American
    Chronicle of Struggle and Schism
    (Salter), 85
Jackson State University, 184
"Jim Crow" laws, 56
Johnson, June, 268

Johnson, Paul B., Jr., 127
Joiner, Vassor, 72
Joliet, Louis, 21
Jones, David, 112
Jones, James Earl, 165
Jones, John Griffin, 220
Jones, Laurence C., 183, 186, 187
Jones, Samuel, 4
Jordan, Buford, 117
Jordan, Cora, 50, 51, 125

Key, V. O., Jr., 126
King, B. B., 170
King, Ed, 76, 84–85, 266
King, Martin Luther, Jr., 67, 266
Kirksey, Henry, 119
Ku Klux Klan, 69, 77

Lamis, Alexander P., 125–26, 128,
    129, 130
La Salle, Sieur de, 21
Leard, Libby, 196–97
Least Heat Moon, William, 22
Leggett, Violet, 117
A Lifetime Burning (Douglas), 216–
    18
"Livvie" (Welty), 30–31, 32, 149–52
Loewen, James W., 58–60, 172–73,
    188–93
Losing Battles (Welty), 142, 146–47
Lott, Trent, 129–30
Louisville, New Orleans, and Texas
    Railroad Company v. Mississippi,
    56
Love, Joe Brown, 200–202
Love, Ruth Winfield: wedding of,
    199–209
"The Lynched Man's Mother Prays"
    (Ragsdale), 57–58
lynching, 56–58, 191

Mabus, Ray, 131–32, 182
McCluhan, Marshall, 161
McComb, Miss., 70
McGrath, Jay, 206
Marquette, Pierre, 20–21

marriage, 194–210
Mars, Florence, 235, 264–65
Mathers, Erma Gay, 33–36; interview with, 36–41
Matherville, Miss., 35
Meredith, James, 13, 72–73, 78, 117
Meridian, Miss., 274–75, 279
Millsaps College, 81
The Miss Firecracker Contest (Henley), 219, 220
Mississippi: aftermath of civil rights movement in, 78–87; artists from, 164–66; changes in, 50–52, 105–6; Chinese-Americans in 58–60; civil rights movement in, 61–78; Democratic party in, 125–32; early explorers of, 20–21; education reform in, 103–4, 182–83; Vaughan Grisham's view of, 87–93; history textbook for, 188–93; Indian history, 25–27; music originating in, 166–73; NAACP in, 116–25; party system in, 125–32; perceptions of, 11–16; race relations in, 53–64; religion in, 264–66, 270–77; Republican party in, 125–30; women as candidates in, 95–96; writers from, 165–66
Mississippi: Conflict and Change (Loewen and Sallis), 188–93
The Mississippi Chinese: Between Black and White (Loewen), 58–60
Mississippi Committee for the Humanities, 106–15
Mississippi Freedom Democratic Party, 76, 78, 127, 266–67
Mississippi Library Commission, 113
Mississippi Sovereignty Commission, 66, 84
Mississippi, University of, 247–51
Mitchell, Dennis, 113, 114
Mobley, Mary Ann, 165, 226, 242
modernism, 159–64
Mondale, Walter, 267
Montgomery, Ala., 67
Moody, Anne, 66, 80–84

Moon, Frank, 200–201
Moore, Ross, 143, 148, 149
Morris, Willie, 227–38
Moses, Robert, 71, 76
"My Mississippi Spring" (Walker), 13

NAACP. See National Association for the Advancement of Colored People
Nashville, Tenn., 69
Natchez Trace Parkway, 16–33; history of, 19–22
National Association for the Advancement of Colored People (NAACP), 66, 68–69, 74–75; in Mississippi, 116–25
National Endowment for the Humanities, 107
Native Son (Wright), 229–30
Norman, Cora, 106–16
Norsworthy, Margaret, 274

Ogletree, Nannie, 264
Ole Miss. See Mississippi, University of
One Writer's Beginnings (Welty), 142, 147–49, 158
The Optimist's Daughter (Welty), 1, 155–57
Oxford, Miss., 133–37

Page, Matthew, 109
Parks, Rosa, 67
Patterson, Steve, 117, 132
Peden, Rachel, 53–54
Pemberton, John D., 260–61
Philadelphia, Miss., 50–52
Phillips, Bob, 113
Phillips, Rubel, 127
Piney Woods Country Life School, 183–87
"Place in Fiction" (Welty), 14
plantations, 55
Plessy v. Ferguson, 56
Pontotoc, Miss., 90

postmodernism, 159–64
Powdermaker, Hortense, 69
Prenshaw, Peggy Whitman, 112,
    113, 144, 239–45
Presley, Elvis, 159–64, 173
Price, Cecil, Sr., 235
Price, Cecil, Jr., 235
Price, Leontyne, 164–65, 173

quilting, 174, 177–82

race relations: in Mississippi, 53–64;
    see also civil rights movement;
    Dupree, Marcus; Hamer, Fannie
    Lou; National Association for the
    Advancement of Colored People;
    Prenshaw, Peggy Whitman;
    Wright, Richard
Ragsdale, Tallulah, 57
Rainey, Ma, II, 170
Ray, Martha, 211
reading, importance of, 10–11, 101
Reagan, Ronald, 129
Reed, John Shelton, 89
religion, 263–66, 270–77; and Fannie
    Lou Hamer, 267–69
Republican party, 125–30
Revels, Hiram R., 56
Rhodes, Leila, 114
Richardson, Willie, 117
Riddell, Rom, 128
The Robber Bridegroom (Welty), 31–
    32, 146
Robinson, Jackie, 81, 82
The Rock Cried Out (Douglas), 88–91
Rodgers, Jimmie, 172–73
Rood, John, 141
A Room of One's Own (Woolf), 1
Rouse, Sarah, 108, 113
Ruleville, Miss., 268–69
Rush, Julian, 211–15, 273, 274
Russell, Bill, 113
Russia: similarity of to American
    South, 161–62

Sallis, Charles, 56, 172–73, 188–93
Salter, John, 84, 85

Sandeen, Ernest, 134–37
Sansing, David, 72
school desegregation, 65–66
Schwerner, Michael, 51, 77
Seawright, Toni, 227
segregation: in Mississippi, 56–58;
    see also civil rights movement;
    race relations
Selah, W. B., 266
sexuality, 196–97, 213–19
Sillers, Walter, 102
slavery, 55
Smith, Estus, 111
Smith, Orma, 192
SNCC. See Student Nonviolent Co-
    ordinating Committee
The Sound and the Fury (Faulkner),
    137–40
Southern Legacy (Carter), 92
Southern Politics (Key), 126
Speakes, Larry, 129
Star, Miss., 41
Stennis, John C., 92, 129, 130
Stockwell, Joe, 113–14
Student Nonviolent Coordinating
    Committee (SNCC), 70–71
sugar cane, 27–30
Sweringen, Bethany, 144
Sylvester, Jeannette, 84

Tannehill, Courtney, 115
Tate, Allen, 2
Tellis, Vivian, 111
Thomas, James, 274
Thomas, James "Son," 169
Thompson, Katie, 240
Thurmond, Strom, 126
Till, Emmett, 66–67
Tunica County, Miss., 165
Tupelo, Miss., 160–61, 162–64
Turner, Gerald, 117
The Two-Party South (Lamis), 125–26

Uncle Tom's Children (Wright), 229
Understanding Media (McCluha), 161

Vicksburg, Miss., 257–63

Wahlman, Maude Southwell, 179
Waits, Jim, 273, 274
Walker, Alice, 268
Walker, Herschel, 234
Walker, Margaret, 13, 114, 118, 123–
    25, 232
Waller, William, 127
Warner, Darryl, 180
Warren, Robert Penn, 141
Washington, Walter, 110
weddings, 198–210
Welty, Eudora, 1, 14, 30–32, 75,
    141–44; interview with, 145–59
Wheatley, Melvin, 214–15
"Where Is the Voice Coming From?"
    (Welty), 75
White Citizens Councils, 66, 69
Whitten, Jamie, 117
Wiedie, Wayne, 114

Williams, Arthur Lee, 169
Williams, John Bell, 99, 127
Wilson, Charles Reagan, 89, 253–57
Wilson, Woodrow, 256
Winfrey, Oprah, 165
Winter, Elise Varner, 100
Winter, William, 94–95, 97–106, 129,
    130, 182
Witness from Philadelphia (Mars),
    235
Wolfe, Karl, 141, 165
Wolfe, Mildred, 165
Woodward, C. Vann, 64
Woolf, Virginia, 1
Wright, Fielding, 126
Wright, Richard, 228–32, 233

Yates, Wilson, 73
Yi-Fu Tuan, 12
Young, Andrew, 266, 268–69